CONTENTS

EUROPEAN LAW SERIES

Series Editor: Professor John A. Usher

Published titles

International Relations Law of the European Union Dominic McGoldrick

EC Public Procurement Law Christopher Bovis

EC Insurance Law Robert Merkin and Angus Rodger

EC Consumer Law and Policy Stephen Weatherill

EC Tax Law David Williams

General Principles of EC Law John A. Usher

EC Environmental Law Joanne Scott

EU Law and Human Rights Lammy Betten and Nicholas Grief

EC Institutions and Legislation John A. Usher

European Social Law and Policy Tamara Hervey

Civil Jurisdiction and Judgments in Europe Peter Stone

EC Media Law and Policy David Goldberg, Tony Prosser and Stefaan Verhulst

EC Social Security Law Robin White

EC Law in the UK Christine Boch

EU Justice and Home Affairs Law Steve Peers

Law of the Common Agricultural Policy Joseph A. McMahon

EC Labour Law Erika Szyszczak

EC LABOUR LAW

ERIKA SZYSZCZAK

An imprint of Pearson Education

Harlow, England · London · New York · Reading, Massachusetts · San Francisco
Toronto · Don Mills, Ontario · Sydney · Tokyo · Singapore · Hong Kong · Seoul
Taipei · Cape Town · Madrid · Mexico City · Amsterdam · Munich · Paris · Milan

Pearson Education Limited

Edinburgh Gate
Harlow
Essex CM20 2JE
England

and Associated Companies throughout the world

Visit us on the World Wide Web at:
www.pearsoneduc.com

_____

First published 2000

ISBN 0-582-30814-3

British Library Cataloguing-in-Publication Data
A catalogue record for this book is available from the British Library.

Set by 7 in 10/13 pt Sabon.
Printed in Great Britain by Henry Ling Ltd, at the Dorset Press, Dorchester, Dorset.

SERIES PREFACE

The Longman European Law Series is the first comprehensive series of topic-based books on EC law aimed primarily at a student readership, though I have no doubt that they will also be found useful by academic colleagues and interested practitioners. It has become more and more difficult for a single course or a single book to deal comprehensively with all the major topics of Community law, and the intention of this series is to enable students and teachers to 'mix and match' topics which they find to be of interest: it may also be hoped that the publication of this Series will encourage the study of areas of Community law which have historically been neglected in degree courses. However, while the Series may have a student readership in mind, the authors have been encouraged to take an academic and critical approach, placing each topic in its overall Community context, and also in its socio-economic and political context where relevant.

Labour law is one of the few substantive areas of EC law to have undergone major changes as a result of the Treaty of Amsterdam, in particular by the incorporation of the Social Protocol into the main body of the EC Treaty and by the introduction of a new chapter on Employment. In a sense, therefore, this book is about a new topic, but it is also a topic which involves long-established principles set out in the original version of the Treaty, such as free movement of workers, and equal pay for equal work as between men and women. Professor Szyszczak brings this material together into a manageable whole presented in a wider context. Even if her conclusion is that there cannot yet be said to be a coherent or complete system of EC labour law, and that its development is subject to political and economic challenges, Professor Szyszczak points out that it involves important substantive and procedural legal rights at both the individual and collective level.

John A. Usher

AUTHOR'S PREFACE

When asked to write a book 'just on EC labour law' I was delighted. No longer would I have to agonise on where the conventional 'social policy' of the European Union began and ended. I have had the luxury of focusing upon a more precise project. The signing of the Treaty of Amsterdam made my task even easier. Now there is a clear legal base to develop a more coherent EC labour law *and* a chapter on 'Employment'. Is it now possible to identify a discrete area of labour law and policy: an 'EC labour law'? The answer, of course, is no. For over a decade, labour lawyers have had to grapple with the academic (and social) response to changes in industrial relations practices, labour market behaviour, the institutions and practices of actors in the field, as well as challenges made to conventional academic discourse, particularly by critical legal studies and feminist theory. A debate has emerged among labour lawyers as to the problem of the 'conception' of labour law as an autonomous academic subject. One of the aims of this book, therefore, is to explore the parameters and boundaries of the evolving EC labour law and employment strategy. Like most divorces, a clean break between social policy and labour law is not easy to achieve. At times it is still necessary to retreat to referring to social policy as a way of explaining and contextualising issues and developments.

This book is an introductory text. As a result of the publisher's constraints, some issues are dealt with in a superficial way, but the reader is referred to the footnotes, where there is detailed referencing. The text is organised around the substantive issues of EC labour law and the themes running through EC labour law. The book has had to be selective in its coverage. Overall, the aim of the book is to begin a discussion of where the boundaries of EC labour law lie, to discuss the parameters of the developing EC labour law, to analyse the dynamics of decision making and ask whether there is a distinctive EC labour law and policy and what its role is in the new European polity.

Alongside the new conceptual problems created by The Treaty of Amsterdam, the renumbering of the Treaty Articles creates hardship for those of us, as Catherine Hoskyns remarked to me, 'for whom Article 119 EC will always be Article 119 EC in our hearts and minds' and for those who are new to the area. Since many of the cases and academic articles referred to discuss particular Treaty provisions, I have referred to both the old and new numbering of the EC Treaty and I have italicised the new numbering.

Finally, my thanks to Richard, Jamie, Larissa and William. At least I shall not be spending the next millennium worrying about when I am going to finish *that* book.

Erika Szyszczak
January 2000

TABLE OF CASES

Judgments of the Court of First Instance

Judgments of the Court of Human Rights

Judgments of the House of Lords

TABLE OF LEGISLATION

TABLE OF EQUIVALENCE

Treaty Establishing the European Community

Previous Numbering	New Numbering	Previous Numbering	New Numbering
Article 3	Article 3	Article 100(4)	Article 94(4)
Article 5	Article 10	Article 100a	Article 95
Article 6	Article 12	Article 103	Article 99
Article 12	Article 25	Article 103a	Article 100
Article 18	repealed	Article 105	Article 105
Article 28	Article 26	Article 110	Article 131
Article 30	Article 28	Article 113	Article 133
Article 36	Article 30	Article 117	Article 136
Article 37	Article 31	Article 118	Article 137
Article 38	Article 32	Article 118A	Article 138
Article 39	Article 33	Article 118B	Article 139
Article 40	Article 34	Article 119	Article 141
Article 41	Article 35	Article 130a	Article 158
Article 42	Article 36	Article 130r	Article 174
Article 43	Article 37	Article 130s	Article 175
Article 44	repealed	Article 130u	Article 177
Article 45	repealed	Article 130v	Article 178
Article 46	Article 38	Article 155	Article 211
Article 85	Article 81	Article 201	Article 269
Article 86	Article 82	Article 215	Article 288
Article 90	Article 86	Article 226	repealed
Article 92	Article 87	Article 228	Article 300
Article 93	Article 88	Article 234(1)	Article 307
Article 94	Article 89	Article 235	Article 308
Article 100	Article 94		

ABBREVIATIONS

CEEP	Centre Européen d'entreprise publique
CFI	Court of First Instance
EC	European Community
ECHR	European Convention on Human Rights and Fundamental Freedoms
ECJ	European Court of Justice
ECSA	European Community Shipowners' Association
EES	European Employment Strategy
EFBWW	European Federation of Building and Wood Workers
EIB	European Investment Bank
EMTU	European Metal Worker Trade Unions
EMU	Economic and Monetary Union
ERM	Exchange Rate Mechanism
ESF	European Social Fund
ETD	Equal Treatment Directive
ETUC	European Trade Union Confederation
EU	European Union
EWC	European Works Council
FST	Federation of Transport Workers' Unions
GATS	General Agreement on Trade in Services
GATT	General Agreement on Tariffs and Trade
GDP	Gross Domestic Product
IGC	Intergovernmental Conference
ILO	International Labour Organization
NAP	National Action Plan
NGO	Non-governmental organisation
OECD	Organisation for Economic Co-operation and Development
SAP	Social Action Programme
SEA	Single European Act
SPA	Social Policy Agreement
TCN	Third-country national
TEU	Treaty on European Union
UEAPME	Union Européenne de l'Artisanat et des Petites et Moyennes Entreprises

UNICE   Union des conféderations d'industrie et des employeurs
                d'Europe
WTO   World Trade Organization

CHAPTER 1

The impact of the Treaty of Amsterdam

1.1 The boundaries and content of EC labour law and employment policy

The Treaty of Amsterdam is a significant legal tool in the history of EC labour law and introduces a new dynamic to labour law thinking. For the first time, there is a clear, though perhaps not coherent, legal base for the enactment of labour law measures at the Community level using the 'social partners' as political actors in the decision-making process. There is also recognition in the EC Treaty of the role of the Community, not only in directing macro-economic labour market policies, but also the capacity to make Recommendations to individual Member States on how to run their labour markets. The link between employment measures and fiscal policy, always in the shadows at EC level, has now been brought into the full glare of political decision making and economic debate. It has come as a surprise to labour lawyers and labour economists 'that for the first time in a long time the big issues in economic policy are about the labour market'.[1] The major issue is the search for the 'right model' to run the European economy by focusing upon the institutions and rules that govern labour markets: wage differentials and earnings inequality; the structure of unemployment, under-employment and unemployment insurance; centralised or decentralised collective bargaining; labour mobility; and modes of compensation. All these issues, which are currently centre stage, have rarely been addressed so openly in the formation of policy in EC labour and social policy law. This substantial shift in philosophy and legal competence can only be appreciated if we contextualise it in an exploration of the previous development of EC labour law.

---

[1] Freeman, R., 'War of the Models: Which Labour Market Institutions for the 21st Century?' (1998) 5 *Labour Economics* 1; Marsden, D. *Theory of Employment Systems* (OUP, Oxford, 1999).

1.2 The new legal base

The Treaty of Amsterdam provides for two strategies for the development of an EC labour law and an EU employment policy.[2] The principal legal base for labour law measures will be the new *Title XI* which is entitled, 'Social Policy, Education, Vocational Training and Youth'. This Title begins with *Article 136 EC,* which sets the context of an EC labour law within a teleological framework of human rights thinking, but also respects the diverse traditions of the Member States and the need to maintain competitiveness in the Community economy. *Article 136 EC* states a belief that the development of a social policy will ensue not only from the functioning of the common market but also from intervention at the Community level. *Article 137 EC* provides a broad legal base for the enactment of 'social policy' measures and, in the particular context of this book, a number of *labour law measures.* The importance of *Article 137 EC* lies in the fact that it allows for *qualified majority voting* in the Council using the co-decision procedure with the European Parliament (as set out in *Article 251 EC*) in areas relating to improvement of the working environment in order to protect workers' health and safety; working conditions; information and consultation of workers; the integration of persons excluded from the labour market;[3] equality between men and women with regard to labour market inequalities and equal treatment at work. In relation to the last heading, it should be noted that the new *Article 141 EC* amends the equal pay provisions originally found in the old Article 119 EC by consolidating some of the Court of Justice's case law in this area, providing a new legal base for equal pay and equal treatment measures and allowing the Member States to retain and introduce positive action measures in relation to pay inequalities between men and women.[4]

---

[2] For an earlier discussion of the relationship between an employment policy and employment law in the EU, see Freedland, M., 'Employment Policy' in Davies, P. *et al.* (eds) *European Community Labour Law: Principles and Perspectives, Liber Amicorum Lord Wedderburn* (OUP, Oxford, 1996).

[3] Such measures must not prejudice the application of *Article 127 EC* which provides:
'1. The Community shall contribute to a high level of employment by encouraging co-operation between Member States and by supporting and, if necessary, complementing their action. In doing so, the competences of the Member States shall be respected.
2. The objective of a high level of employment shall be taken into consideration in the formulation and implementation of Community policies and activities.'

[4] Compare the Declaration on *Article 141 EC* annexed to the Treaty of Amsterdam where the Member States contradict the neutral wording of *Article 141 EC*: 'Member states, in the adoption of measures mentioned in Article 141(4) EC, have to aim primarily, to improve the situation of women in their working life.' See Betten, L. and Shrubshall, V., 'The Concept of Positive Sex Discrimination in Community Law – Before and After the Treaty of Amsterdam' (1998) 14 *The International Journal of Comparative Labour Law and Industrial Relations* 65.

Any Directives adopted under the new legal base of *Article 137 EC* must be aimed at imposing *minimum requirements* which are in harmony with the national conditions and rules of the Member States and the new Directives must avoid imposing administrative, financial and legal constraints in a way which would hold back the creation and development of small and medium-sized (SMEs) undertakings. Inherent within this new legal base are two limitations of EC competence in labour market regulation which represent the cornerstones of the Member States' reluctance to hand over national competence completely to market integration principles. The first is the distinct, and sometimes divergent, industrial practices found in each of the Member States. The second is the underlying belief that regulation of labour law and of labour markets can result in excessive fixed costs and create rigidities in national labour markets which prevent flexibility, and ultimately competitiveness, in not only an open European market but also a global market.

Using the same procedure (that is, qualified majority voting and the co-decision procedure of *Article 251 EC*) the Council may also adopt measures designed to encourage *co-operation* between the Member States through initiatives aimed at improving knowledge, developing exchanges of information and best practices, promoting innovative approaches and evaluating experiences to combat social exclusion.

Using a *unanimous* vote, the Council may adopt Directives in a wider range of labour law areas: social security and social protection of workers; protection of workers where the contract of employment is terminated; representation and collective defence of the interests of workers; conditions of employment for third-country nationals legally resident in the EU; and financial contributions for promotion of employment and job creation. The European Parliament is to be consulted, as is the the Economic and Social Committee and the Committee of the Regions.

Many of the central issues of collective labour law remain, by and large, outside the competence of the Community. The new *Article 137(6) EC* excludes pay, the right of association, the right to strike or the right to impose lock-outs from Community competence. However, as we will see in Chapter 2, some aspects of collective labour may be affected by Community competence.[5]

---

5 See Ryan, B., 'Pay, Trade Union Rights and European Community Law' (1997) 13 *The International Journal of Comparative Labour Law and Industrial Relations* 305; Betten, L., 'Fundamental Rights (Human Rights) after the Adoption of the Treaty of Amsterdam' in Hertzfeld Olsson, P. *et al.* (eds) *Transnational Trade Union Rights in the European Union* (Arbetslivsisstituut, Stockholm, 1998); Betten, L. and MacDevitt, D. (eds) *The Protection of Fundamental Social Rights in the European Union* (Kluwer, The Hague, 1996).

1.2.1 New legal actors

Two new Treaty provisions, *Articles 138 EC* and *139 EC,* create jurisdiction over collective bargaining at the European level. An earlier attempt to make Community intervention into labour law issues more acceptable for some Member States and the two sides of industry had met with opposition from the British government at the time of the signing of the Single European Act in 1986 and had resulted in the much watered-down clause of Article 118B EC.[6] The opposition of the UK government also resulted in the UK being excluded from the processes of the Social Policy Agreement which formalised the role for the social partners to be involved in decision making at the Community level.

There has been a long history of *consultation* of the social partners at all levels of Community decision making[7] but *Articles 138 EC* and *139 EC* go much further by providing a Treaty obligation on the part of the Commission to consult the social partners before making any labour law proposals and secondly to give the social partners the opportunity to replace any Commission initiatives with a Community-wide collective agreement. Thus, the social partners are elevated to the role of political and institutional *actors* in the Community decision-making process. This wider involvement of actors has been criticised for not going further and introducing a 'civic dialogue' alongside the 'social dialogue'.[8] In contrast, as Bercusson points out, the use of the social partners in the decision-making process of the EU provides a 'striking example of the fundamental change in European labour law, reflecting transnational private regulation by private actors'.[9]

1.2.2 A new legal base for equal pay issues

The Treaty of Amsterdam consolidates the Court's case law under Article 119 EC by including the concept of equal pay for work of equal value into *Article 141 EC*. This new Article also provides a legal base for the Council – using a qualified majority vote and the co-decision procedure – to adopt measures to ensure the application of the principles of equal opportunities and equal treatment for men and women in employment and occupation

---

[6] Article 118B EC stated: 'The Commission shall endeavour to develop the dialogue between management and labour at European level which could, if the two sides consider it desirable, lead to relations based on agreement.'

[7] See *Communication on the Development of the Social Dialogue at Community Level,* COM (96) 448 final.

[8] Schulte, B., 'Juridical Instruments of the European Union and the European Communities' in Beck, W. *et al.* (eds) *The Social Quality of Europe* (Kluwer, The Hague, 1997).

[9] Bercusson, B., 'Globalizing Labour Law: Transnational Private Regulation and Countervailing Actors in European Labour Law' in Teubner, G. (ed.) *Global Law without a State* (Dartmouth, Aldershot, 1997), p. 139.

including the equal pay for work of equal value principle. Unlike the procedures of *Article 137 EC*, there is no need for the Commission to involve the social partners in the decision-making process. Read with the competence in *Article 137 EC*, there is now Treaty recognition of the fact that the *causes* of wages inequalities need to be tackled, perhaps through operating on the structure of labour markets, as well as allowing an individual right of litigation to tackle existing wage disparities. To this end, *Article 141(4) EC* introduces the radical and controversial possibility of *allowing* the Member States to adopt positive action measures to redress past disadvantages suffered by men or women in the labour market. From the Court's case law on a positive action provision found in Article 2(4) of the Equal Treatment Directive,[10] the Court will scrutinise such measures closely to ensure that they are not too general and deal with specific instances of inequality and underrepresentation of one sex.[11] The definition of what constitutes sex discrimination embraces discrimination against transsexuals,[12] but not discrimination on the ground of sexual orientation.[13] Given the fact that any new measures taken under the new legal base of *Article 137 EC* will be secondary legislation which cannot alter the scope of primary legislation found in the Treaty, *Article 141 EC* will continue, like its predecessor, Article 119 EC, to be a focus for exploring the constitutional boundaries of sex discrimination in Community law largely through the use of vertical and horizontal direct effect.

1.3 The history of EC labour law in the context of the Treaty of Amsterdam

1.3.1 Legal base issues

The Treaty of Amsterdam is a major turning point in the development of EC labour law for a number of reasons.[14] First of all, it consolidates a

---

[10] Council Directive 76/207/EEC, OJ 1976 L 39/40.

[11] In Case C-450/93 *Kalanke* v *Freie Hansestadt Bremen* [1995] ECR I-3051 the Court stated that the predecessor provision, Article 6(4) of the Social Policy Agreement (SPA) should, for the sake of consistency, be interpreted in accordance with Article 2(4) Equal Treatment Directive (ETD). However, in the light of the *Kalanke* ruling, *Article 141 EC* uses different, neutral wording.

[12] Case 13/94 *P* v *S and Cornwall CC* [1996] ECR I-2143. See also Case T-264/97 *D* v *Council*, judgment of 28 January 1999 (appeal lodged by *D*: Case C-122/99P, OJ 1999 C188/13 and Sweden has also commenced an independent action: Case C-125/99P, OJ 1999 C188/14).

[13] Case C-249/96 *Grant* v *SW Trains* [1998] ECR I-621.

[14] See Davies, P., 'The Emergence of European Labour Law' in McCarthy, W. (ed) *Legal Interventions in Industrial Relations* (Blackwell, Oxford, 1992); Barnard, C., 'EC "Social Policy"' in Craig, P. and De Burca, G. (eds) *The Evolution of EU Law* (OUP, Oxford, 1999).

number of political arrangements where unanimity between the Member States has been difficult to achieve. The development of a discrete area of EC labour law has been difficult because of a lack of political will to intervene in labour market regulation since 1957.[15] After receiving a report from a group of experts,[16] the framers of the original Treaty of Rome 1957 kept EC intervention to a minimum, focusing only upon the principle of non-discrimination on the grounds of nationality (Article 6 EC, now *Article 12 EC*), the free movement of workers (Article 48 EC, now *Article 39 EC*) and the establishment of a Social Fund to assist disadvantaged states in order to equalise labour costs, training and welfare costs. At the insistence of France, an equal pay provision (Article 119 EC, now *Article 141 EC*) was included as a competition measure rather than an employment protection measure.[17] There was no legal base to develop EC labour law other than the generic Articles 100 EC (now *Article 94*) and 235 (now *Article 308 EC*). Both Articles demanded unanimity voting in the Council and were triggered by showing a necessity for any proposed measures to fulfil the aims of the Common Market. In relation to Article 235 EC (*Article 308 EC*), it has to be the case that there is no other suitable legal base within the Treaty to generate the measure.[18]

In 1957 there was firstly a belief that the developed labour law/industrial relations systems of the Member States could continue intact without conflicting with the aims of European integration, and secondly an assumption that the functioning of the Common Market would bring about a raised standard of living of workers in the EC. This is seen in the Preamble to the Treaty, Article 2 EC, which sets out the aims of the Common Market and Article 117 EC which sets out the principles and aims of the rather limited Social Policy Chapter of the original Treaty of Rome 1957. These provisions can be compared with the wording of *Article 136 EC* which recognises an *explicit* role for the Community to bring about changes in the social policy arena. It is notable that the only provision in the original Social Policy Chapter of the Treaty of Rome 1957, Article 118 EC, speaks of the Commission promoting 'close co-operation' between the Member

---

[15] Summaries can be found in *Social Europe* 1/87 pp. 51–62; *Social Europe* 1/88 pp. 19–20.

[16] The Ohlin Report, International Labour Office; 'Social Aspects of European Economic Co-operation' (1956) 74 *International Labour Review* 99.

[17] See Szyszczak, E. 'Sex Inequalitites and Equal Value Claims' (1985) 48 *Modern Law Review* 139; *Cf.* Hoskyns, C. *Integrating Gender* (Verso, London, 1996).

[18] But see Chalmers, D. *European Union Law, Volume One. Law and EU Government* (Dartmouth, Aldershot, 1998) p. 212, who notes that Article 235 EC (now *Article 308 EC*) was used expansively and that no judicial limit was placed on its ambit until *Opinion 2/94, Accession to the European Convention for the Protection of Human Rights and Freedoms* [1996] ECR I-1759.

States in a number of areas relating to labour law: employment, working conditions, basic and advanced vocational training, social security, prevention of occupational accidents and diseases, occupational hygiene, labour law, the right of association and collective bargaining between employers and workers. The Court did rule that the Commission could take legally binding measures to give effect to its duties under Article 118 EC.[19]

The Court enhanced the role of Article 117 EC in that, while it could not give rise to direct effect,[20] it could be used as a teleological tool for interpreting other EC law provisions.[21] This is seen, for example, in one of the early equal pay cases, *Defrenne* v *Sabena (No. 2)*,[22] where the Court argued that where a pay inequality was due to sex discrimination, the lower wages should be raised to the level of the higher wages in order to comply with the aims of Article 117 EC.

As a result of the limited political commitment and fragile legal base on which to develop labour law measures, there was little legislative action in this field in the early years of the Common Market, outside of the development of an embryonic health and safety programme[23] and the development of one of the 'core freedoms' of the Common Market, the free movement of workers.

At the political level, a turning point in this *laissez-faire* position, can be traced back to 1972 when, on the eve of the first enlargement of the Common Market, the heads of state or government issued a Declaration after the Paris Summit wherein they outlined an attachment to developing the social as well as the economic side of the Common Market.[24] The Court of Justice emphasised the social side to the Common Market in one of its most famous rulings in *Defrenne* v *Sabena (No. 2)* where, in paragraph 10, it stated that the equal pay provision of Article 119 EC:

---

[19] Joined Cases 281/85, 283-85/85 and 287/85 *Germany and Others* v *Commission* [1987] ECR 3203.

[20] Joined Cases C-72/91 and C-73/91 *Firma Sloman Neptun Schiffahrts AG* v *Seebetriebsrat Bodo Ziesmer der Sloman Neptun Schiffahrts AG* [1993] ECR 887.

[21] Case 126/86 *Zaera* v *Instituto Nacional de la Seguridad Social y Tesorería General de la Seguridad Social* [1987] ECR 3697.

[22] Case 43/75 [1976] ECR 455.

[23] The Commission established an Industrial Health and Safety division in 1962, but out of three proposals put forward, only one was accepted by the Council: a harmonising measure dealing with the classification, labelling and packaging of certain dangerous substances, Council Directive 67/543/EEC, OJ 1967 L 196/1.

[24] There is some academic disagreement as to the reasons for this change in policy. Lodge argues that economic and fiscal crises were contributing factors (Lodge, J., 'Towards a Human Union: EEC Social Policy and European Integration' (1978) 4 *British Review of International Studies* 120. In contrast, Shanks argues the political upheavals of the 1960s led to a greater questioning of the underlying assumptions of the Treaty of Rome 1957 (Shanks, M., *European Social Policy Today and Tomorrow* (Pergamon Press, Oxford, 1977)).

... forms part of the social objectives of the Community, which is not merely an economic union, but at the same time intended, by common action, to ensure social progress and seek the constant improvement of the living and working conditions [of the people of Europe].[25]

The Commission issued a Social Action Programme 1974–6 which focused upon employment protection, industrial democracy and the rights of third-country nationals (TCNs) in the EC.[26] However, with the exception of sex equality[27] and health and safety initiatives,[28] only three core areas of labour law were addressed in hard law measures: redundancies,[29] acquired rights of workers on a transfer of a business[30] and insolvency rights.[31] By the end of the 1970s, a number of economic, political and social factors mitigated against any expansion of EC competence into the area of labour law. The recession, high unemployment, competition from unregulated labour markets of the Far East and the 'flexible' labour markets of the United States led to a change in attitude at the national level, with the restructuring of industry taking place across Europe. Thus, for most of the 1980s, Member States were only prepared to commit themselves to soft law measures and even in the more politically acceptable areas of intervention, such as health and safety[32] and sex equality,[33] EC action was minimal and *ad hoc*.[34]

During the late 1970s and 1980s the Court of Justice played a crucial role in keeping labour law issues alive. The willingness of national courts to refer cases to the Court under Article 177 (now *Article 234 EC*) created a dialogue at the Community level, not only in relation to the substantive content of EC labour law, but also aspects relating to procedural law and remedies.[35]

---

[25] Case 43/75 [1976] ECR 455.

[26] Bulletin of the EC, Supp. 2/74, 8.

[27] See Chapter 4.

[28] See Neal, A. and Wright, F. *European Communities Health and Safety Legislation* (Chapman Hall, London, 1992).

[29] Council Directive 75/129/EEC OJ 1975 L 48/29, amended by Council Directive 92/56/EC, OJ 1992 L 245/3.

[30] Council Directive 77/187/EEC, OJ 1977 L 61/26, amended by Council Directive 98/50/EC, OJ 1998 L 201/88.

[31] Council Directive 80/987/EEC, OJ 1980 L 283/23.

[32] The major concern of this era was with the control of dangerous substances.

[33] Only two pieces of 'hard law' were enacted during the 1980s: Council Directive 86/378/EEC on occupational social security and Council Directive 86/613 on equal treatment for the self-employed.

[34] See Hepple, B., 'The Crisis in EEC Labour Law' (1987) 18 *Industrial Law Journal* 129.

[35] See Szyszczak, E., 'Future Directions in European Union Social Policy Law' (1995) 24 *Industrial Law Journal* 31; Szyszczak, E., 'Social Rights as General Principles of Community Law' in Neuwahl, N. and Rosas, A. (eds) *The European Union and Human Rights* (Nijhoff, The Hague, 1995).

Jacques Delors, the visionary architect of the Internal Market programme (promoted through the Commission's White Paper[36]) saw a way of developing the social dimension of the Internal Market by arguing that equivalence of social laws was necessary in order to minimise 'social dumping' whereby Member States with low levels of employment costs and social protection would not only gain a competitive edge but would also be attractive for investors who could then either produce goods at lower costs or 'post' workers to other Member States to carry out contracts, thereby disrupting the smooth functioning of the Internal Market.[37] This fear of a 'race to the bottom', which the Internal Market programme supposedly fosters, can be challenged. It can be argued that some competition between different labour markets is necessary to foster a competitive climate. Where there are high sunk costs or special needs (for example, a skilled workforce, location factors) businesses may not have much flexibility in where they locate. Equally, employment laws will not be the only factor determing production location.

The resulting Single European Act 1987 (SEA) brought about development on three fronts. First, Delors promoted the idea of a 'social dialogue' whereby the two sides of industry could develop a dialogue which would focus upon a convergence of objectives and policies implemented through the Member States' existing industrial relations framework. It was hoped this would be more palatable than 'intervention from above'. The 'Val Duchesse' intersectoral social dialogue was launched on 31 January 1985, bringing together the European Trade Union Confederation (ETUC), the Union of Industrial Employers' Confederation of Europe (UNICE) and the European Centre of Enterprises with Public Participation (CEEP).[38]

The social dialogue was formalised in Article 118B EC, introduced by the SEA 1987. Although the social dialogue process was informal and voluntary, it resulted in a number of joint opinions, declarations, a couple of agreements and a number of 'summits' with the President of the Commission. In retrospect, it had great conceptual value in paving the way for widening the consultative role of the social partners, increasing the number of political actors in the legislative process and introducing the idea that

---

[36] COM(85) 310 final.

[37] This is perceived of as a real problem requiring Community intervention: Council Directive 97/1/EC, OJ 1997 L 18/1; Proposal for a Council Directive Extending the Freedom to Provide Cross-Border Services to Third-Country Nationals Established Within the Community COM (99) 3 final (OJ 1999 C 67/17) and Proposal for a Directive of the European Parliament and of the Council on the Posting of Workers Who are Third Country-Nationals for the Provision of Cross-Border Services COM (99) 3 final (OJ 1999 C 67/3).

[38] See Chapter 2 for details.

collective bargaining and collective agreements could have a role in the Community legal structure.

A second development was to break the use of unanimity voting (or, in other words, the threat of a veto to stall progress of Commission initiatives) for labour law issues. Article 118A EC granted express power to the Community to enact legislation, using qualified majority voting and the co-operation procedure with the Parliament in areas concerning the working environment, particularly in the field of health and safety measures. Looking back, this was an ingenious device. On the one hand, it allowed for further progress in the field of health and safety, which was relatively uncontentious. On the other hand, it introduced a wider concept of the 'working environment'. In Nordic law this was a wide-ranging concept which could go beyond pure health and safety matters to embrace the organisation of work and aspects of contractual employment protection rights.[39] Neal argues that the area of health and safety has proved to be one of the most high-profile examples of an interface between the 'social' as contrasted with the 'economic' dimension of the single market envisaged in the Single European Act 1987.[40] This period is called a 'programmatic' phase by Neal.[41] One key to the success of the programme lies in the use of a 'Framework Directive'[42] to establish general principles followed by a series of 'daughter Directives' addressing specific risks.[43] During the period of 1989–92, the initiatives from the Commission 'flowed thick and fast'[44] as it sought to implement the health and safety ideas of the 1989 Social Charter (discussed below). In 1992 the Commission designated the year as the 'European Year of Safety, Hygiene and Health Protection at Work'. This idea had originally been suggested in 1987 in a Council Resolution[45] and was intended to raise public awareness of the European programme.[46] The Commission also made a proposal for a European Safety, Hygiene and Health Agency which was established in 1994.[47]

The Commission moved cautiously in its proposals based on Article 118A EEC, which were not directly part of the health and safety pro-

---

[39] See Hydén, H., 'IV. Working Environment' in Bruun, N. *et al.* (eds) *The Nordic Labour Relations Model* (Dartmouth, Aldershot, 1992).

[40] Neal, A., 'Regulating Health and Safety at Work: Developing European Union Policy for the Millennium' (1998) 14/3 *The International Journal of Comparative Labour Law and Industrial Relations* 17.

[41] *Ibid.*

[42] Council Directive 89/391/EEC, OJ 1989 L 183/1.

[43] See Nielsen, R. and Szyszczak, E. *The Social Dimension of the European Union* (Handelshøjsklens Forlag, Copenhagen, 1997) pp. 336–44.

[44] Neal, *supra* n. 40.

[45] OJ C 1988 28/1.

[46] COM (93) 627 final.

[47] Council Regulation (EC) No. 2062/94 of 18 July 1994, amended.

gramme. The scope of Article 118A EC was enhanced by the ruling of the Court of Justice in *UK v Council*.[48] The United Kingdom brought a long-threatened infringement action using *Article 230 EC* (ex Article 173 EC) for annulment of Council Directive 93/104/EEC,[49] which regulates working time. The UK argued that the Directive was *ultra vires* since it went beyond the scope of Article 118A EC. In his Opinion, Advocate General Léger relied upon the Danish interpretation of the concept of the 'working environment' arguing that the concept was broad enough to embrace the performance of work, conditions at the workplace, technical equipment and substances used at work. Thus, in Denmark, legislation covered measures concerning working hours, psychological factors, the way work is performed, training in hygiene and safety, protection of young workers, worker representation, and security against dismissal or any other attempt to undermine working conditions. He argued further that the concept of the working environment is not immutable but reflects the social and technological evolution of society.

The Court looked to see if the principal aim of the Working Time Directive was to protect the health and safety of workers. If this was so, Article 118A EC was an appropriate legal base even if the Directive might have ancillary effects on the functioning of the Internal Market. Following the Advocate General, the Court ruled that the recitals to the Directive gave a clear indication that the regulation of working time did have an impact upon workers' physical and psychological health.

In addition to Article 118A EC, the SEA 1987 also introduced a new legal base for the enactment of general measures affecting the function and establishment of the Internal Market, Article 100A EC (now *Article 95*). Again qualified majority voting and the co-operation procedure with the European Parliament were designed to ease the introduction of more EC legislation. From a labour law perspective, Article 100A EC (*Article 95 EC*) has limited potential since, while Article 100A(3) EC (now *Article 95(3) EC*) provides that where health and safety measures are proposed, the Commission must take as a base a high level of protection; Article 100A(2) EC (now *Article 95(2)EC*) provides that unanimity voting is required for, *inter alia*, measures relating to the free movement of persons and the rights and interests of employed persons. Because of this ambiguity between Article 100A(1) EC and 100A(2) EC, the Commission moved cautiously in presenting proposals based on Article 100A(1) relating to matters of labour law. In determining the correct use of Article 100A(1) EC, the Court will look to see if the

---

[48] Case C-84/94 [1996] ECR I-5755. See Fitzpatrick, B., 'Straining the Definition of Health and Safety' (1997) 26 *Industrial Law Journal* 115.
[49] OJ 1993 L 307/18.

principal aim of the measure is of market liberalisation or whether its focus is upon another policy, such as health and safety protection. The Member States may continue to apply national provisions even where harmonising legislation has been passed by a qualified majority vote under Article 100A(1) EC. The Member States must notify the Commission under Article 100A(4) EC (now *Article 95(4) EC*) and show that the national provisions are not a method of arbitrary discrimination or a disguised restriction on trade between Member States. Denmark and Germany, in particular, have considered the use of *Article 95(4) EC* (ex Article 100A(4) EC) where EC measures relating to the working environment, particularly the use of dangerous substances at work, fall below the standards set at the national level.[50] Two of the most important labour law measures to be enacted in the technical harmonisation field are the Machinery Directive[51] and the Directive on the marketing of personal protective equipment.[52]

Finally, the third development from the SEA 1987 was the reform and realignment of the Community's Structural Funds as a result of Article 130 a–e EC (now *Articles 158–162*) which identified economic and social cohesion as one of the six priority areas in the completion of the Internal Market.[53] As we will see, the use of the structural funds is an adjunct to the development of a number of Community labour market policies.

1.3.2 Social rights issues

An attempt to make social rights an integrated part of Community policy was made during 1988/1989. A working party of the Commission proposed a set of minimum social provisions which were formulated as a Charter of the Fundamental Social Rights of Workers in 1989.[54] On 9 December 1989, 11 out of the then 12 Member States approved the Charter. The government of the United Kingdom refused to accept it. As a result, the 1989 Social Charter could not be integrated into the EC Treaty and its legal status is obscure. It is a political declaration accepted by the

---

[50] See Case C-41/93 *Commission* v *France* [1994] ECR I-1829; Case C-127/97 *Burstein* v *Freistaat Bayern* [1998] ECR I-6005.

[51] Council Directive 89/392/EEC, OJ 1989 L 183/9.

[52] Council Directive 89/686/EEC, OJ 1989 L 399/18.

[53] Such measures must not prejudice the application of *Article 127 EC* which provides:
1. The Community shall contribute to a high level of employment by encouraging co-operation between Member States and by supporting and, if necessary, complementing their action. In doing so, the competences of the Member States shall be respected.
2. The objective of a high level of employment shall be taken into consideration in the formulation and implementation of Community policies and activities.

[54] See Hepple, B., 'The Implementation of the Community Charter of Fundamental Social Rights' (1990) 53 Modern Law Review 64; Bercusson, B., 'The European Community's Charter of Fundamental Social Rights For Workers' (1990) 53 *Modern Law Review* 624.

majority of Member States. The 1989 Social Charter was not particularly dramatic since most of the 'core' set of social rights it identified were familiar ideas in international, EC and domestic law. Equally, it focused upon 'workers' – one of the economic factors in European integration – and did not adopt the wording of the first draft offered by the Commission which used the term 'citizens'.[55] The most disappointing aspect of the 1989 Social Charter was that it did not offer a new legal base upon which this core set of social rights could be developed.[56] As a result, the Commission adopted an Action Programme[57] to implement the 1989 Social Charter in which it was obliged to make do with the existing legal bases of Article 118, Article 118A, Article 100, Article 100A and Article 235 EC (as well as specific bases within the free movement of persons provisions).

The legislative labyrinth of the EC Treaty was used by the Council to stall Commission initiatives.[58] Combined with the inherent caution of the Commission's approach, very few measures were enacted under the 1989 Social Charter, and Nielsen and Szyszczak[59] have argued that this era of EC Labour Law is now closed.[60] The Charter was useful in refocusing labour law issues around social/fundamental rights issues and the starting up of a dialogue on labour law intervention at the EC level after a decade of stagnation. Outside of the area of health and safety legislation, only six major labour law Directives were enacted under the 1989 Social Charter Action Programme. These were a Directive on an employer's obligation to inform employees of the conditions applicable to the contract of employment/employment relationship,[61] a revision of the 1975 Directive on collective redundancies,[62] a Directive giving rights of employment protection to pregnant women and women who have recently given birth or who are breastfeeding,[63] a Directive on the organisation of working time,[64] a

---

[55] See Bercusson, B. *European Labour Law* (Butterworths, London, 1996), Ch. 37.

[56] See Vogel-Polsky, E., 'What Future Is There for a Social Europe Following the Strasbourg Summit?' (1990) 19 *Industrial Law Journal* 65.

[57] COM(89) 568 final, Brussels.

[58] See *First Report on the Application of the Community Charter of the Fundamental Social Rights of Workers*, COM (91) 511 final.

[59] Nielsen, R. and Szyszczak, E. *op. cit.*, p. 37.

[60] The Charter is quoted in the Preamble to a number of Directives: Council Directive 91/533/EEC (information on the employment contract); Council Directive 92/56/EC (amendment to collective redundancies); Council Directive 93/104/EC (working time); Council Directive 94/45 (European works councils); Council Directive 96/34/EC (parental leave); Council Directive 97/81 (part-time work); Council Directive 98/59 (amended collective redundancies).

[61] Council Directive 91/533/EEC, OJ 1991 L 288/32.

[62] Council Directive 75/129/EEC, OJ 1975 L 48/29 amended by Council Directive 92/56/EEC, OJ 1992 L 245/3.

[63] Council Directive 92/85/EEC, OJ 1992 L 348/1.

[64] Council Directive 93/104 EC, OJ 1993 L 307/18.

Directive regulating the employment of young people,[65] and a Directive on the posting of workers.[66] The newer Directives agreed under the Social Dialogue process also refer to the Social Charter in their recitals or Preambles and the future use of the Charter will also be that of a teleological role as a result of *Article 136 EC*.

1.3.3 Maastricht: a labour law of bits and pieces

Thus, while the SEA 1987 introduced only minor, cosmetic changes, it was a turning point in the development of attitudes towards EC labour law. The Treaty on European Union 1993 also introduced a number of changes which have affected the development of EC labour law, for example the introduction and formalisation of the principle of subsidiarity in Article 3b EC (now *Article 5*), the introduction of a concept of citizenship of the Union in Article 8 EC (now *Articles 17–22 EC*), as well as changes to the Titles on education, social policy and vocational training.[67] An attempt to introduce a coherent social policy/labour law chapter to the EC Treaty was opposed by the UK government. In a rather ugly, legally contentious move the proposals were withdrawn from the main body of the Treaty and attached by a Protocol as a Social Policy Agreement (SPA).[68] This provided for a novel procedure in EC law-making by allowing the then 11 Member States to use the EC Institutions under the SPA to proceed where it was clear that the United Kingdom would block any Commission proposals for new labour laws. The idea of a 'Social Chapter' and the ensuing SPA were problematic for the United Kingdom since, for the first time, a clearly defined legal base for Community labour law could be found and, in some areas, allowed for qualified majority voting. As if this were not enough, it also provided a role for the social partners to take over Commission proposals and develop a European-wide collective agreement. Furthermore, labour rights were linked to fundamental rights ideas as a result of the 1989 Social Charter. There is, therefore, little wonder that the then Conservative government of the United Kingdom wanted such approaches to labour law regulation consigned to the outer realms of Community responsibility, or better still, left to the other Member States to pursue.

---

[65] Council Directive 94/33/EC, OJ 1994 L 216/12.

[66] Council Directive 96/71/EC, OJ 1997 L 18/1, discussed in Chapter 3.

[67] See Shaw, J., 'Social Policy after the Treaty of Maastricht' (1992) 3 *The Journal of Social Welfare and Family Law* 255.

[68] See Curtin, D., 'The Constitutional Structure of the Union: A Europe of Bits and Pieces' (1993) 30 *Common Market Law Review* 17; Szyszczak, E., 'Social Policy: a Happy Ending or a Re-Working of the Fairy Tale?' in O'Keeffe, D. and Twomey, P. (eds) *Legal Issues of the Maastricht Treaty* (Chancery/Wiley, Chichester, 1993).

1.4 The importance of the Treaty of Amsterdam

Despite the novel approach of side-lining the United Kingdom government,[69] at Maastricht very few measures were enacted under the SPA: by the signing of the Treaty of Amsterdam only one collective agreement had been reached on parental leave[70] and one Directive adopted on Works Councils.[71] The difficulties of incorporating collective bargaining into the decision-making process of the EU are discussed in Chapter 2. Again, it was only in the area of health and safety that labour law measures were adopted.[72]

Fortuitously for the EU, the General Election on 1 May 1997 ushered in a new Labour Party government in the United Kingdom with a more positive approach to the EU. This led to the new arrangements in the Treaty of Amsterdam as well as interim measures to allow the Directives on works councils,[73] the burden of proof[74] and parental leave[75] to apply to the United Kingdom. However, the United Kingdom is moving cautiously adopting a new approach to labour market regulation alongside a reluctance to embrace a wholesale platform of individual employment protection rights or to reform collective labour law.[76]

---

[69] Other Member States were reluctant to allow the Community to take competence over social policy issues: Binyion, M., 'EC Voices Doubts on the Social Charter', *The Times*, 27 November 1990. The Commission tried to keep the UK involved for as long as possible by using the old legal bases of the EC Treaty to propose measures and only resorting to the SPA as a last resort. As a result, some of the Commission's proposals were watered down, seen, for example, in Council Directive 92/85/ EC (pregnant workers' Directive) discussed in Chapter 5.

[70] Council Directive 96/34/EC, OJ 1995 L 145/4. Amended and extended to the UK in Council Directive 97/75, OJ 1998 L 10/24. The first measure to pass through the SPA, the Directive on European Works Councils, Council Directive 94/45/EC, failed to utilise the social dialogue effectively and it was enacted by a Council Directive.

[71] Council Directive 94/45/EC, OJ 1994 L 254/64, amended and extended to the United Kingdom, Council Directive 97/74, OJ 1997 L 10/22.

[72] A new action programme on safety, hygiene and health and work (1996–2000) provides a framework. Five Directives have been adopted: on chemical agents (98/24/EC); chemical, physical and biological agents (96/94/EC); biological agents (97/59/EC) and (97/65/EC); and protection of workers from the risks related to exposure to carcinogens (97/42/EC). In addition, there are proposals for Directives on protection of risks from explosive atmospheres, exposure to physical agents and on transport activities and workplaces on transport.

[73] *Supra* n. 71.

[74] Council Directive 97/80/EC, OJ 1998 L 14/6, as amended and extended to the United Kingdom, Directive 98/52/EC, OJ 1998 L 14/205.

[75] Council Directive 96/34/EC, OJ 1996 L 145/9, as amended and extended to the United Kingdom, Directive 97/75/EC, OJ 1998 L 10/24.

[76] See Kenner, J., 'The EC Employment Title and the "Third Way": Making Soft Law Work?' (1999) *The International Journal of Comparative Labour Law and Industrial Relations* 33.

1.4.1 The Treaty of Amsterdam: a summary

The Treaty of Amsterdam is important because it brings the United Kingdom back into the fold by incorporating into the main body of the EC Treaty the notorious 'Social Chapter' of Maastricht.

A second aspect of the Treaty of Amsterdam is to consolidate a number of developments in Community labour law as a result of interventions by the Court of Justice. This is seen in the amendments made to the existing equal pay provision found in Article 119 EC by *Article 141 EC* and in the addition of the words 'equality between men and women' to the list of purposes of the Community found in *Article 2 EC*.

A third change brought about by the Treaty of Amsterdam is the most dramatic and represents a radical shift in Community law thinking about labour market issues. At Maastricht, Article 2 EC (also now *Article 2 EC*) was revised to include the words 'and a high level of employment' in the list of aims of the Union, and now in *Article 2* 'employment and social protection' are subtly moved up from fourth place to second place in the list of purposes of the Union. Competitiveness has joined convergence. In the ruling in *Albany International BV*[77] the Court of Justice recognises the equivalence of the social and economic objectives of the Treaty:

> ... it is important to bear in mind that, under Article 3(g) and (i) of the EC Treaty (now, after amendment, Article 3(1)(g) and (j) EC), the activities of the Community are to include not only a 'system ensuring that competition in the internal market is not distorted' but also 'a policy in the social sphere'. Article 2 of the EC Treaty (now, after amendment, Article 2 EC) provides that a particular task of the Community is 'to promote throughout the Community a harmonious and balanced development of economic activities' and 'a high level of employment and of social protection'.

It is the new indent to *Article 3 EC* which establishes a new co-ordinated employment strategy as an activity of the Community which paves the way for a new *Title VIII* of the EC Treaty which has the most impact on labour law strategies for the Member States. Within this Title there is now explicit acceptance of Community responsibility for the co-ordination of macro-economic policy *vis-à-vis* national labour markets. A new *Article 125 EC* charges the Member States *and the Community* with the task of working towards developing a co-ordinated strategy for employment, in particular for promoting a skilled, trained adaptable workforce and labour markets which are responsive to economic change and which achieve the objectives set out in the new *Article 2 EC* and *Article 2 TEU*.

---

[77] Case C-67/96 *Albany International BV v Stichting Bedrijfspensioenfonds Textielindustrie*, judgment of 21 September 1999, para 54.

The need for flexible labour markets was a view promoted by the new British Labour government but not all of the Member States take such a broad view of flexibility and the French government has maintained a different approach. *Article 126(2) EC* states that the task of promoting employment is a matter of common concern with the proviso that national practices related to the responsibilities of management and labour should be taken into account. *Article 127 EC* provides that the objective of a 'high level of employment' is a Community task and an objective which must be taken into consideration in the formulation and implementation of Community policies and economic policies is finalised in *Article 126(1) EC* which states that:

Member States, through their employment policies, shall contribute to the achievement of the objectives referred to in *Article 125* in a way consistent with the broad guidelines of the economic policies of the Member States adopted pursuant to *Article 99(2) EC.*

1.5 Why the need for a European Employment Strategy?

At the time of the signing of the Treaty of Amsterdam, EU unemployment stood at an official figure of 18 million people. The level of unemployment varied widely from Member State to Member State with the highest levels of unemployment found in Spain (19%), followed by Finland (13%), France (12.6%) and Italy (12.1%), and the lowest levels were to be found in Luxembourg (3.7%), Austria (4.5%) and Denmark (5.8%).[78]

Meulders and Plasman[79] argue that European unemployment displays a number of characteristics in the form of high, long-term unemployment rates, especially for young people and women, low exit rates from unemployment and a weak relationship between economic growth and the creation of jobs. What worried the EU was that whatever economic growth the completion of the Internal Market and the introduction of Economic and Monetary Union (EMU) might bring, it would never resist massive unemployment in Europe. Another reason for the interest in unemployment is the need to create competitive growth. The Commission has argued that while unemployment is a weakness and the source of a large social cost, the capacity to *create* jobs is an area where the EU has a competitive edge over the United States and Japan.[80] To this end, the

---

[78] *Eurostat*, November 1997.

[79] Meulders, D. and Plasman, R., 'European Economic Policies and Social Quality' in Beck, W. *et al.* (eds) *The Social Quality of Europe* (The Hague, Kluwer, 1997).

[80] *Communication from the Commission to the Council, the European Parliament, the Economic and Social Committee and the Committee of the Regions, Growth and Employment in the Stability-Oriented Framework of EMU Economic Reflections in View of the Forthcoming 1998 Broad Guidelines,* COM (1998) 103 final.

Community began searching for solutions. In a White Paper, *Growth, Competitiveness and Employment*,[81] the Commission explored a number of strategies which led to the Essen Council Meeting 1994 drawing up five priorities around which the Member States were invited to organise their employment policies in order to stimulate job creation. These were known as the Essen Priorities:

1 improving employment opportunities for the working population by promoting investment in vocational training;
2 increasing the employment intensiveness of growth;
3 reducing non-wage labour costs, particularly for non-qualified workers;
4 improving efficiency of employment policies by avoiding measures that negatively affect the availability for work and by replacing passive policies with active ones;
5 improving measures to affect groups most affected by unemployment (women, young people, older employees, long-term unemployed).

There were, however, underlying tensions in this approach. Firstly, unemployment was twinned with the combating of social exclusion as the two dominant goals of social policy. Secondly, linked to this, was the fact that the Essen Priorities did not dovetail with the Maastricht convergence criteria for EMU and in fact were in direct conflict with them. The convergence criteria are set out in Article 4 of the Protocol on the Convergence Criteria referred to in Article 109j EC. They are firstly, the avoidance of an excessive budgetary deficit (defined as where the planned or actual deficit exceeds 3% of GDP or total government debt exceeds 60% of GDP). Secondly, a Member State's currency must remain within the narrow margins of the ERM for two years without devaluation or severe tensions. Thirdly, long-term interest rates of a Member State must not exceed by more than 2% the average of the three Member States with lowest rates of inflation. The need to constrain budgets and reduce public debt inevitably led to cuts – some drastic – in the Member States' public spending, but also, as Meulders and Plasman point out, at least three of the Essen Priorities challenge the twin policy of social exclusion being put forward by the EU; for example, the flexibilisation of work and salaries may lead to increased job insecurity and poverty, the reduction of non-salary costs is a euphemism for reducing social security contributions, and Priority Number 4 inevitably leads to lower unemployment compensation.

The Commission urged the Member States to take account of the Essen Priorities in their convergence programmes and made a number of propos-

---

[81] COM (93) 700.

als for Decisions in the employment field,[82] but there was no means to compel the Member States to co-ordinate their action. A number of questions hang over the introduction of EMU; in particular, what structural mechanisms will take the place of exchange-rate mechanisms?[83] Many of the responses from economists are negative. Feldstein[84] argues that imposing a single interest rate and an inflexible exchange rate on the Member States which are characterised by different economic shocks, inflexible wages, low labour mobility and separate national fiscal systems without significant cross-border cyclical transfers will in fact raise the overall rate of cyclical unemployment among EMU members. Equally, he argues, the emphasis upon common economic and social policies will reduce the scope for experimentation and competition that would otherwise lead to reductions in the current high levels of structural unemployment. In contrast, the Commission argues that the macroeconomic policies of EMU enhance the prospects of avoiding the obstacles which have, on repeated occasions, brought economic growth and job creation to a halt.[85] This is because exchange-rate turbulence will be prevented among participating Member States, stability conflicts will be avoided and a more stable and less risk-prone environment for investment will be created.

These issues help to explain why the Treaty of Amsterdam created the employment chapter of *Title VIII*, and help to explain the dynamic of its implementation and the linkages with macro-economic policy. Kenner[86] has argued that the nature of the policy being created is dominated by the voices of the revisionist governments of Europe. Its success may be contingent upon the success of those governments in proving to the European electorate that such policies work.

The Member States decided to 'fast-track' these provisions of the Amsterdam Treaty by calling an extraordinary Summit Meeting of the heads of state or government in Luxembourg on 20–21 November 1997.

---

[82] EC Commission, *Follow-up to the Essen Council on Employment* COM (95) 74.

[83] Peters, T., 'Economic and Monetary Union and Labour Markets: What to Expect?' (1995) 134 *International Labour Review* 315; Teague, P., 'Monetary Union and Social Europe' (1998) 8 *Journal of European Social Policy* 117.

[84] Feldstein, M., 'The Political Economy of the European Economic and Monetary Union: Political Sources of an Economic Liability' (1997) 11 *Journal of Economic Perspectives* 23.

[85] Communication From the Commission, Growth and Employment in the Stability-Oriented Framework of EMU, COM (1998) 103 final.

[86] Kenner, J., 'The EC Employment Title and the "Third Way": Making Soft Law Work?' (1999) *The International Journal of Comparative Labour Law and Industrial Relations* 33. See also Tucker, C., 'The Luxembourg Process: the UK view' (2000) *The International Journal of Comparative Labour Law and Industrial Relations* 33.

This has become known as the 'Jobs Summit' and started a series of 'Processes' at the European Union level.[87]

1.6 The fast-track implementation of *Title VIII*

The Commission produced a set of guidelines for Member States' employment policies in October 1997[88] and these were commented upon by the social partners and the European Parliament. Tension was created in that the Commission's original suggestion was that concrete targets for reducing unemployment should be set, whereas the Member States did not want such rigid employment strategies to be established.[89] The Commission conceded that any targets should be for guidance only, and attention was focused on how the Member States could achieve co-ordination of their employment policies to create convergence of labour market policy and employment levels.

The model to be followed seems to be similar to the *convergence* strategy set out to achieve economic and monetary union in the TEU. This is different from the 'co-ordinated strategy for employment' set out in *Article 125 EC*.[90] The Commission describes the strategy as a 'convergence process' but points out that while the reward for compliance was entry to the EURO-club, there is no tangible reward for compliance with the employment strategy:

> ... but at stake is the credibility of employment policy and the political pressure which results from failure to achieve the criteria. Experience has shown that peer pressure can be as effective as legal or market based sanctions.[91]

The Member States were invited to draw up National Employment Action Plans (NAP) on the basis of the Commission's preparatory guidelines by June 1998. The NAPs were organised around what is described as the 'four pillars' of the Luxembourg Jobs Summit of November 1997:

---

[87] At the time of writing in December 1999, there are three processes in operation: the 'Luxembourg' process of the Luxembourg Jobs Summit, November 1997; the 'Cardiff Process' of the Cardiff Summit June 1998, which adopted a comprehensive approach to structural reforms in services, product and capital markets; and the 'Cologne Process' from the Cologne Summit of June 1999, which initiated The European Pact for Employment for closer co-operation and to boost employment and economic reforms.

[88] COM (97) 497 final.

[89] France and Germany subsequently asked the other Member States to rethink this strategy, writing an open letter urging for targets to be set: *Financial Times*, 9 December 1998.

[90] See Biagi, M., 'The Implementation of the Amsterdam Treaty With Regard to Employment Co-ordination or Convergence?' (1998) 14 *The International Journal of Comparative Labour Law and Industrial Relations* 325.

[91] European Commission, *Forum Special 5 Years of Social Policy*, OOPEC, Luxembourg, 1999, p. 13.

employability, entrepreneurship, adaptability and equal opportunities. After assessment of each Member State, Recommendations will be drafted by the Commission and made by the European Council.[92] This policy is based upon voluntarism with no means to compel the Member States to act and no sanctions for failure to implement the European Council's Recommendations. The 1998 Guidelines were adopted at the Council meeting of 15 December 1997 in the form of a Resolution.[93]

The commitment of the Member States to *Title VIII* on employment is remarkable. Within a time frame of only four months, all 15 of the Member States delivered a NAP. These are commented upon by the Commission in a Communication, *From Guidelines to Action: The National Action Plans for Employment*.[94] The NAPs were discussed at the Cardiff Summit in June 1998. One development from this Summit was a discussion as to whether the four pillars defined in the Luxembourg Summit of November 1997 should be reduced to three. It was argued by some Member States that equal opportunities policy should be mainstreamed into the other three pillars. At the Council meeting of October 1998 it was agreed to continue with four pillars but to encourage mainstreaming of equal opportunities into the other three pillars.[95] It was also agreed that equal opportunities should be restricted to sex equality. The Guidelines for 1999 followed the same structure as the 1998 Guidelines arguing for the need for stability and consistency. However, as well as mainstreaming equal opportunities, there are some additions: the analysis of, and possible adjustments to, the compensation and taxation schemes of the Member States and the need to take fuller account of disadvantaged social groups. The 1999 Guidelines are preceded by an introduction stressing the need and importance of common statistical indicators and calling upon the Member States to set themselves national targets which, in some instances, can be quantified. The Guidelines for 2000[96] follow the same structure adding one more Guideline to make a total of 22. From 1999 onwards the Member States will submit only one report (in mid-June) on the implementation of the National Action Plan and the adjustment of the Plan to the latest EU guidelines.

The November 'Jobs Summit' thus gave a foretaste of the obligations set out in the new *Article 128 EC*, which obliges the European Council to consider the employment situation in the Community each year and adopt conclusions on the basis of a joint annual report by the Council. The

---

[92] The first set of Recommendations was produced in 1999, COM (99) 442.
[93] OJ 1998 C 30/1.
[94] COM (98) 316.
[95] In the Commission's Recommendations, COM (99) 442, the Commission notes that very few attempts have been made at gender mainstreaming.
[96] COM (99) 441.

European Council shall draw up an annual set of Guidelines for the Member States acting by a qualified majority on a proposal from the Commission and after consulting the European Parliament, the Economic and Social Committee, the Committee of the Regions and the new Employment Committee established under the new *Article 130 EC*.[97] The Member States are to take account of the Guidelines in their employment policies. Again, the marriage of employment policies and economic policies is confirmed in that the employment Guidelines must be consistent with the broad economic guidelines adopted under *Article 99(2) EC*. The Member States' actions are to be monitored by their presentation of an annual report to the Council and the Commission. This report will provide for a review of the Member States' actions and the most far-reaching intrusion into the Member States' autonomy is to be found in *Article 128(4) EC*, which allows the Council to act by a *qualified majority* on a recommendation from the Commission[98] to make recommendations to a Member State on how to conduct its employment policy. After the review process, the Council and the Commission are to make a joint annual report to the European Council on the employment situation in the Community and on the implementation of the guidelines for employment.[99] Biagi[100] has noted that the fast-track implementation of *Title VIII* has resulted in the Commission pursuing a form of condemnation of various Member States' policies as well as moving Community competence towards *convergence* of employment policies rather than co-ordination. In an interview in the *Financial Times* on 9 November 1999, the new Commissioner for Social Affairs stated that this was a personal policy on the part of the previous Commissioner, Padraig Flynn, and that she will adopt a less aggressive tone.

---

[97] The new *Article 130 EC* states that the Employment Committee's tasks will be to monitor the employment situation and employment policies in the Member States and the Community and, without prejudice to *Article 207 EC,* to formulate opinions at the request of either the Council or the Commission, or, on its own initiative to contribute to the Council meetings referred to in the new *Article 128 EC.*

[98] The draft Recommendations were adopted by the Commission on 8 September 1999. They are seen as part of an 'annual employment package' along with the draft Joint (Council and Commission) Employment Report 1999; Proposal for guidelines for Member States' Employment Policies 2000 examined by the Labour and Social Affairs and ECOFIN Councils. The first debate on the 'annual employment package' took place on 8 October 1999.

[99] The first overview Report on Employment Performance in the EU was adopted on 14 October 1998. In the Report it is argued that the aim of this exercise is to achieve an effective measure of the Member States' economies. The focus is upon employment and the employment potential of the non-employed in the EU pointing to where the Member States can improve their NAPs. One fear which emerges from this first report is the fact that the EU's employment rate has declined in relation to that of the USA.

[100] *Supra* n. 90.

Lawyers are now faced with a new typology of measures at the EU level. Although the European Parliament and the social partners have been consulted, the operation of this new *Title VIII* bears the hallmarks of lawyers' criticisms of the inter-governmental pillars of the EU. Decisions are being taken without full democratic input or accountability and the legal status – and binding nature – of the measures taken has yet to be clarified.[101]

The European Employment Strategy (EES) has had a spill-over effect into the use of the structural funds to support projects which complement the EES.[102]

1.7 The future of the European Employment Strategy

Treating labour market regulation as a macroeconomic policy issue in the same way that fiscal policy has been treated seems, at first sight, a rather naïve 'quick fix' for tackling what is the underlying problem – unemployment. As the Commission's Green[103] and White Papers[104] on social policy reveal, there are underlying tensions between the Member States (and within the Member States) as to whether, and how, labour markets can, and should, be regulated. In attempting to push forward a 'European social model', the Commission is faced with a variety of labour markets in Europe which, when compared with the United States' labour market, are highly regulated, but the degree and method of regulation varies between the Member States: the United Kingdom, bearing the legacy of the Conservative governments and the caution of 'New Labour', is the least regulated 'free market', and Germany is setting the standard for a 'social market' and a 'flexibly co-ordinated approach'. Most of the 'old' continental Member States, the Nordic states as well as the new-found democracies of the Mediterranean states in the 1980s have adopted, to varying degrees, this latter model – tempered with newer ideas of civil liberties.

The major task for the EU will be to find a route which can encompass both highly regulated markets and a *laissez-faire* approach which flexible labour markets demand. The problem facing Europe is that the labour

---

[101] These ideas are explored in Szyszczak, E., 'The Evolving European Employment Strategy' in J. Shaw (ed.) *Social Law and Policy in an Evolving European Law* (Hart, Oxford, 2000).

[102] The rules of the European Social Fund and the European Regional Development Fund have been amended to support projects which complement the EES: Regulation 1260/1999 of 21 June 1999 laying down general provisions on the Structural Funds, OJ 1999 L 161/1 and the European Investment Bank launched the Amsterdam Special Action Plan four weeks after the Amsterdam Summit of June 1997 (http://eib/eu.int/pub/news/asap-ir3.htm).

[103] European Policy Options for the Future, COM (93) 551.

[104] European Social Policy – A Way Forward for the Union, COM (94) 333.

markets also vary widely in terms of wage levels, employment growth, unemployment (both in terms of levels and nature, i.e. the mix of unemployed between skilled/unskilled, male/female, race/ethnic groups) trade union organisation and density. There is a division at the political level as to how far regulation contributes to levels of employment growth and how best to manage employment growth. France, in particular, with the inheritance of the Mitterand philosophy of the 1980s, has a particularly distinctive way of tackling unemployment by using regulatory measures to reduce the *size* of the labour market through measures such as work-sharing, early retirement, and reducing the working week. In contrast, other Member States have reacted against Keynsian macroeconomic policies and focused attention upon microeconomic strategies. At the forefront of this policy is the British attempt to use the European stage to push home the need for *co-ordinated deregulation*.

1.8 Widening the concept of discrimination

The Treaty of Amsterdam creates a new legal base for further measures to combat wider forms of discrimination in *Article 13 EC*. Acting on a Commission proposal and after consulting the European Parliament, the Council, voting unanimously, may take 'appropriate action to combat discrimination based on sex, racial or ethnic origin, religion or belief, disability, age or sexual orientation'. This new Treaty provision is in response to wider lobbying and test-case litigation strategies within the Member States.[105] Competence to address race discrimination has long been a contentious issue at the Community level[106] and while there has been much soft law in this area in the form of Resolutions and Recommendations, the Member States and the Commission have maintained that there was no legal base in Community law to develop race discrimination legislation. Article 6 EC (new *Article 12 EC*) which forbids discrimination on the ground of nation-

---

[105] See Szyszczak, E., 'Building A European Constitutional Order: Prospects For A General Non-Discrimination Standard' in Dashwood, A. and O'Leary, S. (eds) *The Principle of Equal Treatment in EC Law* (Sweet and Maxwell, London, 1997).

[106] See Szyszczak, E., 'Race Discrimination: The Limits of Market Equality?' in Hepple, B. and Szyszczak, E. (eds) *Race Discrimination: The Limits of Law* (Mansell, London, 1992); Gregory, J., 'Racial Discrimination and the EC' (1993) 22 *Industrial Law Journal* 59; Bindman, G., 'Europe Against Racism: An Uncertain Future' in Konstadinidis, S. (ed.) *A People's Europe Tuning a Concept into Content* (Dartmouth, Aldershot, 1999); Gearty, C., 'The Internal and External "Other" in the Union Legal Order: Racism, Religious Intolerance' in Alston, P. (ed.) *The EU and Human Rights* (OUP, Oxford, 1999); Hervey, T., 'Putting Europe's House in Order: Racism, Race Discrimination and Xenophobia' in O'Keeffe, D. and Twomey, P. (eds) *The Treaty of Amsterdam* (Hart, Oxford, 1999).

ality has been confined by the more specific Treaty provisions and secondary legislation protects only nationals of one of the Member States. Similarly, the Citizenship of the Union provisions found in the old Article 8 EC (new *Article 17 EC*) are confined to citizens holding the nationality of the Member States.[107] The Court has, however, moved the concept of sex discrimination to embrace the protection of transsexuals. In *P v S*[108] a transsexual claimed that the termination of her contract of employment was contrary to the Equal Treatment Directive. She claimed that the dismissal was motivated because of her sex. The Court accepted that the Equal Treatment Directive could not be confined simply to discrimination based on the fact that the person is of one sex or another and went on to rule on the constitutional importance of the case by stating that if discrimination against transsexuals was tolerated it would be:

> ... tantamount, as regards such a person, to a failure to respect the dignity and freedom to which he or she is entitled, and which the Court has a duty to safeguard.[109]

This ruling sent out signals that the Court was concerned to extend citizenship-type rights beyond equal treatment between men and women and perhaps to protect the interests of other groups denied protection under national law, but the Court declined to build upon this ruling from *P v S* in *Grant v S.W. Trains.*[110] Here a lesbian employee brought a claim based upon Article 119 EC (now *Article 141 EC*) arguing that the denial of travel concessions to lesbian couples was a breach of the principle of sex discrimination contained in Article 119 EC (now *Article 141 EC*) when such concessions were available to married and cohabiting heterosexual couples. The Court ruled that the conditions applied by the employer

---

[107] Although the Member States must exercise their nationality laws to give effect to Community law principles of non-discrimination and free movement: Case 21/74 *Airola v Commission* [1975] ECR 221; Case C-369/90 *Micheletti and Others v Delegación del Gobierno en Canatabria* [1992] ECR I-4239.

[108] Case C-13/94 [1996] ECR I-2143.

[109] Para. 22 of the judgment.

[110] Case C-249/96 [1998] ECR I-621. See also T-264/97 *D v Council*, judgment of 28 January 1999. Here, under the staff regulations, the Court of First Instance (CFI) confirmed a decision of the Council not to recognise a registered same-sex marriage under Swedish law arguing that Community law does not as yet assimilate stable relationships between two persons of the same sex to relationships between married persons. D has appealed the decision of the CFI to the Court of Justice and Sweden has initiated its own action. There has been extensive coverage of *Grant* and *P v S*; see: Barnard, C., 'The Principle of Equality in the Community Context: *P, Grant, Kalanke* and *Marschall:* Four Uneasy Bedfellows?' (1998) 57 *Cambridge Law Journal* 352; Bell, M., 'Shifting Conceptions of Sexual Discrimination at the Court of Justice: from *P v S* to *Grant v SWT* (1999) 5 *European Law Journal* 63.

applied regardless of sex. Travel concessions would be refused to a male worker if he were living with a person of the same sex, just as they were in Ms Grant's case to a female worker living with a partner of the same sex. The Court argued this was a matter for legislation and that *Article 13 EC* provided a legal base for measures to protect lesbian and gay rights if the political will of the Member States was behind this.[111] The Court may have to consider its position in a case on appeal from the Court of First Instance. In *D* v *Council*[112] an official of the Council lodged an appeal against a decision of the Council refusing to recognise his registered same-sex marriage in Sweden for the purposes of a family allowance under the staff regulations. The CFI followed the *Grant* ruling. However, a recent ruling of the Court of Human Rights in Strasbourg has recognised that homosexual rights may be protected under Article 8, ECHR (European Convention on Human Rights).[113] This may influence the ECJ to rethink the ruling in *Grant*.

There is some disappointment with *Article 13 EC*[114] since earlier proposals[115] had pressed for a wider range of social rights to be included in the new Treaty with a broad general non-discrimination clause which would fulfil the same role which Article 6 EC currently occupies.[116] The need for unanimity in the new *Article 13 EC* may result in slow progress with either watered-down measures or the adoption of soft law. On 4 December 1998 the then Commissioner for Social Affairs, Padraig Flynn, announced a new anti-discrimination package. There are to be three key strands to this package. First, a horizontal Directive addressing all grounds of discrimination in employment. Second, a Directive addressing race discrimination. This will extend beyond employment matters to cover goods, services, health education and sport. Third, an Action Programme to strengthen co-operation

---

[111] For a discussion of the limitations of the legal protection of discrimination see Waaldijk, K. and Clapham, A. (eds) *Homosexuality: A European Community Issue* (Martinus Nijhoff, The Hague, 1993).

[112] Case T-264/97 [1999] ECR II-11; On appeal, Case C-122/99P OJ 1999 C 188/13. Sweden has commenced an independent action Case C-125/99P, OJ 1999 C 188/14.

[113] *Lustig-Prean and Beckett* v *The United Kingdom, Smith and Grady* v *United Kingdom*, ruling of 25 September 1999.

[114] See Waddington, L., 'Testing the Limits of the EC Treaty Article on Non-Discrimination' (1999) 28 *Industrial Law Journal* 133; 'Throwing Some Light on Article 13 EC Treaty' (1999) 6 *Maastricht Journal* 1; 'Article 13: Mere Rhetoric or a Harbinger of Change?' (1998) 1 *The Cambridge Yearbook of European Legal Studies* 175.

[115] The most wide-ranging proposals are to be found in a report presented by the Comité des Sages (established by the Commission) entitled 'For a Europe of Civic and Social Rights', March 1996.

[116] See Szyszczak, E., 'Building a European Constitutional Order: Prospects for a General Non-Discrimination Standard' in Dashwood, A. and O'Leary, S. (eds) *The Principle of Equal Treatment in EC Law* (Sweet and Maxwell, London, 1997).

with Member States and 'civil society'. The purpose of this Directive is to create frameworks leading to partnerships between public bodies and the private sphere, the aim being to deepen knowledge and exchange and disseminate best practice.[117] It took until 24 November 1999 for this package to meet with approval within the Commission. The resulting package was a Communication from the Commission with only two proposals, one for a General Framework Directive for Equal Treatment in Employment and Occupation and the second for a Directive implementing the principle of equal treatment between persons irrespective of racial or ethnic origin.

1.9 The external dimension of EC labour law[118]

We have discussed how part of the rationale for developing an EC labour law was to avoid social dumping. That rationale has also motivated the Community's interest in developing an *external* dimension. The current focus of the external dimension is to examine how the new accession states in the Agenda 2000 enlargement strategy measure up to the EU's labour and social law standards.[119] The external dimension is also concerned in looking at the impact of globalisation, the capacity of the EC and the EU to enter into agreements concerning labour and social law at the international level and promoting international labour standards or 'social clauses' in international trade agreements.

The Community's competence in the field of external relations has had as rough a ride as have the debates over its internal competence in the field of social policy. *Article 300 EC* (old Article 228(1) EC) authorises the Council to authorise the Commission to open the necessary negotiations with third states or international organisations where the Treaty of Rome so provides.[120] In the *ERTA*[121] case the Court of Justice introduced the idea of 'parallelism' in the area of external relations competence. This allows for co-extensive competence in the external relations sphere with competence in the internal sphere. Thus the new legal bases for an employ-

---

[117] See Waddinghton, L., 'Throwing Some Light on Article 13 EC Treaty' (1999) 6 *Maastricht Journal* 1; Bell, M., 'The New Article 13 EC Treaty: A Sound Basis for European Anti-Discrimination Law?' (1999) 6 *Maastricht Journal* 5; Article 13 EC: the EC Commission's Anti-Discrimination Proposals' (2000) 29 *Industrial Law Journal* 79.

[118] See Barnard, C., 'The External Dimension of Community Social Policy: The Ugly Duckling of External Relations' in Emiliou, N. and O'Keeffe, D. (eds) *The European Union and World Trade Law After the GATT Uruguay Round* (Wiley, Chichester, 1996).

[119] COM (95) 163 final; EC Commission, *Social Action Programme 1998–2000*, COM (98) 259.

[120] See McGoldrick, D., *International Relations Law of the European Union* (Longman, Harlow, 1997).

[121] Case 22/70 *Commission v Council* [1971] ECR 263.

ment law and an employment policy in the Treaty of Amsterdam are significant in determining competence in external relations issues.

In *Opinion 2/92*,[122] concerning ILO Convention No. 170 on safety in the use of chemicals at work, a dispute arose as to whether the Convention fell within the exclusive competence of the Community. The aim of the ILO Convention was to prevent and reduce the risks associated with the use of chemical substances at work by evaluating the hazards associated with use of certain chemicals. The Court held that the Community held internal competence in the field of health and safety measures and that the subject matter of ILO Convention No. 170 coincided with Community Directives already enacted under the old legal base of Article 118A EC. The Court distinguished between situations where the Community could establish *minimum requirements* and situations where the Community could *harmonise legislation*. In the former situation Member States retain competence in the area and may lay down more stringent rules. This entailed *concurrent competence* between the Community and the Member States in the field of external relations. In relation to the latter situation, the Community had *exclusive competence* to conduct an external relations policy.

In this Opinion the Court concluded that in matters dealing with co-operation between the two sides of industry (the 'social dialogue') concurrent competence was the norm, although account had to be taken of the objective pursued by the social dialogue. The Court pointed to Article 118 B EC which charged the Commission with promoting a social dialogue at the Community level. However, with the new *Articles 138* and *139* inserted by the Treaty of Amsterdam, the social dialogue has now become an integral part of Community competence and policy.

There are problems with the Community's relationship with the ILO.[123] The Community has only observer status at the ILO and cannot conclude Conventions. To achieve the conclusion of a Convention, the Community must act through the Member States. Thus, the Court ruled that there must be a close association between the Community institutions and the Member States.[124]

---

[122] [1993] ECR I-1061. See Nielsen, R. and Szyszczak, E., 'ILO Convention 170' (1994) *Journal of Social Welfare Law* 401.

[123] See Mancini, F., 'The European Court of Justice and External Competences of the Community' in Davies, P. *et al.* (eds) *European Community Labour Law Principles and Perspectives Liber Amicorum Lord Wedderburn* (Clarendon Press, Oxford, 1996).

[124] The problem is addressed, but remains unresolved, in the Commission's White Paper COM (94) 333.

In a later Opinion[125] the Court was asked to rule on whether the Community had competence to conclude all parts of the World Trade Organisation (WTO) Agreement. The Court ruled that the Community had exclusive competence to conclude the Multilateral Agreements on Trade in Goods, but that there was concurrent competence to conclude the General Agreement on Trade in Services (GATS). The Commission had argued that Articles 100A (*Article 95 EC*) and 235 EC (*Article 308 EC*) gave it exclusive competence in respect of GATS. The Court ruled that only where internal powers had been exercised under Articles 100A (*Article 95 EC*) and 235 EC (*Article 308 EC*) would exclusive external powers be available to the Community.

Given that the Community has become a major actor on the world stage, there are strong incentives to allow the Community to be a party to international and regional Conventions, particularly to ensure uniformity and reciprocity of standards. In relation to developing labour law rights as fundamental rights, this is particularly important given that that in 1998 the ILO reaffirmed the fundamental nature of a number of its Conventions relating to labour law issues.[126] The Court has ruled out the possibility of the Community acceding to the European Convention on Human Rights[127] and there have been instances where a Member State's domestic obligations under the ILO may contravene EC Law. One example is the issue of the ban on night work for women which was imposed by ILO Conventions 4, 41 and 89. Cases appeared before the Court claiming that such a ban was contrary to the EC Equal Treatment Directive 76/207/EEC.[128] For Member States adhering to the ILO Convention before the entry into force of the EC Treaty Article 234(1) EC (new *Article 307*) allows the international obligation to continue but the Member States should take all appropriate steps to iron out any incompatibilities between the preceding international obligation and Community law. Differences in international rules – and their application – thus create problems of estab-

---

[125] *Opinion 1/94* [1994] ECR I-5267. See Emiliou, N., 'Towards A Clearer Demarcation Line? The Division of External Relations Power Between The Community and the Member States' (1994) 19 *European Law Review* 76.

[126] ILO Declaration on Fundamental Principles and Rights At Work, adopted by the Conference at its eighty-sixth session, Geneva, 18 June 1998.

[127] *Opinion 2/94* [1996] ECR I-1759. *Cf.* Betten, L. who argues that there is some mileage in the ruling of the Court in Case 249/86 *Commission* v *Germany* [1986] ECR I-263 where the principles of the ECHR were recognised as principles of Community law with Ewing, K., 'Human Rights' (1997) 10 *Wig and Gavel London Law Review* 8 and 'The Human Rights Act and Labour Law' (1998) 27 *Industrial Law Journal* 275. Ewing points out that none of the rulings of the Court of Human Rights have had favourable outcomes for workers' interests.

[128] See, for example, Case C-158/91 *Levy* [1993] ECR I-4287.

lishing 'a level playing field' within the EC. In the disappointment following the adoption of the Charter of the Fundamental Social Rights of Workers 1989, Hepple[129] and Vogel-Polsky[130] have suggested that the use of labour law monitoring bodies might be introduced, along the lines of the ILO system.[131]

The Community has, however, been at the forefront of incorporating human rights and democracy clauses in its own international trade agreements with third states.[132] Despite the Commission's support of a 'social clause' in the Uruguay Round of the GATT negotiations in 1994, this was not included in the Final Act.[133] Another dimension has been the use of the social dialogue at the European level to develop codes of practice either with individual multinational companies or at a sectoral level within certain industries.

1.10 Conclusion

This introductory chapter has shown the significance of the Treaty of Amsterdam for the development of EC labour law and policy. The next chapter will examine how collective labour law issues have been managed at the Community level, followed by chapters looking at a number of areas where the Community has developed a discrete body of labour law. The final chapter will examine some of the themes that run through EC labour law.

---

[129] 'The Implementation of the Community Charter of Fundamental Social Rights' (1990) 53 *Modern Law Review* 643.

[130] 'What Future Is There for a Social Europe Following the Strasbourg Summit?' (1990) 19 *Industrial Law Journal* 65.

[131] See Nielsen, H., 'The Supervisory Machinery of the International Labour Organization' (1995) 64 *Nordic Journal of International Law* 129.

[132] See the Commission Communication, *European Union and the External Dimension of Human Rights Policy: From Rome to Maastricht and Beyond,* COM (95) 567 final; Barnard, C., 'The External Dimension of Community Social Policy: the Ugly Duckling of External Relations' in Emiliou, N. and O'Keeffe, D. (eds) *The European Union and World Trade Law* (Wiley, Chichester, 1996); Brandtner, B. and Rosas, A., 'Human Rights and the External Relations of the European Community: An Analysis of Doctrine and Practice' (1998) 9 *European Journal of International Law* 468. There are several essays in Alston, P. (ed.) *The EU and Human Rights* (OUP, Oxford, 1999): Simma, B., Beatrix Aschenbrenner, J. and Schulte, C., 'Human Rights Considerations in the Development Co-operation Activities of the EU'; Brandtner, B. and Rosas, A., 'Trade Preferences and Human Rights'; Riedel, E. and Wil, M., 'Human Rights Clauses in External Agreements of the EC'.

[133] COM (96) 402 final.

CHAPTER 2

Collective labour law

2.1 Difficult issues

In Chapter 1 we explored how EC intervention in labour law and labour market regulation permeates a number of areas of national labour law creating different systems of multi-level decision making using a variety of actors. One of the greatest challenges for the evolution of an EC labour law is how, and in what form, should aspects of national collective labour law be accommodated in the Community system? All of the Member States recognise (and often create the framework to promote and protect) the role of collective labour law in the national legal order. Collective labour law rights have also been addressed at the international level, particularly through the International Labour Organization (ILO). Recently the ILO reaffirmed the status of a core of collective labour law rights as fundamental rights in a Declaration on Fundamental Principles and Rights At Work.[1] Yet, until recently, Community law provided few guarantees, either to secure the use of collective labour law as a source of Community law obligations or as a means of implementing Community law at the national level. Community law has also been slow in developing transnational structures to protect and facilitate collective labour law rights to accommodate the increasing fragmentation of national boundaries as a result of the success of the Internal Market project.

Traditionally, collective labour law issues have been marginalised in Community labour law, reflecting a widely held political belief that collective labour law issues are better left to national competence in line with the principle of subsidiarity. However, *Article 137 EC*, following the Social Policy Agreement, brings issues of information and consultation of workers within the remit of agreements between the social partners (or, in default, qualified majority voting in the Council and co-decision with the European Parliament). Matters relating to 'representation and collective defence of the interests of workers and employers' fall within the unanim-

---

[1] http://www.ilo.org. See the articles in (1998) 137/2 *International Labour Law Review* Special Issue: Labour Rights Human Rights.

ity vote in the Council. A major stumbling block for collective labour is *Article 137(6) EC* which appears to exclude a wide range of collective labour law issues from the scope or competence of EC labour law.[2] For some commentators this is seen as a major weakness of Community labour law.[3] Bercusson's analysis of the labour law texts[4] concludes that there is a 'conceptual disarray'[5] as to the nature of the law affecting collective labour law issues in the EU. His analysis fails to appreciate the fact that some texts reflect the mixture of individual and collective labour law issues covered by the substantive provisions of Community law rather than a rigid division of collective and individual labour law issues.

The failure to appreciate the inroads of Community law upon collective labour law issues has led to pessimism on the part of some academic commentators. Streeck,[6] for example, has cast doubts as to whether the EU can construct a feasible system of industrial relations. Sciarra[7] argues that social policy in general lacks an 'identity' and cannot lay claim to an obvious constituency in the EU. She argues that no generous and far-sighted initiative of the social partners could compensate for the lack of a solid constitutional basis on which to found the development of collective rights at Community level. In particular, she notes that EU law may often be at odds with national collective labour law, particularly where individuals may challenge rights protected at the national constitutional level or in terms of a collective agreement against individual rights provided for in EU law. In Chapter 6 we will also look at how collective labour law rights may come into conflict with the rules and principles of Community law generally. In contrast, Bercusson[8] is more positive, arguing that there is a 'spill-over' effect of reflections of national collective labour law into the

---

[2] For a counter view, see Betten, L., 'Fundamental Rights (Human Rights) After the Adoption of the Amsterdam Treaty' in Olsson, P. *et al.* (eds) *Transnational Trade Union Rights in the European Union* (Arbetslivinstitutet, Stockholm, 1998); Ryan, B., 'Pay, Trade Union Rights and European Community Law' (1997) 13 *The International Journal of Comparative Labour Law and Industrial Relations* 305.

[3] See, for example, Lord Wedderburn, 'Consultation and Collective Bargaining in Europe: Success or Ideology?' (1997) 26 *Industrial Law Journal* 1; ' European Community Law and Workers' Rights: Fact or Fake?' (1991) 13 *Dublin University Law Journal* 1.

[4] Bercusson, B., 'European Labour Law in Context: A Review of the Literature' (1999) 5 *European Law Journal* 87.

[5] Bercusson, B., 'The Collective Labour Law of the European Union' (1995) *European Law Journal* 157, 158.

[6] Streeck, W., 'Neo-Voluntarism: A New European Policy Regime' (1995) 1 *European Law Journal* 31.

[7] Sciarra, S., 'Collective Agreements in the Hierarchy of European Community Sources' in Davies, P. *et al.* (eds) *European Community Labour Law Principles and Perspectives Liber Amicorum Lord Wedderburn* (Clarendon Press, Oxford, 1996).

[8] *Supra* n. 5.

legislative proposals of the Community and the case law of the Court of Justice. Bercusson hails the Social Policy Agreement introduced at Maastricht as 'the founding constitutional basis for the collective labour law of the EU'.[9]

Collective labour law differs quite fundamentally between the Member States and this divergence has been seen as a major barrier for securing even a degree of harmonisation or convergence measures at the Community level.[10] Much of the debate within the academic literature has focused upon the perceived existence of a set of internally homogeneous national systems (sometimes displaying enough common transnational characteristics to be grouped into 'families'[11]) and how these will react to the pressures of European integration. From the classic 'harmonisation' perspective of Community law, it seemed as though collective labour law could not be touched by Community intervention without altering or interfering with the delicate balance of power established at the national level and sometimes protected by constitutional guarantees. If we begin to unpick the areas in which the Community has penetrated aspects of labour law, we begin to see that the barriers between Community concerns and national concerns are not so solid and that there have been a number of inroads into the collective labour law arena.

The Social Action Programme 1974–6[12] addressed worker participation, calling for the progressive involvement of workers or their representatives in the life of undertakings in the Community *and* the promotion of the involvement of management and labour in the economic and social decisions of the Community. These embryonic ideas of citizenship rights have again gained currency as a result of a number of different factors towards the end of the last century. The interest in, and moves towards, industrial democracy are shaped by the interest in, and discussions of, ways of involving citizens in democratic and participative decision-making processes in the different layers of Community decision-making processes. There are, however, other factors too. For example, there are economic aspects to this discourse. Long-term management strategies are beginning to realise that openness, transparency and involvement of workers or their representatives in decision making affects the economic viability and success of an enterprise. Also, changes in organisational practices and global

---

[9] *Supra* n. 5 and 'Maastricht: A Fundamental Change in European Labour Law' (1992) 20 *Industrial Law Journal* 177.

[10] See EC Commission, *Comparative Study on Rules Governing Working Conditions in the Member States*, Brussels, 1989.

[11] See Nielsen, R. *Employers' Prerogatives in a European Nordic Perspective* (Copenhagen, Copenhagen Business School Press, 1996).

[12] *Bulletin of the EC*, Supp 2/74, 8.

competition have taken on board new practices which recognise worker autonomy. Vertical disintegration of employment relationships has created an expectation that workers are now expected to take risks. The concomitant obligation is that workers need information on which to base their risk assessment and need to have some control over decision making. Another factor is the success of the Internal Market programme. Restructuring of industry and greater internal cross-border trade has resulted in the growth of a number of new transnational actors. In 1972 Wedderburn argued that it was much harder for workers to organise themselves collectively at the international level in order to match the international power of multinationals.[13] But since 1987, as a response to the imperative of establishing transnational actors to operate within the Internal Market, there have been a number of institutional and procedural reconfigurations of collective labour law; some are based upon Community structures but others are developing an independent dynamic of their own. Marginson and Sisson[14] argue that employers are reluctant to establish supranational organisations with the capacity to engage in sector-wide negotiations. Employee representatives are also reluctant to yield power to supranational bodies, particularly in crucial areas such as negotiations over pay and working conditions. Marginson and Sisson identify an emerging process which they call 'virtual collective bargaining', whereby decentralised collective bargaining arrangements are growing based on the transnational economy. This chapter will attempt to organise this range of developments into a structure which makes them more comprehensible for the newcomer to the subject.

2.2 Collective rights and migrant workers

Article 8 of Regulation 1612/68[15] sets out the principle of equal treatment between migrant workers and workers of the host state in relation to membership of trade unions and the exercise of trade union rights.[16] There is an exception where migrant workers may be excluded from the management of bodies governed by public law, but a migrant worker may still sit on workers' representative bodies in such fields.[17]

---

[13] Wedderburn, K., 'Multinational Enterprise and National Labour Law' (1972) 1 *Industrial Law Journal* 12.

[14] Marginson, P. and Sisson, K., 'European Collective Bargaining: A Virtual Prospect?' (1998) 36 *Journal of Common Market Studies* 505.

[15] OJ Sp. Ed. 1968, No. L 257/2, 475.

[16] Evans, A., 'Development of European Community Law Regarding the Trade Union Rights and Related Rights of Workers' (1979) 26 *International and Comparative Law Quarterly* 354.

[17] Case C-213/90 *Association de Soutien aux Travailleurs Immigrés* v *Chambres des Employés Privés* [1991] ECR I-3507; Case C-118/92 *Commission* v *Luxembourg* [1994] ECR I-1891.

2.3 Collective bargaining as a source of Community labour law

Until recently, collective bargaining, as a source of EC labour law, had a limited role. Collective involvement in Community decision-making processes had taken the form of participation on a purely consultative basis on cross-industry advisory committees and joint committees. The turning point and realisation that a dialogue between the social partners would be a useful way of pushing forward Community-based initiatives can be traced back to the Delors initiative of the Val Duchesse talks which began on 31 January 1985. During the initial period of the social dialogue from 1986–7, three joint Opinions were adopted by the social partners on the Annual Economic Reports for 1986/87 and 1987/88 and on training motivation, informing and consultation of workers. A new period of social dialogue began on 12 January 1989 with the convening of the Egmont II Summit, and between 1989–91 a further five joint Opinions were adopted.[18] The Egmont Summit has met twice more and three further texts or joint Opinions have been adopted.[19]

At the Community level, collective bargaining is found in three principal forms.[20] The first concerns the development of European-wide framework agreements establishing basic principles which are then translated into national collective agreements. These agreements are dependent upon national principles and regulations for their implementation and enforcement. As a result of the low level of international organisation of trade unions in the past, there are few of these framework agreements and their content is vague.[21]

The second type of European collective agreement is at the enterprise level in cross-border collective agreements in multinationals. These types of agreements are more popular than the framework agreements discussed above. The Commission has shown an interest in these types of agreements and would like to encourage them in its plans for a 'European Company', which have not yet materialised into concrete action.

---

[18] These covered the creation of an area of geographical and occupational mobility and improvement of the European labour market; basic education, initial training and vocational training for adults, transition from school to working life, procedures to maximise training, new technologies and work organisation.

[19] On women and training, recommendation on the implementation of the Agreement attached to the Social Policy Protocol at Maastricht and an outline plan for the general shape of economic policies.

[20] See Sciarra, S., *supra* n. 7.

[21] See Treu, T., 'European Collective Bargaining Levels and the Competences of the Social Partners' in Davies, P. *et al.* (eds) *European Community Labour Law. Principles and Perspectives* (Clarendon Press, Oxford, 1996).

The third type of collective agreement is the new form of agreement between the social partners introduced under the Social Policy Agreement at Maastricht[22] and now found in *Article 138 EC*. This type of agreement is introduced as a binding piece of Community law by means of a Council Directive.

2.4 Collective bargaining after the Treaty of Amsterdam

The new role for the social partners after the Maastricht and Amsterdam Treaties has two dimensions under *Articles 138* and *139 EC*: one consultative and one of negotiation. Fredman[23] argues that the legitimacy given to the social dialogue as a form of lawmaking outside of the usual institutional structures of the EU can be derived from a model of industrial relations which portrays the social dialogue as a form of collective bargaining. Seen in this light, the opportunities for social dialogue at the European level are immense, but, as Fredman notes, there are two factors which militate against seeing the social dialogue as a European level of industrial relations collective bargaining. First, the outcome: an Agreement adopted as a Directive by the Council is a binding form of legislation, and it has far-reaching consequences beyond a collective agreement as understood in the traditional sense. Secondly, the nature of the sanctions available to the parties, particularly the unions, is far weaker than under collective bargaining. There is no power to compel negotiation and there are few bargaining tools to influence the nature of the bargaining. Trade Unions cannot call a strike or engage in traditional forms of industrial action when they do not have the full attention of the employers' representatives in the bargaining process. This is what Bercusson has described as 'bargaining in the shadow of the law'.[24]

Paradoxically, in a set of consultation and negotiation rounds under the Social Policy Agreement we see that it is the employers' representatives who have emerged the worse from their unwillingness to negotiate. In 1995 the Commission issued a Communication on Worker Information and Consultation and encouraged the social partners to identify the arrangements for a general framework for the information and consultation of employees in the European Community. The Communication was

---

[22] See Bercusson, B. *European Labour Law* (Butterworths, London, 1996) who shows how the role of collective bargaining was up-graded in the final version of the Social Policy Agreement.

[23] Fredman, S., 'Social Law in the European Union: The Impact of the Lawmaking Process' in Craig, P. and Harlow, C. (eds) *Lawmaking in the European Union* (Kluwer, The Hague, 1998).

[24] Bercusson, B. *European Labour Law* (Butterworths, London, 1996).

responded to by the social partners and on 5 November 1997 the Commission launched the second stage of the social dialogue. While ETUC and CEEP indicated their willingness to enter into Community-level negotiations, UNICE declined to do so.[25] The resulting draft proposal[26] has some draconian terms and the Commission is committed to seeing it through. In its present form it will apply to all undertakings employing more than 50 people. Article 4 contains a broad set of issues on the development of an undertaking and its economic and financial situation over which consultation and information must take place. Article 7(3) states that where there is a serious breach of the information and consultation provisions of the Directive and the decisions taken by management have direct and immediate consequences in terms of substantial change or termination of the employment contracts/employment relations the decisions shall have no effect on the employment contracts or employment relationships of the employees affected.

The Community has no power to compel collective bargaining and neither the 1989 Social Charter nor the Treaty of Amsterdam facilitates the development of collective bargaining. The Commission has a duty under the EC Treaty to ensure that the social dialogue is initiated. *Article 138 (1) EC* states that the Commission '… shall take any relevant measure to facilitate [the social partners'] dialogue by ensuring balanced support for the parties'. Jacobs[27] has argued that this is an obligation to assist the social partners as much as possible, for example by performing secretarial tasks, providing interpreters, covering the costs of the meetings, organising research, informing the public, training and providing negotiators.

The role of the social partners as 'institutional' actors is now receiving more detailed analysis. Work has been carried out by Mosely, Keller and Speckesser[28] who argue that *state* regulation of the social partners should not be overlooked. This is an important aspect of the new configurations of 'social dialogue' emerging under the European Employment Strategy. Perhaps the most important and detailed work is that of Dølvick[29] who

---

[25] UNICE's reasons were: the principle of subsidiarity, the existence of adequate legal frameworks at national level, the lack of any link between employee information and consultation and job security, the view that labour management should be the exclusive preserve of the company's internal organisation and management and the risks inherent in a measure which would prejudice the company's own management prerogatives.

[26] COM (1998) 612 final, 17 November 1998.

[27] Jacobs, A., 'The Role of EU Institutions' in Olsson, P. *et al.* (eds) *Transnational Trade Union Rights in the European Union.* Arbetslivsrappoter 1998:36 (Arbetslivsistitutet, Stockholm, 1998).

[28] Mosely, H., Keller, T. and Speckesser, S. *The Role of the Social Partners in the Design and Implementation of Active Measures* (ILO, Geneva, 1998).

[29] Dølvik, J. *Re-drawing The Boundaries of Solidarity* (Oslo, FAFO, 1998).

argues that '... the social partners have been recognised and integrated in a modest but new kind of co-regulatory regime of international labour market governance at Community level which has no counterpart any other place in the world'.[30] The introduction of new institutional actors is sometimes viewed as a step towards participative democracy in the EU.

If we look more closely at the dynamics of the social dialogue, we see that it is not without problems. It is clear that the power of the two sides of industry is not symmetrical. The main *negotiating* partners have been UNICE, CEEP and ETUC. ETUC was established in 1973. It is an umbrella organisation rather than a negotiating structure, which in turn reflects the weaknesses of most of its confederation members. It has limited resources and has in the past been obliged to delegate responsibility for lobbying to sectoral organisations. For example, in the lobbying around the introduction of the Posting of Workers Directive (discussed in Chapter 3), the lobbying was led by the European Federation of Building and Wood Workers. ETUC has little experience of mandated negotiations, its work to date being confined to networking and lobbying. ETUC has to come to terms with how national mandates can be sent quickly and also adapted to changes in the negotiating process.

Similarly, UNICE – the employers' representative body – is composed of national employers' federations. It requires a unanimous vote to proceed with negotiations. This inflexibility prevents adjustments to changes in the social dialogue process as the negotiations proceed.[31]

The public sector is very underrepresented in the social dialogue. Yet, with some 25%–30% of all employment located in the public sector of the Member States, it has a substantial and strategic role to play in the development of EC labour law.[32] While enterprises and management structures are already supranational, the 'internationalisation' of worker representation is still at a formative stage.[33] Where there are supranational collective

---

[30] Dølvik, J. *The ETUC and Development of Social Dialogue and European Negotiations after Maastricht*. Arena Working Paper No. 2 1997 (Arena, Oslo, 1997) p. 76.

[31] See Jensen, C. *et al.*, 'The Voice of European Business and Industry – The Case of UNICE. A Study of an Employer Organisation on the European Labour Market' in Flood, P. *et al.* (eds) *The European Union and the Employment Relationship, Fifth IIRA European Industrial Relations Congress* (Dublin Oak Tree Press, Dublin, 1997).

[32] Freedland argues that there is now a distinct and rapid evolution of a third sector which is labelled the 'public-service sector' which can be distinguished from the state sector and the private sector: Freedland, M., 'Law, Public Services, and Citizenship – New Domains, New Regimes?' in Freedland, M. and Sciarra, S. (eds) *Public Services and Citizenship in European Law Public and Labour Law Perspectives* (Clarendon Press, Oxford, 1998).

[33] See Treu, T., 'European Collective Bargaining Levels and the Competences of the Social Partners' in Davies, P. *et al.* (eds) *European Community Labour Law, Principles and Perspectives* (Clarendon Press, Oxford, 1996).

agreements in existence, they are at the enterprise level, following management initiatives, and the content and scope of such agreements relate specifically to the activities of the enterprise.

The fragmented nature of trade unionism in the EU has made it difficult to draw up appropriate criteria for the inclusion of social partner representatives in the consultation process. The Commission organised a study of the representatives of the various European-level organisations and from this drew up a set of criteria which trade unions/employees' representatives must satisfy in order to be consulted under *Article 138 EC*. The results of this study were analysed in a Communication from the Commission.[34] In order to qualify for inclusion in the consultation process the organisations must: be cross-industry, consist of organisations which are an integral and recognised part of Member State social-partner structures, have the capacity to negotiate agreements, and be representatives of all the Member States as far as is possible. They must have adequate structures to ensure their participation in the consultation process.[35] The Commission must keep the list of organisations to be *consulted* under review and linkages must be made between the social partners and small and medium-sized undertakings.

This Communication has taken on a normative status and has been endorsed by the Court of First Instance. In the consultations over the introduction of the Parental Leave Directive, a number of representatives of the social partners criticised the Commission when they were left out of the negotiations. This, they argued, undermined the validity of the Agreement, and one organisation, UEAPME, initiated a judicial review action before the Court of First Instance.[36] The Commission responded to the criticisms by arguing that 'information meetings' of the organisations which had been consulted on the proposal had been held and that the negotiations of the social partners (UNICE, ETUC, CEEP) fulfilled the criteria necessary to make the agreement valid. The judgment of the Court is significant since it shows a willingness on the part of the Court to take jurisdiction over the social dialogue and also endorses, by implication, the Commission's view of the legitimacy of the way it has chosen the new institutional actors. Some commentators have argued that the Treaty should be revised so that

---

[34] *Communication of the Commission, concerning the application of the Agreement on Social Policy*, COM (93) 600 final.

[35] For a critique of these criteria, see Keller, B. and Sörries, B., 'The New Social Dialogue: Procedural Structuring, first results and perspectives' (1997) *Industrial Relations Journal* 77.

[36] Case T-135/96 *Union Européenne de l'Artisanat et des Petites et Moyennes Entreprises (UEAPME)* v *Council* [1998] ECR II-2335.

the issue of representativity of the social partners is addressed,[37] for example in the creation of a 'Committee of Wise Persons' consisting of high-level impartial experts to give guidance on the matter of representativity. Other commentators argue that the lack of comprehensive representation puts the onus upon the EC institutions to ensure that unrepresented interests are adequately reflected in measures adopted at the Community level.[38]

The issue of sectoral collective bargaining has not been addressed squarely at the Community level. Treu[39] argues that sectoral collective bargaining represents the backbone of the collective bargaining structure in most continental Member States yet, paradoxically, until 1998[40] there was no attempt at a formal projection of sectoral collective bargaining at the Community level. Sectoral bargaining tends to focus upon employment conditions, pay and hours of work, and seems too sector-specific to be transferred to the supranational stage.

It may be that the flexibility of the social dialogue, relying on subsidiarity and close involvement of the social partners at the national level, using national collective bargaining processes will result in more sectoral EU legislation. For example, An Agreement on Working Time in the Maritime Sector was agreed on June 1999 involving the European Community Shipowners' Association (ECSA) and the Federation of Transport Workers' Unions in the European Union (FST).[41] The trade-off is that the resulting legislation is of a looser nature than the traditional rights-based employment legislation of the 1970s.

---

[37] Franssen, E. and Jacobs, A., 'The Question of Representativity in the European Social Dialogue' (1998) 35 *Common Market Law Review* 1295. Bernard, N. 'Legitimising EU Law: Is the Social Dialogue the Way Forward? Some Reflections Around the UEAPME Case' in Shaw, J. (ed.) *Social Law and Policy in an Evolving European Law* (Hart, Oxford, 2000).

[38] Schmidt, M. (1999) 'Representativity – A Claim not Satisfied: The Social Partners' Role in the EC Law-Making Procedure for Social Policy', *The International Journal of Comparative Labour Law and Industrial Relations* 259.

[39] *Supra* n. 21.

[40] COM (98) 322. See also the Commission Decision of 20 May 1998 on the establishment of Sectoral Dialogue Committees Promoting the Social Partners at European Level, OJ 1998 L 225/27. Keller, B. and Sörries, B., 'The Sectoral Social Dialogue and European Social Policy – less facts, more fantasy' (1998) 4 *European Journal of Industrial Relations* 331.

[41] Council Directive 1999/63/EC of 21 June 1999 concerning the agreement on the organisation of working time of seafarers concluded by the European Community Shipowners' Association (ECSA) and the Federation of Transport Workers' Unions in the European Union (FST), OJ 1999 L 167/33.

40

2.5 New forms of collective organisation

Changes are occurring where transnational sectoral bargaining is beginning to create new strategies. For example, the European Metal Worker Trade Unions have developed a joint collective bargaining strategy in response to the introduction of the euro on 1 January 1999. The EMTU accused the employers of using the euro to fragment wage bargaining at company, regional and national level, and responded by creating a common bargaining agenda at the EMTU level while leaving affiliated unions in each Member State scope for local flexible bargaining on specific issues.[42] In March 1999 the European Metalworkers' Federation adopted a solidarity pact which provides for cross-border rights for its members and trade union officials affiliated to the EMF.[43] The intersectoral approach to the social dialogue is still embyronic, although 'High Level' Groups in the car industry and on restructuring generally were established as part of the 'Luxembourg Process' after the Jobs Summit in Luxembourg in November 1997. This shows how far the 'quantum leap' of Maastricht created a yawning gap between the different systems of national collective bargaining structures and the Community system.

2.6 Exclusion of pay issues from EC labour law

A major weakness for the social dialogue is that *Article 137(6) EC* appears to exclude one of the central issues of collective bargaining from the scope of Community competence: pay. Ryan[44] has argued that the exclusion of pay and trade union rights from Community competence is remarkable since one of the main arguments put forward by the Commission for Community intervention in the field of social policy is to forestall competitive deregulation and social dumping.

Ryan argues the exclusion of pay from Community law competence reveals the 'political' or 'presentational' function of European Community labour law. As we have seen, one motivation for the inclusion of social rights in the Treaty has been to make European integration acceptable to European citizens. Thus, Ryan concludes that in the period since 1989, the inclusion of individual social rights has made the Single Market project palatable, whereas the exclusion of pay and trade union rights reflects the cost of such rights and the political weakness of European trade unions.

---

[42] *Financial Times*, 6 November 1998.
[43] (1999) 307 *European Industrial Relations Review and Report* 2.
[44] Ryan, B., 'Pay, Trade Union Rights and European Community Law' (1997) 13 *The International Journal of Comparative Labour Law and Industrial Relations* 305.

Community labour law addresses issues of pay in Article 5 of the Social Charter 1989, which provides that 'all employment shall be fairly remunerated', and that workers shall be assured of an equitable wage. There is soft law in this area. In 1993 the Commission issued an *Opinion on Equitable Wage*.[45] This was a particularly weak piece of soft law since the Commission refused to be drawn into specifying either the level or the mechanisms by which an equitable wage should be established and enforced.

The Commission did not offer up any proposals for legislative action in the field of pay and trade union rights in the Action Programme to implement the Social Charter.[46] The reasons given by the Commission for inaction in these areas were, *inter alia*, the principle of subsidiarity and the principle of diversity of national systems, cultures and practices. Ryan has subjected these arguments to rigorous analysis. The inclusion of subsidiarity implies a narrow interpretation of the principle which Ryan argues is likely to mask basic beliefs about the legitimacy or necessity of a European labour law. In relation to the diversity arguments, Ryan argues that there are precedents in the ILO machinery whereby a normative rule can be implemented at the national level in the context of national arrangements and contexts. The example given by Ryan is the 1928 ILO Convention 26 on Minimum Wage-Fixing Machinery where a minimum wage should be fixed as a percentage of median wages or income in the signatory states. Again, in relation to the reasons of diversity and specific culture, there are several ILO Conventions which address collective rights which have been ratified by the Member States.

2.7 New configurations of the social dialogue

The advent of EMU and the development of a formal European Employment Strategy have found new uses for the social dialogue. At the national level, the Member States have been obliged to rethink the role of labour market institutions, particularly those connected with wage bargaining. This has been achieved by social pacts. There have been calls for *European* Social Pacts since the Member States have aligned or shadowed wage agreements in other Member States bringing about convergence of such policies. Thus, the traditional social corporatist arrangements are giving way to a weaker social agenda whereby trade unions and employers

---

[45] COM (93) 388. See also the follow-up report: *Equitable Wages – A Progress Report*, COM (96) 698.
[46] COM (89) 568.

are engaged in negotiations to keep to the Stability Pact and to improve domestic competiveness.[47]

While *Title XI* gives the social partners a formal role in decision-making processes, the new *Title VIII* does not mention the social partners. Their involvement in the European Employment Strategy is therefore informal with no legal guarantees. The social partners have been consulted on the 'Luxembourg Process' and are invited to the Social and Labour Affairs Council meetings. They do not participate in these meetings but mention is made in the Press Releases of the Council 'having lunch', 'meeting the social partners before or after lunch' or in the 'margins of the Council', and of keeping the social partners fully informed of the agenda items. In analysing the National Action Plans (NAPs), almost all the Member States recognise a role for the social partners. The exact nature of their participation at the national level is often left vague with little indication as to the nature of the consultation or participation in the evolution and the implementation the NAPs.

At the Vienna Council Meeting of December 1998, the German government suggested a plan for closer co-operation to boost employment and economic reforms. The European Pact for Employment was initiated at the Cologne Summit of June 1999 (the 'Cologne Process'). The purpose of this process is to create a new dialogue between all actors responsible for wage negotiations, monetary, budgetary and fiscal policies with enhanced roles for the social partners and the European Central Bank. The continuity and consistency of the Luxembourg and Cologne Processes is to be achieved by a second Jobs Summit in 2000. These new configurations of political actors are emerging in an *ad hoc* manner, with no legal base or legal guarantees. Sciarra has described the processes as a loose and open sequence of actions which are nebulous and uncertain as to when they start and how they should be completed.[48]

While the independence and autonomy of the various actors is to be respected, latent issues can appear legitimately on the European level of the economic governance agenda: for example, the appropriate level of wage bargaining; the organisation of collective bargaining; labour market reforms; the appropriate level and uses of employment and measures of social protection; and the modernisation of the organisation of work.[49]

---

[47] See Rhodes, M., 'Competitive Corporatism' (EUI/Robert Schumann Centre, Florence, 1997); Teague, P., 'Monetary Union and Social Europe' (1998) *Journal of European Social Policy* 117.

[48] Sciarra, S., 'The Employment Title in the Amsterdam Treaty. A Multi-Language Legal Discourse' in O'Keeffe, D. and Twomey, P. (eds) *The Treaty of Amsterdam* (Hart, Oxford, 1999). See also Goetschy, J. and Pochet, P., 'The Treaty of Amsterdam: A New Approach to Employment and Social Affairs' (1997) 3 *Transfer* 607.

[49] For details of this new agenda, see European Central Bank, *Annual Report, 1999*, Frankfurt.

These issues are maintained on a European agenda by Commission soft law policy documents.[50]

2.8 Employee consultation, information and participation

Recent legislation has given the social partners an important status in implementing new areas of EC labour law at the national level.[51] Yet, worker consultation and information has had an important place on the EC labour law agenda since the Social Action Programme of 1974.[52] A number of the employment protection Directives have specific provisions relating to employee consultation.[53] There are elaborate obligations regarding worker information and consultation set out in the Framework Directive on the Working Environment.[54] The Charter of Fundamental Rights of Workers 1989 sets out some general principles concerning freedom of association and collective bargaining, including the right to participation of workers in strategic planning. It is the latter concept which has been the stumbling block in developing collective EC labour law.[55] The social dialogue was the process whereby the political deadlock over the various proposals for works councils was broken. In the final stages, when the proposal was initiated under the Social Policy Agreement, the negotiations between the social partners broke down quickly and the idea was introduced into Community law[56] by a Council Directive.[57] The Directive

---

[50] For example, see the following European Commission publications: *Public Investment in the Framework of the Economic Strategy* COM (1998) 682; *Social Action Programme 1998–2000* COM (98) 259; *Community Policies in Support of Employment* COM (1999) 167; *Modernising the Organisation of Work* COM (1998) 592; *Modernising Public Employment Services to Support the European Employment Strategy* COM (98) 641.

[51] See Council Directive 97/81, OJ 1998 L 14/9 (part-time work) and Council Directive 1999/70/EC, OJ 1999 L 175/43 (fixed-term work).

[52] Docksey, C., 'Employee Information and Consultation Rights in the Member States of the European Communities' (1985) 6 *Comparative Labour Law* 32; Kolvenbach, W., 'EEC Company Law Harmonization and Worker Participation' (1990) *University of Pennysylvania Journal of International Business Law* 709.

[53] For example, the Redundancies Directive, and Transfer of Undertakings Directive, discussed in Chapter 5.

[54] Council Directive 89/391/EC.

[55] The Commission has also received reports highlighting the fact that employee involvement in strategic decision making is good for productivity contributing to a highly skilled and productive workforce: Davignon Report, *European Systems of Worker Involvement, With Regard to the European Company Statute and Other Pending Proposals*; Gyllenhammar Report, *Interim Report of the High Level Expert Group on the Economic and Social Impact of Industrial Change*.

[56] Hall, M., 'Behind the European Works Council Directive: The Commission's Legislative Strategy' (1992) 30 *British Journal of Industrial Relations* 547.

[57] Council Directive 94/45/EC, OJ 1994 L 254/64, as amended and extended to the United Kingdom by Council Directive 97/74/EC, OJ 1997 L 10/22.

has been extended to the United Kingdom and from 15 December 1999 applied throughout the EU and the European Economic Area. It has been estimated that the Directive covers some 1,325 transnational undertakings, affecting a significant part of the economy.[58] The success of getting the Directive accepted lies in the fact that it has flexibility. Unlike previous proposals, it only applies where there is a transnational element. The aim of this Directive is to improve employees' rights to information and consultation within Community-scale undertakings. The Directive only applies where the undertakings or a group of undertakings have operations in more than one Member State and employ more than 1,000 employees in the EU. At least two of the undertakings must employ at least 150 employees.

Under the Directive, a body representing interests of all the workers in the undertaking, or group of undertakings, in the Community can be established.[59] This will be called the European Works Council (EWC). A complicated procedure is used to establish this body. The employees' representatives in each establishment or group undertaking must create a special negotiating body composed of representatives from each Member State in which the undertaking employs at least 100 employees. An EWC can be established by written agreement between, on the one side, the central management of the Community-scale undertaking (or the controlling undertaking of the group) and the special negotiating body on the other. The agreement must determine specific matters: the nature and composition of the EWC; its functions and powers; the procedure for consulting and informing the EWC; the place, frequency, duration of its meetings; and the financial and material resources to be allocated to the EWC. This agreement is flexible; its contents are to be determined by the central management and the special negotiating body. The special negotiating body can decide (by a two-thirds majority) not to request an agreement. If the central management refuses to start negotiations within six months of receiving a request to do so, or if after three years of negotiations the two sides do not reach agreement, then subsidiary requirements which are set out in the Annex to the Directive apply.

The EWC competence is restricted to information and consultation on matters which affect the transnational working of the undertaking or at least two subsidiaries of the undertaking in different Member States. The subsidiary requirements also lay down the organisation structure of the EWC. A specific committee consisting of at most three members is

---

[58] (1996) 268 *European Industrial Relations Review and Report* 15.
[59] For details, see Blanpain, R. and Windey, P. *European Works Councils* (Peters, Leuven, 1994).

provided for. The EWC must be informed and consulted at least once a year on general aspects of the undertaking's/group's policy. However, if measures with significant disadvantages for employees are at stake, additional information and consultation of the committee is required before such measures can be carried out. The members of the EWC who represent workers affected by a particular measure are allowed to participate in this meeting. The provisions also allow for the support of experts if necessary and all costs are to be supported by central management, but the Member States may impose limits on the amount of funding made available.

The Directive also contains what is known as the 'Article 13 clause'. The Directive does not apply to undertakings or groups of undertakings which had an agreement on transnational information and consultation covering the entire workforce or which concluded one by certain dates. The content of such an agreement is left to the parties.

2.9 Collective rights as fundamental rights

At the time of writing, a Bill of Rights for the European Union is being discussed. The Comité des Sages proposed that the right to associate, the right of collective bargaining and the right to take collective action should be recognised explicitly at Community level.[60] In 1996, four leading European labour law professors solicited the support of some 110 other labour and social law experts within the EU calling for the repeal of then Article 2(6) of the SPA and the inclusion in the new Social Chapter at the Amsterdam Intergovernmental Conference (IGC) of rights such as the right to an equitable wage, the right to associate, to organise, to bargain collectively and to resort to collective action in the event of a conflict of interests between management and labour.[61] *Article 136 EC* provides a teleological role for the application of fundamental rights principles, particularly the rights contained in the 1989 Social Charter.

The role of social rights as fundamental rights in international law has assumed importance in Community law since the Court of Justice has used such standards in order to draw inspiration for a set of Community-based social rights. In a Declaration on Fundamental Principles and Rights At Work, June 1998, the ILO has advanced the normative foundation of core labour standards.[62] It is interesting to note, however, that out of the 179

---

[60] Commission of the European Communities, *For a Europe of Civic and Social Rights: Report by the Comité des Sages* (1996) 50. See Neal, A. *Fundamental Social Rights at Work in the European Community* (Ashgate, Aldershot, 1999).

[61] Blanpain, R., Hepple, B., Sciarra, S. and Weiss, M. *Fundamental Social Rights: Proposals for the European Union* (Peeters, 1996).

[62] http://www.ilo.org

Conventions of the ILO, only seven are raised to the constitutional status of 'human rights' Conventions.

In a number of cases the Court has recognised international social law conventions and standards as providing inspiration for *sources* of Community law social rights.[63] In contrast to the disintegrative effects of Community law which writers such as Wedderburn and Sciarra point to, this approach uses Community law for integrative purposes, drawing upon common principles and values found in the Member States.

The Court seems to move between arguing that such rights cannot be directly transposed into Community law to looking to see how far a particular right has now gained acceptance in the international sphere as an indicator of whether such a right should be recognised in Community law. In the *Nold* [64] case the Court stated:

> ... fundamental rights form part of the general principles of law, the observance of which it ensures. In safeguarding these rights the Court is bound to draw inspiration from constitutional traditions common to the Member States. It cannot uphold measures which are incompatible with the fundamental rights recognised and protected by the Constitutions of those States.

In 1986 the Court modified this statement in *Commission* v *FRG*[65] stating that principles of the ECHR are recognised as principles of Community law.

The Advocates General have gone further and looked to other jurisdictions, notably the United States, for inspiration as to how to tackle issues raised before the Community Court.[66] Thus, lawyers presenting cases before the Court have drawn upon other jurisdictions in their arguments to develop (and, of course, to prevent) the recognition of social rights as fundamental rights.

In an Opinion of Advocate General Jacobs in *Albany International*,[67] we

---

[63] Case 149/77 *Defrenne* v *Sabena (No. 3)* [1978] ECR 1365 (European Social Charter 1961) Convention No. 111, ILO 1958); Case C-262/88 *Barber* v *GRE* [1990] ECR 1889 (ECHR 1950, International Covenants concluded within the framework of the United Nations Organization on Civil and Political Rights and on Economic and Cutural Rights 1966); Case 24/86 *Blaizot* v *University of Liège* [1988] ECR 379 (European Social Charter 1961); Case 222/84 *Johnston* v *Chief Constable of the RUC* [1988] ECR 379 (ECHR); Case C-249/96 *Grant* v *SW Trains* [1998] ECR I-621 (International Covenant on Civil and Political Rights, ECHR).

[64] Case 4/73 *Nold* v *Commission* [1974] ECR 491, para 13.

[65] Case 249/86 [1986] ECR 1263.

[66] See Case C-450/93 *Kalanke* [1995] ECR I-3051.

[67] Case C-67/96 *Albany International BV* v *Stichting Bedrijfspensioenfonds Textielindustrie*, Joined Cases C-115/97, C-116/97 and C-117/97 *Brentjens' Handelsonderneming BV* v *Stichting Bedrijfspensioenfonds voor de Handel in Brouwmaterialen* and Case C-219/97 *BV Maatschappij Drijvende Bokken* v *Stichting Pensioenfonds voor de Vervoer-en Havendedrijven*, Opinion of 28 January 1999.

see the methodology used to develop aspects of social rights which are not necessarily evident in the legislative provisions of Community law. In looking to see if there was a fundamental right to bargain collectively in Community law, the Advocate General identified three kinds of collective rights: the right of individuals to form and join a trade union or an association of employers; the general right of a trade union or association to take collective action in order to protect occupational interests; and thirdly the right of trade unions and employers' associations to bargain collectively. The Advocate General then drew upon the Community Charter of Fundamental Social Rights of Workers 1989, the ECHR, the European Social Charter, the International Covenant on Economic, Social Cultural Rights, the Freedom of Association and Protection of the Right to Organise Convention and the Right To Organise and Collective Bargaining Convention of the ILO in order to come to a number of conclusions concerning the recognition by Community law of a right to collective bargaining. The conclusions were that the Community legal order protects the right to form and join trade unions and employers' associations which Advocate General Jacobs describes as 'at the heart of freedom of association'.[68] In his view, the right to take collective action in order to protect occupational interests in so far as it is indispensable for the enjoyment of freedom of association is also protected by Community law. However, the Advocate General came to the conclusion that there was not sufficient convergence of national legal orders and international instruments on the recognition of a specific fundamental right to bargain collectively. The Advocate General argued that the collective bargaining process:

> like any other negotiation between economic actors, is in my view sufficiently protected by the general principle of freedom of contract. Therefore, a more specific fundamental right to protection is not needed. In any event the justified limitations on the alleged right to bargain collectively would arguably be identical to those on freedom of contract.[69]

These comments reveal the drawbacks of not having a specific recognition of collective social rights and the difficulties inherent in treating collective social rights in the same way as fundamental rights generally.

---

[68] Para 158.
[69] Para 161.

2.10 Conclusions

This chapter shows that Community law impinges upon a number of areas of collective labour law. Actions of trade unions and collective agreements are not immune from the principle of supremacy of Community law and can be set aside even in situations where the national constitution does not provide for this or respects the autonomy of the social partners. In Chapters 3 and 4 we will also see how trade union rights are subject to the principle of non-discrimination in the provisions of Community law concerning equal treatment and the free movement of persons.

We are also beginning to see the Europeanisation of collective bargaining systems at the Community level, through institutional structures and processes created in Community law and also as a result of the dynamics of the Internal Market. Bercusson is optimistic about these developments,[70] though even he admits to being cautious of 'bargaining in the shadow of the law'. Other commentators have pointed to the ambivalence of the social partners to the social dialogue. In particular, Treu[71] argues that the social dialogue cannot proceed simply through either an imitation or an extension of national institutions but that there must be a mixture of innovation and adaptation, perhaps through flexible and limited *ad hoc* experiments. At the moment, the social dialogue under the EC Treaty is too rigid.

Questions also hang over the social dialogue as to how representative[72] it is and whether it is a good model for other forms of participative democracy in the EU. Betten[73] illuminates a paradoxical aspect of the social dialogue. *Article 138 EC* is the first area of Treaty-level decision making where there is real participation in the law-making processes by non-EC institutional actors, yet it is also one of the few areas in the law-making process where the European Parliament is marginalised.[74] Betten argues that this is in conflict with the attempts post-Maastricht to open up EC decision-making processes to greater transparency and democracy with a wider input from a citizenship perspective. The Commission has consulted the European Parliament on the social dialogue and keeps it informed of

---

[70] For example, he points out that the acceptance of the Works Council Directive was inspired by the social dialogue route in 'European Labour Law and Sectoral Bargaining' (1993) *Industrial Relations Journal* 257.

[71] *Supra* n. 21.

[72] Betten, L., 'The Role of the Social Partners in the Community's Social Policy Law-making' in Engels, C. and Weiss, M. (eds) *Labour Law and Industrial Relations at the Turn of the Century. Liber Amicorum Roger Blanpain* (Kluwer, The Hague, 1998).

[73] Betten, L., 'The Democratic Deficit of Participatory Democracy in Community Social Policy' (1998) 23 *European Law Review* 20.

[74] See the European Parliament's Resolution, OJ 1998 C 187/229.

the consultations and negotiations with the social partners. It is hard to see how *Article 138 EC* could be amended to give the European Parliament a formal role in the decision-making process.

Finally, the use of a social dialogue is emerging in the various 'Processes' taking place at the intergovernmental level, lending some legitimacy to crucial decisions on the future direction of EU policy. Voruba[75] and others have criticised this kind of use of the social dialogue as the legal introduction of 'Euro-corporatism' which brings with it a trend towards specific selectivity as regards choice of topics which can, and will, be handled in a Euro-corporatist fashion on the European stage. This in turn gives preferential treatment to work and production-related topics, to the disadvantage of 'citizen' or 'social' topics.[76]

---

[75] Voruba, G., 'Social Policy for Tomorrow's Euro-Corporatist Stage' (1985) 24 *Journal of European Social Policy* 182.

[76] The concern with citizenship rights focusing upon work-oriented matters is explored in a number of critiques of the citizenship model adopted in Community law: see, *inter alia*, Schulte, B., 'Juridical Instruments of the European Union and the European Communities' in Beck, W. *et al.* (eds) *The Social Quality of Europe* (The Hague, Kluwer, 1997); Shaw, J., 'The Many Pasts and Futures of Citizenship' (1997) 22 *European Law Review* 554; Moebius, I. and Szyszczak, E., 'Of Raising Pigs and Children' (1998) *Yearbook of European Law* 125.

CHAPTER 3

The free movement of labour

A national of one of the Member States may move around the Community in order to work in a number of ways. He or she might be a frontier worker; for example, a Swedish waiter might cross over to Copenhagen from Malmö every day to work in a Copenhagen bar and return home each evening. A person may move to another Member State as a 'posted worker' either to complete a particular contract or to work for a temporary period in the employment of the employer abroad. Alternatively, a person may decide to emigrate temporarily or permanently to another Member State. He or she may work as an employee (or under an employment relationship) or as a self-employed person, perhaps interrupting his/her working life on either a voluntary or involuntary basis and also settling there on retirement. All these situations are covered by EC labour law.

The free movement of persons is a fundamental aspect of the Internal Market. It also has relevance for EC labour law. The right to free movement is one of the rights attached to Citizenship of the Union and is a fundamental right in Community law.[1] Community law provides for the idea of equal treatment or non-discrimination[2] of migrant workers (who hold the nationality of one of the Member States) with the treatment of host-state nationals.[3] This has contributed to the formation of a European social citizenship.[4] The Court of Justice has enhanced the concept of non-

---

[1] It is recognised as such in the Community Charter of Fundamental Rights of Workers 1989, *Article 18 EC* and in the ECJ case law. For a powerful discussion of human rights/citizenship rights, see the Opinion of Advocate General Jacobs in Case C-168/91 *Konstantinidas* [1993] ECR I-1191.

[2] See Hilson, C., 'Discrimination in Community Free Movement Law' (1999) 24 *European Law Review* 445.

[3] See Case C-369/90 *Micheletti and Others* v *Delegación del Gobierno en Canatabria* [1992] ECR I-4239; Case C-238/98 *Hocsman* v *Ministre de l'emploi et de la Solidarité*, pending.

[4] Ball, C., 'The Making of a Transnational Capitalist Society: The Court of Justice, Social Policy, and Individual Rights Under the European Community's Legal Order' (1996) 37 *Harvard International Law Journal* 314.

discriminatory barriers to free movement in the *Bosman* case.[5] This could have an impact upon a number of national employment practices which may deter or prevent a person moving between the Member States in order to engage in paid work.[6]

3.1 Free movement of labour as a fundamental tenet of the Internal Market

Building upon the success of the free movement of labour provisions of the Benelux Union, the original Treaty of Rome 1957 created the right to free movement of workers in Article 48 EC (now *Article 39 EC*)[7], the free movement of services in Article 59 EC (now *Article 49 EC*) and the freedom of establishment in Article 52 EC (now *Article 43 EC*).

There has been a tendency to create flexibility in the Member States' labour markets by a process of what Collins has described as the vertical disintegration of the firm.[8] This has been achieved by creating or encouraging more self-employment as well as 'atypical' working arrangements in the form of out-sourcing, temporary, part-time, and home-work. One reason for these new forms of working relationships is to reduce labour costs for employers – and thus to transfer some of the risks of non-employment or under-employment on to workers. The 1980s saw a growth in the service sector, not only in professional services but also in education, healthcare, personal services as well as a number of new forms of services, particularly in what Esping-Andersen calls the 'fun and food' sector.[9] The Treaty of Rome 1957 addressed the issue of self-employment from the very limited and classic angle of securing the freedom to operate in other Member States without suffering from discrimination on the ground of nationality. Until 1987, this area of law was underdeveloped. Professional

---

[5] Case C-415/93 [1995] ECR I-4705.

[6] The Citizenship provisions may also apply when a person is out of the paid labour market in another Member State: see Case C-85/96 *Martínez Sala* v *Freistaat Bayern* [1998] ECR I-2691. *Cf.* Case C-275/96 *Anne Kuusijarvi* v *Riksforsakringsveret* [1998] ECR I-3419.

[7] Ancillary measures were also introduced to develop a genuine employment market in Council Regulation 1612/68/EEC (Part II) to exchange information on job vacancies within the Member States, with the idea being to give 'Community preference' where there were work shortages. See also Council Regulation 2434/92 of 27 July 1992 amending Part II of Regulation (EEC) No. 1612/68, OJ 1992 L 245/1, and Commission Decision 93/569/EEC of 22 October 1993 on the implementing of Council Regulation (EEC) No. 1612/68 freedom of movement for workers within the Community, as regards, in particular, a network entitled EURES, OJ 1993 L 274/32.

[8] Collins, H., 'Independent Contractors and the Challenge of Vertical Disintegration for Employment Protection Laws' (1990) 10 *Oxford Journal of Legal Studies* 353.

[9] Esping-Andersen, G. *The Three Worlds of Welfare Capitalism* (Princeton University Press, Princeton, 1990).

qualifications and regulatory rules were the two principal barriers to full liberalisation of the professions, but the Commission's approach of sectoral harmonisation was slow and piecemeal. As the Internal Market programme developed, so did a renewed interest in addressing liberalisation for the self-employed, particularly service providers.[10]

The rights to free movement were organised around the exercise of an economic activity and by so doing created rights to 'market citizenship'.[11] There is now a divorce from linking the right of free movement to the exercise of an economic activity, firstly by allowing a right of residence in another Member State where a person is retired,[12] or a student[13] or has sufficient funds to be economically independent;[14] secondly, by creating a right to free movement as one of the rights of citizenship of the Union to be found in the new *Article 18 EC* (ex Article 8a EC).

The provisions on the free movement of persons extend to nationals of the EEA states and to members of the migrant's family, even if they are third country nationals (TCNs). TCNs are covered by the free movement provisions of international agreements if they can show they are economically active or a member of a migrant worker's family.[15] The rights to citizenship of the Union are only granted to EU nationals.

Article 42 EC (ex Article 51 EC) allows for the continuity of social security protection when a person moves between Member States. Three principles underpin the way the continuity of social security protection is approached. The first is the principle of co-ordination.[16] EC law does not seek to harmonise or create a supranational system of social security law but instead seeks to co-ordinate the various divergent Member States' systems. The second principle is that of aggregation. For the purposes of acquiring, retaining and calculating social security benefits, there is an

---

[10] The Commission has revealed that employment in the services sector accounts for only 39.2% of working age population in the EU, while it accounted for 54.2% in the USA: European Commission Press Release on the 1999 Employment Guidelines, 14 October 1998.

[11] See Everson, M., 'The Legacy of the Market Citizen' in Shaw, J. and More, G. (eds) *New Legal Dynamics of European Union* (Clarendon Press, Oxford, 1995).

[12] Council Directive 90/365/EEC, OJ 1990 L 180/28.

[13] Council Directive 93/96/EEC, OJ 1993 L 317/59.

[14] Council Directive 90/364/EEC, OJ 1990 L 180/26.

[15] Peers, S., 'Towards Equality: Actual and Potential Rights of Third-Country Nationals in the European Union' (1996) 33 *Common Market Law Review* 7.

[16] The Court has not provided a definition of co-ordination. The Member States are free to determine the rules of national social security systems, to decide who is to be insured, benefits to be granted and the principles upon which these benefits are to be based. Such rules must meet the criteria of non-discrimination on the grounds of sex as laid down in Community law discussed in Chapter 4. See White, R., *EC Social Security Law* (Longman, Harlow, 1999).

aggregation of all periods under the laws of the Member States where the person resides. The final principle is that of exportability. This speaks for itself. A person may export the benefits acquired under the laws of the Member States to the Member State where he/she is resident. The principal Regulation, 1408/71/EEC, implementing these principles has been amended several times. It is felt that the Regulation is outdated. It fails to address newer forms of social security and the wave of privatisation of social security risks across Europe. Its rules are inordinately complex and often inconsistent.[17] Another problem is that TCNs are excluded from its scope[18] unless they fall within the definition of the claimant's family in Article 2(1) of Regulation 1408/71.[19] The Commission is currently undertaking a review of the Regulation with a view to replacing it.[20]

Even with this array of provisions, the number of EC nationals who take advantage of the free movement provisions is still extremely small.[21] The Commission has argued that *Article 14 EC* establishing the Internal Market concept in which the free movement of persons is a fundamental tenet, has direct effect.[22] The Commission set up a working group under the chairmanship of Simone Weil to investigate the barriers to the full realisation of the free movement of persons in the EU.[23] In the Commission's Social Action Programme 1998–2000,[24] the Commission states that removing the remaining obstacles to the free movement of workers and improving labour market flexibility is a key employment objective of the EU. An Action Plan for free movement of workers has been drawn up.[25] One of the first proposals to emanate from the working group was for a Directive on safeguarding the supplementary pension rights of employed and self-employed persons moving within the EU.[26]

---

[17] See Council Recommendation 92/442/EC on the convergence of social policy objectives, OJ 1992 L 245/49, and Council Recommendation 92/441/EC on common criteria concerning sufficient resources and social assistance, OJ 1992 L 245/46.

[18] Case 94/84 *Office National de l'Emploi* v *Josezef Deak* [1985] ECR 1873. *Cf.* Case C-277/94 *Z Taflan-Met* [1996] ECR I-4085.

[19] Case C-308/93 *Cabanis-Issarte* [1996] ECR I-2097; Case C-126/95 *Hallouzi-Choho* v *Bestuur van de Sociale Verzekeringsbank* [1996] ECR I-4807.

[20] See COM (97) 561 final (extension to TCNs); COM (97) 378 final (miscellaneous) amended by COM (97) 158 final.

[21] On the gender dimension see Ackers, L. *Shifting Spaces: Women, Citizenship and Migration Within the European Union* (Polity Press, Bristol, 1998).

[22] SEC (92) 877 final. *Cf.* Case C-378/97 *Wijsenbeek*, judgment of 21 September 1999.

[23] The Weil Report is at http://europa.eu.int/comm/dg15/enpeople/hlp/summ/htm

[24] COM (1998) 259 final.

[25] COM (97) 128.

[26] Now Council Directive 98/49/EC; OJ 1998 L 209/46.

3.2 The complex legal base of the right to free movement

The gradual expansion of the right to free movement under Community law has resulted in a multiplicity of legal bases under which the right can be exercised. In the Commission's First Report on Citizenship,[27] it was announced that a new unitary legal text would be forthcoming which would codify the Court's case law on the free movement of persons and residence. Yet, no amendments to the legal base of the economic/ Citizenship rights to free movement were made at Amsterdam. From 1 May 1999, the elimination of border controls will take place within the framework of *Article 62 EC*. Until there is harmonisation of measures concerning the crossing of external frontiers, Member States retain the right to check the identity and nationality of persons entering their territory.[28] In the Commission's XVIth Report on Monitoring the Application of Community Law,[29] the Commission reiterates an earlier view that more information is needed to allow citizens of the EU to exercise their rights to free movement, as well as to training and information for those involved in the exercise of free movement.[30]

The broadest right to free movement is contained in *Article 18 EC* (ex Article 8a EC) which states:

 Every citizen of the Union shall have the right to move and reside freely within the territory of the Member States, subject to the limitations and conditions laid down in this Treaty and by the measures adopted to give it effect. ✳

The Court has declined to rule upon whether *Article 18 EC* creates direct effect. *Article 18(2) EC* envisages further implementing legislation which would seem to deny direct effect. Another issue is whether *Article 18 EC* improves upon the economic rights to free movement since it does not contain any limitations. Questions remain as to whether the Member States' ability to control who enters and remains within their territory under the economic rights to free movement should be read across into *Article 18 EC*. A number of cases have come before the Court where the issue of the scope of *Article 18 EC* has arisen. In *Skanavi*[31] the Court ruled that *Article 18* EC is a residual right and not the basis or starting point for an analysis of the constitutional nature of the right to free movement

---

[27] COM (93) 702 final, 5. The plethora of legal bases may account for the Member States' poor record of transposition of Directives in this field. See *XVIth Report on Monitoring the Application of Community Law* COM (1999) 301 final.
[28] Case C-378/97 *Florus Ariel Wijsenbeek*, judgment of 21 September 1999.
[29] COM (1999) 301 final.
[30] COM (1998) 403 final.
[31] Case C-193/94 *Skanavi and Chryssanthakopoulos* [1996] ECR I-929.

under EC law. Two Advocates General[32] have argued for an expansive interpretation of *Article 18 EC,* but the Court until recently has been cautious and refused to address the significance of *Article 18 EC* directly. The Court gave hints of a limited role for *Article 18 EC* in the *Uecker and Jacquet* case.[33] This was a case of reverse discrimination where the Court ruled that Community Law had no application. The Court stated that:

> ... it must be noted that citizenship of the Union, established by Article 8 [now *Article 17*] of the EC Treaty, is not intended to extend the scope of *rationae materiae* of the Treaty also to internal situations, which have no link with Community law.[34]

In a later ruling the Court has provided more positive guidance on the scope of *Article 18 EC.* In Martínez Sala[35] a Spanish woman lived and worked in Germany for a number of years but gave up paid work on the birth of a child. After 1984 her residence permit was not renewed but she received documentation that an extension of her residence permit had been applied for. In 1993 she applied for a child-rearing allowance but this was denied by the German authorities who argued that she was not eligible for the allowance on the ground that she was not in possession of a residence permit. Martínez Sala argued that the German law contravened Article 6 EC (now *Article 12*) which sets out the principle of non-discrimination on the grounds of nationality. She argued that the child-raising allowance fell within the scope of Community law where the non-discrimination principle applied. In order to bring herself within the scope of Community law, Martínez Sala was obliged to prove that she had a right of residence in Germany and/or she was a person covered by the free movement of persons provisions. The Court ruled that Martínez Sala did have a right of residence in Germany although she had been refused a residence permit. It was not necessary, therefore, to examine whether *Article 18 EC* created a new right to reside in the territory of the Member State concerned. But at paragraph 61 the Court states:

> As a national of a Member State lawfully residing in the territory of another Member State, the appellant in the main proceedings comes within the scope of *ratione personae* of the provisions of the Treaty on European Citizenship.

---

[32] See Advocate General La Pergola in Joined Cases C-4/95 and C-5/95 *Stober and Pereira v Bundesanstalt für Arbeit* [1997] ECR I-511; Advocate General Ruiz-Jarabo in Case C-65 and 111/95 *R v Secretary of State for the Home Department, ex parte Shingara* [1997] ECR I-3343.

[33] Joined Cases C-64/96 and C-65/96 *Land Nordrhein-Westfalen v Uecker and Jacquet v Land Nordrhein* [1997] ECR I-3171.

[34] *Ibid.* at para 23.

[35] Case C-85/96. *Martínez Sala v Freistaat Bayern* [1998] ECR I-2691.

The Court then went on to rule that as a 'citizen of the European Union' lawfully resident in a host Member State, Martínez Sala could rely on *Article 12 EC*[36] in all situations which fall within the scope of Community law, including the situation where a Member State delays or refuses to grant a benefit to a national of another Member State who is not in possession of certain documents where such benefits are available to its own nationals without necessitating similar documentation.[37]

The main limitations on the use of *Article 18 EC* as the generic right to free movement in the Community are the fact that it is an individual right; it gives no rights to family migration where the family members are TCNs. Secondly, the right crystallises around the right to be a national of a Member State which is left in the hands of the Member States to determine. The Court has made some inroads into this sovereign right by ruling that the Member States must *exercise* their nationality laws in conformity with Community law.[38]

Given that *Article 18 EC* provides a generic right to free movement of persons, it seems an anachronism that the economic rights to free movement have been retained. The Court has begun to apply some of the general principles of market integration found in the other economic freedoms to the area of the free movement of persons, for example principles of mutual recognition[39] and the tackling of non-discriminatory barriers to market integration.[40] The Court has also stated that Member States cannot raise their own internal classifications of a person's status to deny the principle of free movement to a Community national.[41] Yet, there are still fine distinctions in Community law, particularly as to whether a person is providing a temporary service in another Member State or is permanently established there.[42]

---

[36] See also Case C-274/96 *Horst Otto Bickel, Ulrich Franz* [1998] ECR I-7637 for the Court's expansive use of citizenship right ideas attached to the non-discrimination principle.

[37] *Cf.* Case C-275/96 *Anne Kuusijarvi* v *Riksforsakringsverket* [1998] ECR I-3419.

[38] Case 21/74 *Airola* v *Commission* [1975] ECR 221; Case C-369/90 *Micheletti and Others* v *Delegación del Gobierno en Canatabria* [1992] ECR I-4265.

[39] See for example, Case C-129/92 *Kraus* [1993] ECR I-1663. L. Daniele describes this as a 'global approach': 'Non-discriminatory Restrictions to the Free Movement of Persons' 22 *European Law Review* 191 (1997).

[40] Case C-415/93 *Union Royal Belge des Sociétes de Football Association ASBL* v *Bosman* [1995] ECR I-4921.

[41] Case C-363/89 *Roux* v *Belgium* State [1991] ECR I-273.

[42] See Case C-55/94 *Gebhard* [1995] ECR I-4165 where the Court states that the three sets of provisions relating to workers, services and establishment are mutually exclusive. The provisions of the chapter in the Treaty relating to services are subordinate to those on establishment in so far as Article 59(1) EC (now *Article 49 EC*) assumes that the provider and the recipient of the service are 'established' in two different Member States and Article 60(1) EC (now *Article 50 EC*) specifies that the provisions relating to services apply only if the provisions relating to establishment do not apply.

3.3 Workers and the self-employed

Article 39 EC grants the right of free movement to workers who have the nationality of one of the Member States and who have crossed an internal frontier in order to take up an offer of employment.[43] *Article 39 EC* may also apply to economic activities outside the EU where aspects of the employment relationship are governed by the law of one of the Member States.[44]

Article 39 EC has vertical[45] and, to some extent, horizontal[46] direct effect. The issue of horizontal direct effect of *Article 39 EC* has yet to be fully explored. Cases to date have focused upon regulatory bodies which perform functions very similar to state institutions. A different situation arose in the *Bosman* case.[47] Here a Belgian footballer brought an action against his employer, the football club, as well as the national body which implemented the European regulatory rules governing football. His complaint was that the European regulatory regime governing the transfer of football players between European football clubs was a barrier to free movement, even though it was not discriminatory. The Court agreed, and at paragraph 94 the Court states that the provisions of the Treaty relating to freedom of movement of persons are intended to facilitate all kinds of occupational activities throughout the Community and preclude measures which might put Community citizens at a disadvantage when they wish to pursue economic activities in other Member States.[48]

The *Bosman* case has far-reaching consequences, extending the reach of Community law into national labour law and practices which may act as barriers or deterrents to the right of free movement of persons. One area stems from the lack of tax harmonisation between the Member States. The Community has been slow in harmonising the direct and indirect taxation schemes of the Member States.[49] This is because there is a diversity

---

[43] The Treaty Articles are supplemented by a raft of secondary measures to facilitate free movement: Council Directive 64/221/EEC; Council Directive 68/360/EEC; Council Regulation 1612/68/EEC; Commission Regulation 1251/70/EEC; Council Directive 90/365/EEC.

[44] Case C-214/94 *Boukhalfa* v *Bundesrepublik Deutschland* [1996] ECR I-2253.

[45] Case 167/73 *Commission* v *France* [1974] ECR 359; Case 41/74 *Van Duyn* v *Home Office* [1974] ECR 1337.

[46] Case 36/74 *Walrave and Koch* v *AUCI* [1974] ECR 1405; Case 13/76 *Donà* v *Mantero* [1976] ECR 1333.

[47] Case C-415/93 [1995] ECR I-4921.

[48] *Cf.* the Opinion of Advocate General Alber of 22 June 1999 in Case C-176/96 *Jyri Lehtonen and Castors Canada Dry Namur-Braine* v *Fédération Royale des Sociétés de Basket-ball and Ligue Belge-Belgische Liga*.

[49] See Williams, D. *EC Tax Law* (Longman, Harlow, 1998). As a consequence of the lack of harmonisation, workers seek to rely on Article 39 EC and Regulation 1612/68. See, for example, Case C-18/95 *F.C. Terhoeve* v *Inspecteur van de Balastingdienst/Odernemigen Buitenland* [1999] ECR I-345.

between the taxation structures of the Member States and also because tax and national insurances systems have different structures fulfilling different fiscal goals within the Member States. Yet, these differences may result not only in discrimination against migrant workers but also may be a disincentive for a migrant worker to move.

3.4 Workers

The Court has given a liberal interpretation to the concept of a 'worker' under *Article 39 EC*. Stating that the concept of a 'worker' must be a Community law concept,[50] the Court has provided a flexible definition stating that the work must be 'effective and genuine'.[51] Job seekers are allowed a period of three months in the host state to look for work when they are unemployed.[52] A person may also be classified as a worker after having left the paid labour market where, for example, he/she takes up a vocational training course. If a person can still be classified as a 'worker' in such circumstances, he/she can take advantage of the principle of non-discrimination found in Article 7 of Regulation 1612/68/EEC and *Article 12 EC* and claim the same treatment in terms of fees/grants payable for such vocational training courses. This opens up the free movement principle to possible abuse: a person could move to a Member State and work for a short period and then claim a host of social/tax benefits on the same footing as host state nationals.[53] To limit this potential abuse, the Court has ruled that where a person is *involuntarily* unemployed and legitimately resident in the host state, he may still rely upon the non-discrimination principle contained in Community law, but where a worker *voluntarily* gives up work in order to undertake further training in the host state, there

---

[50] Case 75/63 *Unger* v *Bestuur* [1964] ECR 1977.

[51] Case C-337/97 *C.P.M. Meeusen*, judgment of 8 June 1999; Case 53/81 *Levin* v *Staatssecretaris van Justitie* [1982] ECR 1035. *Cf.* Case 344/87 *Bettray* v *Staatssecretaris van Justitie* [1989] ECR 1621 where work – paid at market rates – on a Dutch rehabilitation scheme was not regarded as effective and genuine since the participants were not selected on their basis to perform certain activities. Arguably, this case is restricted to its own facts since in Case C-1/97 *Mehmet Birden* v *Stadtgemeinde Bremen* [1998] ECR I-7747 the Court has ruled that '... [the *Bettray*] conclusion does not follow the general trend of the case-law ... [and] can be explained only by the particular characteristics of that case...', para 31. Article 39 EC may also be relied upon by an employer: Case C-350/96 *Clean Car Autoservice GmbH* v *Landeshauptmann von Wien* [1998] ECR I-2521.

[52] Case C-292/89 *Antonissen* v *Secretary of State for Home Affairs* [1991] ECR I-745; Case C-344/95 *Commission* v *Belgium* [1997] ECR I-1035.

[53] *Cf.* Case C-85/96 *Martínez Sala* [1998] ECR I-2691 where the Court ruled: 'Once the employment relationship has ended, the person concerned as a rule loses his status of worker, although that status may produce certain effects after the relationship has ended' (para 32).

must be some link between the further studies and the previous employment.[54]

Article 39(4) EC exempts the public service from the free movement of workers provisions on the ground that such work is often sensitive and can therefore be reserved to nationals of the host state. Despite the Court's ruling that because this is a derogation from a fundamental principle of Community law and must, therefore, be interpreted restrictively,[55] there is evidence that discrimination occurs in a number of public-service posts and also in the public sector of many of the Member States. Even with the tide of privatisation across the EU, the public sector comprises around 25% of employment in the EU.[56] To counteract this discrimination, the Commission adopted an Action Plan to eliminate restrictions on the grounds of nationality to public-service/sector posts and has begun a series of infringement actions against Member States which have persisted with direct and indirect discriminatory provisions.[57] In *Commission v Greece*[58] the Court found Greece guilty of a Treaty infringement by failing to take into account time served in the civil service of another Member State. Infringement proceedings are pending against Luxembourg and Spain concerning nationality criteria applied to posts in the civil service.[59] A number of preliminary rulings have also been made; for example, in *Kalliope Schoning-Kougebetopoulou v Freie und Hansestadt Hamburg*[60] a clause in a German collective agreement was held to be null and void by virtue of Article 7(4) of Regulation 1612/68. The clause did not take into account previous periods of comparable employment in the public service of another Member State in calculating promotion opportunity. The Court ruled that the clause was contrary to *Article 39 EC* (ex Article 48 EC) and Article 7(1) of Regulation 1612/68/EEC.

In addition to allowing a migrant worker the right to bring his/her family

---

[54] Case 39/86 *Lair v University of Hanover* [1988] ECR 3161. *Cf.* Case 197/86 *Brown v Secretary of State for Scotland* [1988] ECR 3205.

[55] Case 152/73 *Sotgiu v Deutsche Bundespost* [1974] ECR 153; Case 225/85 *Commission v Italy* [1987] ECR 2625.

[56] See Freedland, M. and Sciarra, S. (eds) *Public Services and Citizenship in European Law* (Clarendon Press, Oxford, 1998).

[57] Even after the Commission's Action Programme, designed to clarify the concept of public service in EC law (OJ C 1988 72/2), a series of *Article 226 EC* (ex Article 169 EC) infringement proceedings has followed: Case C-473/93 *Commission v Luxembourg* [1996] ECR I-3207; Case C-173/94 *Commission v Belgium* [1996] ECR I-3265; Case C-290/94 *Commission v Greece* [1996] ECR I-3285. Luxembourg has not complied with the Court's ruling and the Commission has commenced a further *Article 228 EC* (ex Article 171 EC) action.

[58] Case 187/96 *Commission v Greece* [1998] ECR I-1095.

[59] A reasoned opinion has been sent to Spain.

[60] Case C-15/96 [1998] ECR I-47; Case C-187/96 *Commission v Greece* [1996] ECR I-3207.

to the host state the Community, anxious to avoid the concept of 'guest workers', has made provision for the integration of the migrant and his/her family into the social, cultural and educational fabric of the host state.[61] These ideas are set out in Regulation 1612/68/EEC.[62] Article 10 provides for extensive rights of family migration together with educational and employment opportunities (contained in Articles 11 and 12) for the spouse and dependent children of the migrant worker.[63] Article 7(2) of Regulation 1612/68/EEC grants the migrant worker the same tax and social advantages as national workers. The term 'social advantages' has been given a wide interpretation by the Court[64] to include educational grants and access to vocational training courses for the children[65] and spouses,[66] death grants[67] and child-rearing allowances.[68] The Court declined to rule on whether a permanent right to remain in the host state for a TCN spouse is a social advantage.[69]

Article 8 of Regulation 1612/68/EEC grants equality of treatment to migrant workers in relation to membership of trade unions and the exercise of trade union rights.[70] Article 9 entitles the migrant worker to enjoy all the rights and benefits accorded to national workers, including house ownership. In *Commission* v *Greece*[71] a restriction on foreigners' rights to

---

61 *Cf.* the position of TCNs in Joined Cases 281/85, 283-85 and 287/85 *Germany and Others* v *Commission* [1988] ECR I-3203. See Peers, S., 'Towards Equality: Actual and Potential Rights of Third-Country Nationals in the European Union' (1996) 33 *Common Market Law Review* 7.

62 JO 1968 L257/2, but a number of problems continue; see, for example, Case C-85/98 *Commission* v *Greece*, pending. The Commission has initiated infringement proceedings against Greece for demanding a higher fee for the issue of residence permits to members of a migrant's family who are TCNs than the fee charged to EU nationals.

63 *Cf.* Case 316/85 *Centre Public d'aide sociale de Courcelles* v *Lebon* [1987] ECR 281 with Case C-85/96 *Martínez Sala* [1998] ECR I-2691.

64 Case 207/78 *Ministère Public* v *Even* [1979] ECR 2019. Peers, S., '"Social Advantages" and Discrimination in Employment: Case Law Confirmed and Clarified' (1997) 22 *European Law Review* 157; Allen, QC, R., 'Equal Treatment, Social Advantages and Obstacles: In Search of Coherence in Freedom and Dignity' in Guild, E. (ed.) *The Legal Framework and Social Consequences of Free Movement of Persons in the European Union* (Kluwer, The Hague, 1999).

65 Case C-308/89 *Di Leo* v *Land of Berlin* [1990] ECR I-5185.

66 Case 152/82 *Forcheri* v *Belgian State* [1983] ECR 2323.

67 Case C-237/94 *O'Flynn* v *Adjudication Officer* [1996] ECR I-33.

68 Case C-85/96 *Martínez Sala* v *Freistaat Bayern* [1998] ECR I-2691.

69 Case C-356/98 *Arben Kaba* v *Secretary of State For The Home Department*, Opinion of Advocate General La Pergola of 30 September 1999; judgment of 11 April 2000.

70 Case C-213/90 *Association de Soutien aux Travailleurs Immigrés* v *Chambres des Employés Privés* [1991] ECR I-3507; Case C-118/92 *Commission* v *Luxembourg* [1994] ECR I-1891. See Evans, A., 'Development of European Community Law Regarding the Trade Union Rights and Related Rights of Migrant Workers' (1979) 26 *International and Comparative Law Quarterly* 354.

71 Case C-213/90 [1991] ECR I-74.

own property in Greece was found to be incompatible with the free movement provisions.

By far the greatest litigation has concerned education rights in relation to migrant workers and their families. Article 7(2) grants equality of treatment in the provision of tax and social advantages to migrant workers. Article 7(3) allows a migrant worker to have equality of access to training in vocational schools and retraining centres. Cases have emerged where a person has worked for a short period of time as a worker in another Member State and then attempted to apply for access to a vocational training/education course claiming the same benefits as host state nationals in the form of reduced fees for maintenance grants. Students now have a right of residence in the host state under Council Directive 93/96/EEC,[72] but they must be financially independent. The Court has accepted that as long as the work is effective and genuine, a person employed for as little as ten weeks[73] or on an intermittent 'on call' contract[74] may take advantage of Article 7(3) of Regulation 1612/68/EEC. The Court has qualified this right in that where a person voluntarily gives up work to undertake a vocational training course a maintenance grant would only be available where there is a link between the future studies and the previous work.[75] This qualification prevents abuse of the free movement principle – a person could easily move to a Member State, work for a short period and then claim advantageous education rights in a Member State. It also prevents migrant workers from 'upskilling' and acquiring new skills in order to adapt to economic and labour market change.

3.5 'Posting' of workers

Because of the disparities in labour costs across the Internal Market, there are incentives to 'forum shop' and draw up labour contracts in Member States with the least onerous labour laws. The liberalisation of the free movement of services and procurement has also created incentives to tender for work in other Member States using personnel posted to another Member State in order to fulfil such contracts. In two cases,[76] the Court

---

[72] OJ L 1993 317/59.

[73] Case C-3/90 *Bernini* v *Minister for Education and Science* [1990] ECR I-1071.

[74] Case C-315/94 *Raulin* [1996] ECR I-1417.

[75] Case 39/86 *Lair* [1988] ECR 3161, para 37.

[76] Case C-113/89 *Rush Portuguesa* v *Office National d'Immigration* [1990] ECR I-1417; Case C-43/93 *Vander Elst* v *Office des Migrations Internationales* [1994] ECR I-3803. Any measures which the host state takes to regulate a posted workforce must be proportionate and necessary. The Court will look to see if the sending Member State (the state where the service provider is established) has similar regulations and requirements: Case 279/80 *Criminal Proceedings Against Webb* [1981] ECR 3305; Case C-272/95 *Guiot and*

has ruled that under the free movement of services principles contained in *Article 49 EC* a service provider may use its own workforce even where the workforce is composed of TCNs. In *Rush Portuguesa* a Portugese company won a tender to build a railway in France. At this time there was freedom to provide services for Portuguese nationals but a long transitional period was in force for the free movement of labour. French law gave the defendants a monopoly over the engagement of foreign workers. The Court ruled that the right to provide services in another Member State involved the right of an undertaking to take its own workforce.[77] The Court sought to avoid social dumping by stating that the host state could still insist on the application of its labour laws to the posted workforce. Otherwise, since there are differences in the labour and social laws of the Member States, there is an incentive for business enterprises to establish themselves in Member States with low labour costs.[78] The Court has facilitated the free movement of services by not creating 'double costs' for an employer. An employer is not obliged to pay social security contributions for employees in the host state if they are already paid in the state of establishment.[79]

There is now a Directive on the Posting of Workers, based upon *Article 47(2) EC (*ex Article 57(2) EC) and *Article 55 EC* (ex Article 66 EC).[80] Further Directives are proposed on the posting of TCN workers.[81] The Directive is a derogation from the Rome Convention 1980[82] which allows for party autonomy as the main rule in all contractual matters.[83] However, in individual employment contracts, an employee is protected by the mandatory rules of the law which would govern the individual employment contract in the absence of a choice of law by the parties.[84] This is the law of the country in which the employee habitually carries out his work or the law of the country in which the place of business through which he

---

Climatec [1996] ECR I-1905. See Onslow-Cole, J., 'The Right of Establishment and Provision of Services: Community Employers and Third Country Nationals' in Guild, E. (ed.) *The Legal Framework and Social Consequences of Free Movement of Persons in the European Union* (Kluwer, The Hague, 1999).

[77] Case C-113/89 [1990] ECR I-1417; Case C-43/93 *Vander Elst v OMI* [1994] ECR I-3803 where the workforce included Moroccan nationals.

[78] Joined Cases C-369/96 and C-376/96 *Jean Claude Arblade, Arblade & Fils SARL and Bernard Leloup, Serge Leloup, Sofrage SARL*, judgment of 23 November 1999.

[79] Case C-272/94 SA *Criminal Proceedings Against Guiot and Climatec SA* [1996] ECR I-1905.

[80] Council Directive 96/71/EC, OJ 1997 L 18/1. See Davies, P., 'Posted Workers: Single Market or Protection of National Law Labour Systems?' (1997) 34 *Common Market Law Review* 571.

[81] COM(1999) 3 final.

[82] Convention on the Law Applicable to Contractual Obligations, OJ 1980 L 266/1.

[83] Article 3.

[84] Article 6.

was engaged is situated.[85] Council Directive 96/71/EC makes a 'hard core' of protective rules in the host country mandatory for the provider of the services. This 'hard core' of employment protection rules comprises maximum work periods and minimum rest periods; minimum paid annual holidays; minimum rates of pay (including overtime rates);[86] the conditions of hiring-out of workers, in particular the supply of workers by temporary employment undertakings; health, safety and hygiene at work; protective measures with regard to terms and conditions of employment of pregnant women or women who have recently given birth, and of children and of young people; equality of treatment between men and women; and other provisions of non-discrimination.

The Directive applies to undertakings established in a Member State which, in the framework of the transnational provision of services under *Article 47 EC* (ex Article 57 EC), posts workers to the territory of another Member State to the extent that one of the following transnational elements is triggered:

> workers are posted to the territory of another Member State on their account and under their direction, under a contract concluded between the undertaking making the posting and the party for whom the services are intended, operating in that Member State, provided there is an employment relationship between the undertaking making the posting and the worker during the period of posting

> or

> workers are posted to an establishment or to an undertaking owned by the group in the territory of a Member State, provided there is an employment relationship between the undertaking making the posting and the worker during the period of posting

> or

> being a temporary employment undertaking or placement agency, hire out a worker to a user undertaking established or operating in the territory of a Member State, provided there is an employment relationship between the temporary employment undertaking or placement agency and the worker during the period of posting.

In the case of initial assembly and/or first installation of goods, where this is an integral part of a contract for the supply of goods and necessary for taking the goods supplied into use and carried out by the skilled and/or specialist workers of the supplying undertaking, the Directive does not apply if the period of posting does not exceed eight days, except in relation to temporary employment undertakings.

---

[85] Article 6(2).
[86] But not supplementary occupational retirement pension schemes.

The Directive must also be considered in the light of ILO Convention, Labour Clauses (Public Contracts Convention), No. 94 of 1949.[87] This Convention requires public contracts to include clauses which ensure certain clauses are observed relating to wages and allowances, hours of work and other conditions of labour which are not less favourable than those established for work in the local area where the public contract is to be carried out (Article 2). The Convention does not establish a set of minimum standards but aims to ensure that workers are not exploited or displaced in public-contract tendering procedures.

3.6 Free movement of services

Articles 49–55 EC (ex Articles 59–66 EC) provide for the freedom to supply services in another Member State. The Court has extended this to the right to freedom to *receive* services.[88] 'Services' are defined in the Treaty as 'those normally provided for remuneration' in so far as they do not fall under the other provisions of the Treaty relating to goods, persons, services and capital. They include specifically activities of an industrial character, of a commercial character, of craftsmen and the professions. The Court has brought services relating to tourism, medical care and education within the scope of the free movement provisions.

Service providers – and receivers – have rights of entry into the host state and a right of residence coincidental with the period in which the service is provided. The principle of non-discrimination applies to the service provider and receiver. In order to enhance the free movement of services, the Court has applied the principles of 'home-state control' and 'mutual recognition' developed from *Cassis de Dijon*[89] in the area of free movement of goods to services. If a person has to qualify twice, once in the home state and again in the host state (which may be more than one Member State) in order to supply a service, this may take time and increase costs and make the service uncompetitive. There are several sectoral Directives applying to different professions, and the Community has also

---

[87] Eight Member States have ratified this Convention: Belgium, Denmark, Finland, France, Italy, The Netherlands, Spain, Austria. The UK ratified it in 1950 but denounced it under the Thatcher government in 1982. See Nielsen, H., 'Public Procurement and International Labour Standards' (1995) 4 *Public Procurement Law Review* 94; Krüger, K. *et al.*, *European Public Contracts in a Labour Law Perspective* (DJØF Publishing, Copenhagen, 1998).

[88] Case 186/87 *Cowan* v *Trésor Public* [1989] ECR 195; Cases 286/82, 26/83 *Luisi and Carbonne* v *Ministero del Tesero* [1984] ECR 377. See also Case C-120/95 *Decker* v *Caisse de Maladie des employés privés* [1998] ECR I-1831 and Case C-158/96 *Kohll* v *Union des caisses de maladie* [1998] ECR I-1931.

[89] Case 120/78 *Rewe-Zentrale* v *Bundesmonopolverwaltung für Branntwein* [1979] ECR 649.

enacted general 'mutual recognition' Directives in the field of Community[90] higher education qualifications.[91]

In *UNECTEF* v *Heylens*[92] the Court ruled that, in the absence of Community harmonisation, the Member States are entitled to stipulate the knowledge and training required for a particular post or profession. However, where employment was dependent upon possession of a diploma, Community law required the Member States to make judicial review available against a decision of the Member State's authorities in order to challenge the refusal to recognise the equivalence of the diploma. The Court has also ruled that the direct effect of *Article 43 EC* (ex Article 52 EC) may be used to facilitate the free movement of persons. The Member States owe a duty under *Article 10 EC* (ex Article 5 EC) to co-operate in the recognition of such educational qualifications by supplying the necessary information.[93] There are difficulties where a national of one of the Member States has obtained qualifications or experience outside of the EU. While such qualifications may be recognised by one Member State, that process of recognition cannot be imposed upon other Member States.[94]

Similarly there are barriers and increased costs where a person is subject to two sets of regulations. The Court has ruled that where a person is regulated in the home state, the host state may not impose its own regulations upon the service provider unless these are justified and proportionate and not covered by the home-state regulation. In areas such as the insurance sector, the EU has moved faster and adopted the concept of a 'single licence' which allows the holder to practise anywhere in the EU. A number of cases are pending before the Court concerning the incorrect transposition of mutual recognition Directives as well as discriminatory rules relating to freedom to provide tourist services.[95]

---

[90] C-154/93 *Tawil-Albertini* v *Ministre des Affaires Sociales* [1994] ECR I-451; Case C-319/92 *Haim* v *Kassenzahnarztliche Vereinigung Nordrhein* [1994] ECR I-425; (note Case C-424/97 *Haim II* pending where Haim is seeking damages from the German state in respect of restrictions placed on his career by the refusal to authorise him to practise in the German social security system, Opinion of Advocate General Mischo 19 May 1999); Case C-238/98 *Hugo Fernado Hocsman* v *Ministre de l'emploi et de la solidarité*, Opinion of Advocate General Jacobs, 16 September 1999.

[91] Council Directive 89/48/EEC OJ 1989 L 19/16; Council Directive 92/5/EEC OJ L 1992 L209/25; Directive 1999/42/EC of the European Parliament and of the Council of 7 June 1999 establishing a mechanism for the recognition of qualifications in respect of the professional activities covered by liberalisation and transitional measures and supplementing the general systems for the recognition of qualifications OJ 1999 L201/77.

[92] Case 222/86 [1987] ECR 4097.

[93] C-340/89 *Vlassopoloulou* v *Ministerium für Justiz, Bunes und Europeangelegenheiten Baden-Württemberg* [1991] ECR 295; Case C-104/91 *Colegio Oficialde Agentes de la Propriedad Inmobiliaria* v *Aguirre Borrell and Others* [1992] ECR I-3003.

[94] See the cases cited in n. 90 *supra*.

[95] See, for example, Case C-375/92 *Commission* v *Spain* [1994] ECR I-923.

3.7 Freedom of establishment

Article 43 EC (ex Article 52(1) EC) prohibits restrictions on the freedom of establishment. The principle of non-discrimination applies and Directive 73/148/EEC provides for rights of entry and residence in the host state. The Court has not gone as far as applying home-state control to freedom of establishment. Freedom of establishment connotes a permanent association with a Member State. It would thus be easy to move around in the Member States and evade regulation.[96]

3.8 Reverse discrimination

The Court has refused to extend the substantive rights relating to free movement, particularly the principle of non-discrimination, to situations which are considered to be purely internal to a Member State, that is, where there is no Community element. This issue represents the interface between Community competence to create an Internal Market and the role of EC labour law in the Internal Market. Cases have arisen under the free movement of workers[97] and the freedom of establishment and services provisions.[98] Where there is a Community element, then the free movement rules may apply, especially where the actions of the home state (including the action of public bodies or other binding rules, such as collective agreements[99]) may be a deterrent to exercising the right to free movement. In *Knoors* v *Secretary of State for Home Affairs*[100] a Dutch plumber had worked in Belgium for a number of years and then wished to return to The Netherlands to practise his trade. The Dutch authorities argued that Knoors did not have the necessary qualifications to practise as a plumber in The Netherlands. There was, however, a Community Directive (64/427/EEC) which allowed for the mutual recognition of qualifications and experience, which Knoors satisfied. The Court ruled that, given the lengthy qualifying periods (the minimum amount of time was six years), there was little possibility of the abuse of the Directive (the Dutch were afraid workers would go

---

96 See Case 81/87 *HM Treasury and Commissioners of Inland Revenue, ex parte Daily Mail and General Trust plc* [1988] ECR 5483. *Cf.* Case C-212/97 *Centros Ltd* v *Erhvers-og Selskabsstyrelses*, judgment of 9 March 1999.

97 Case 180/83 *Moser* [1994] ECR 2539; Joined Cases 35/82 and 36/82 *Morson and Jhanjan* v *Netherlands* [1982] ECR 3723; Joined Cases C-64/96 and C-65/96 *Land Nordrhein-Westfalen* v *Uecker and Jacquet* [1997] ECR I-171.

98 Case C-61/89 *Criminal Proceedings Against Bouchacha* [1990] ECR I-355; Case C-238/98 *Hocsman*, pending, Opinion of 16 September 1999.

99 Case C-234/97 *Bobadilla* v *Museo Nacional del Prado, Comite de Nacional del Prado, Comite de Empresa del Museo Nacional del Prado, Ministerio Fiscal*, judgment of 8 July 1999.

100 Case 115/78 [1979] ECR 399.

abroad to evade the requirements of Dutch law) but Dutch nationals might be deterred from pursuing their trade in another Member State if they could not return home and continue to use their skills in the home state. Where a Member State has knowledge that the migrant worker has not been in another Member State acquiring the alleged skills and experience, it can refuse mutual recognition of the alleged experience or skills.[101]

In *Surinder Singh*[102] an Indian national married to a British national had accompanied his spouse to Germany where the couple had worked. On return to the United Kingdom, the marriage broke down and the British immigration authorities issued a deportation notice against the Indian spouse. The marriage had not been formally dissolved. The Indian spouse invoked the protection of Community law. The Court had ruled in *Diatta*[103] that it may be necessary for spouses to live apart in order for a spouse to work in the host state. The Court accepted that the free movement provisions had been triggered and that a potential migrant might be deterred from moving to another Member State if his or her conditions of entry and residence – and those of the family – to the *home* state were not equivalent to those he/she would enjoy in the host state. The Court recognised that the Community rules could be abused and ruled that where such abuse was evident a person could not claim the protection of Community law. This is a major limitation upon the right to free movement since a migrant worker may bring his or her third-country-national family members into the EU by triggering the free movement provisions. The Council has adopted a Resolution on the combating of marriages of convenience.[104] There is concern that the free movement provisions, as they impinge upon TCNs, may infringe basic human rights and they may have a gendered effect upon family life.[105] This is shown in *Kadiman*[106] where a spouse of a Turkish worker lost the right to stay in Germany because she was not living with her husband who had been violent and deceptive towards her.

---

[101] Case 130/88 *Van de Bijl* v *Staatssecretaris van Economische Zaken* [1989] ECR 3039.

[102] Case C-370/90 [1992] ECR I-4265.

[103] Case 267/83 *Diatta* v *Land of Berlin* [1986] ECR 567.

[104] OJ 1997 C 382/1. The Commission's earlier attempt to protect widows and deserted spouses by an amendment to Article 11 of Regulation 1612/68/EEC to allow rights to continue after the death of the migrant worker or on dissolution of marriage has not been taken up. Regulation 1251/70/EEC (OJ Sp. Ed 1970 L 142/24) gives the migrant and his/her family a right to remain only on retirement or permanent incapacity to work.

[105] See Blake, QC, N., 'Family Life in Community Law: The Limits of Freedom and Dignity' and Hantrais, L., 'What is a Family or Family Life in the European Union?' in Guild, E. (ed.) *The Legal Framework and Social Consequences of Free Movement of Persons in the European Union* (Kluwer, The Hague, 1999).

[106] Case C-351/95 [1997] ECR I-2133.

3.9 Limitations on the free movement of labour

All three provisions relating to the free movement of persons contain provisos or limitations on the right to free movement. In relation to workers,
Article 39(3) EC (ex Article 48(3) EC) provides that a Member State may
limit the right to free movement for workers on the grounds of public
health, public security and public policy.

Limitations on the right to residence are also found in the three residence
Directives.[107] There is no proviso/limitation written into *Article 18 EC* (ex
Article 8a EC) and it is questionable as to whether the limitations found in
the economic rights to free movement should be read into *Article 18 EC*
(ex Article 8a EC).

Council Directive 64/221/EEC[108] gives definitions on how the proviso
should be applied by the Member States. Article 4(1) of Council Directive
64/221/EEC provides that the public health proviso may be invoked only to
refuse entry to the Member State or to refuse the issue of a first residence
permit and only if the applicant has one of the diseases listed in Annex A to
the Directive.[109] This list has not been revised since 1964 and there are
problems in handling new illnesses, such as Aids.[110] In List B of the Annex
the health risks of drug addiction, profound mental disturbance, manifest
conditions of psychotic disturbance with agitation, delirium, hallucinations
or confusion may be used to raise the public policy/public security proviso.
Member States must respect fundamental human rights when applying
Treaty derogations, and the derogations must be interpreted in accordance
with the EC law principle of proportionality.[111] The provisos relating to
public policy and public security have tended to be conflated in their application, with the emergence of a generic concept of 'public policy'.[112] In *Van*
Duyn v Home Office[113] the Court ruled that provisions of the Directive
could create direct effect. In this case the issue was one of vertical direct
effect against a Member State. In *Bosman*[114] the issue of whether *Article*

---

[107] Council Directives 90/364/EEC, 90/365/EEC, 93/96/EC, *supra* nn. 12, 13, 14.

[108] OJ 1964 L 56/850.

[109] These are TB, syphilis, diseases subject to quarantine as listed in the International Health
Regulation No. 2 of the WHO of 25 May 1951 and other infectious, contagious parasitic
diseases if they are subject to provisions to protect nationals of the host state. Note that
Aids/HIV positive infection is not included in this list.

[110] Pais Macedo van Overbeek, J., 'Aids/HIV Infection and the Free Movement of Workers
within the European Economic Community' (1990) 27 *Common Market Law Review* 791.

[111] Case 36/75 *Rutili* v *Minister for the Interior* [1975] ECR 1219; S. Hall, 'The ECHR and
the Public Policy Exceptions to the Free Movement of Workers Under the EEC Treaty'
(1991) 16 *European Law Review* 466.

[112] See Peers, S., 'National Security and European Law' (1996) 16 *Yearbook of European
Law* 363.

[113] Case 41/74 [1974] ECR 1337.

[114] Case C-415/93 [1995] ECR I-4705.

39(3) EC (ex Article 48(3) EC) could deny horizontal direct effect was discussed by the Court but was not found to be an obstacle.

In *Van Duyn* the Court ruled that the concept of public policy found in *Article 39 (3) EC* (ex 48(3) EC) and Directive 64/221/EEC was a concept of Community law. Furthermore, because it was a derogation from a fundamental right, it should be interpreted restrictively. The Court went further in *Rutili*[115] by ruling that a Member State cannot restrict the right to free movement unless the presence of the individual in the territory of the host state constitutes a 'genuine and sufficiently serious threat to public policy'. Any restrictions on the right to free movement must be interpreted in accordance with the principle of proportionality and the Court also invoked Articles 8–11, ECHR 1950 as guidance for applying the Community law proviso. In *Bouchereau*[116] the Court tightened up the room for manoeuvre by the Member States even more by ruling that the concept of public policy must always presuppose a genuine and serious threat affecting one of the fundamental interests of society.

Article 3(1) of Council Directive 64/22/EEC provides that any measures taken on the grounds of public policy or public security must be based exclusively on the personal conduct of the individual concerned, and Article 3(2) provides that previous criminal convictions do not in themselves constitute grounds for invoking the proviso. In *Van Duyn*[117] the Court was asked whether membership of an organisation can be regarded as 'personal conduct' within the meaning of Article 3(1). The Court ruled that past association with an organisation cannot be considered as 'personal conduct', whereas present association, as a voluntary act, represented an identification with the aims of the association and could be regarded as 'personal conduct'.

In *Adoui and Cornuaille* v *Belgian State*[118] the Court ruled that a Member State could not deny residence to non-nationals for committing acts (in this instance, prostitution) which were not the subject of repressive (or other genuine/effective measures) for host-state nationals. The Court also ruled that a Member State may not take general or repressive measures to discourage anti-social behaviour of migrants.[119] Each case must be considered individually to assess the threat to public policy.

More recently, an Italian tourist was able to rely upon the free movement provisions to challenge a Greek law which provided for expulsion from its

---

[115] Case 36/75 [1975] ECR 1219.
[116] Case 30/77 *R* v *Bouchereau* [1977] ECR 1999.
[117] Case 41/74 [1974] ECR 1337.
[118] Joined Cases 115 and 116/81 [1982] ECR 1665.
[119] See also Case 6/74 *Bonsignore* v *Obserstadtdirektor of the City of Cologne* [1975] ECR 297.

territory for life of any person found guilty of drug offences.[120] The Court found that the law did not take any account of the personal conduct of the offender or the danger which the offender posed to Greek society for the requirements of the public policy proviso.

3.10 Remedies

Community law provides a set of remedies derived from the general principles of Community law and Articles 5–9 of Council Directive 64/221/EEC. In *Rutili*[121] the Court ruled that an authority of a Member State making an immigration decision must give a migrant a precise and comprehensive statement of the grounds of the decision to allow the migrant to take effective steps to prepare his/her defence. A migrant cannot be deported until appeal processes have been exhausted, except where there is an emergency situation where the migrant's presence would pose a threat to public security. The Directive also secures the review of immigration decisions either by a court of law or a 'competent authority'.

The main procedural controls are set out in Articles 8 and 9 of the Directive. Article 8 provides that the migrant shall have the same rights of judicial review concerning any measure taken under *Article 39(3) EC* (ex Article 48(3) EC) as are available to nationals of that state in respect of acts of the administration. Since Member States cannot expel their own nationals, the comparison should be made with general rights of judicial review.[122]

The role of the competent authority is discussed in *Gallagher*.[123] Here an exclusion order was made against an Irish national who worked in England. Gallagher chose to leave England voluntarily but asked for an interview with a person nominated by the Home Secretary. An interview took place in the British Embassy in Dublin but the interviewer did not reveal his identity or give any information on the grounds of exclusion. After reconsidering Gallagher's case, the Home Secretary did not alter his initial decision. Gallagher argued that the procedure adopted was contrary to Article 9. The Court ruled that the competent authority can be appointed by the same administrative authority as takes the decision ordering expulsion, provided that the competent authority can perform its

---

120 Case C-348/96 *Donatella Calfa* [1999] ECR I-11.
121 Case 30/77 [1977] ECR 1999.
122 Joined Cases C-65/95 and C-111/95 *R v Secretary of State for the Home Department, ex parte Shingara and Radiom* [1997] ECR I-3343. See also Case C-357/98 *R v Nana Koadu Yiadom, ex parte Secretary of State for the Home Department,* pending, Opinion of 30 March 2000.
123 Case C-175/94 *R v Secretary of State for the Home Department, ex parte Gallagher* [1995] ECR I-4253.

duties in absolute independence and is not subject to any control by the authority empowered to take the measures provided for in the Directive.

Article 7 of the Directive states that a person must be notified officially of any decision to refuse the issue or renewal of a residence permit or expulsion from the territory of a Member State. A period of time must elapse between the notification and expulsion, except in cases of urgency; the period shall not be less than 15 days for persons who do not have a residence permit and not less than one month in other cases. By virtue of Article 6, the migrant must be informed of the grounds upon which the decision was made unless this is contrary to the interests of state security. The notification must be made in such a way as to enable the person concerned to comprehend the content and effect of the decision.[124]

3.11 Third-country nationals

In the early years of the Common Market, many of the Member States relied upon immigrant labour from outside the EU either to shore up expanding economies with labour shortages[125] or to fill jobs which indigenous workers no longer were prepared to undertake.[126] Germany was at the forefront of establishing a 'guest worker' system whereby non-EC workers, particularly Turks and Yugoslavs, were allowed entry to work in a Member State but were not allowed the right to bring their families with them, to stay within the host state after they had ceased their economic activity or to move freely to other Member States to look for work. Other Member States, particularly France and Italy, even turned a blind eye to illegal migration. TCNs thus had neither the right of free circulation within the Common Market nor derived any social, political, economic or citizenship rights from Community law. In fact, at the Community level, a special regime was deliberately created whereby nationals of the Member States should receive priority over TCNs in the labour market of other Member States.[127] TCNs were left to be regulated by each Member State. The Community began to show an interest in the regulation of TCNs when the recession began to bite in the 1970s.[128] There was some early discussion as

---

[124] Joined Cases 115 and 116/81 *Adoui v Belgian State and City of Liège* and *Cornuaille* v *Belgian State* [1982] ECR 1665.

[125] Claude-Valentin, M., 'Entre économie et politique: le "clandestin", une figure sociale à géométrie variable' (1988) 47 *Pouvoirs* 75; Collinson, S. *Europe and International Migration* (Pinter, London, 1993).

[126] Castles, S. and Kosack, G. *Immigrant Workers and Class Structure in Western Europe* (OUP/Institute for Race Relations, Oxford, 1973).

[127] Article 43 of Regulation 15/61 JO 1961 1073. See the discussion by Advocate General Mancini in Joined Cases 281, 283–5 and 287/85 *Germany and Others* v *Commission* [1988] ECR I-3203.

[128] See the first social action programme, OJ 1976 C-277/2.

to whether Article 6 EC (now *Article 12 EC*) which forbids discrimination on the ground of nationality could be applied to TCNs since, on a literal reading of the Article, it is not confined to EC nationality,[129] but the Court has confined its application to EC nationals since the more specific provisions of the Treaty, such as *Article 39(2) EC* (ex Article 48(2) EC), and the secondary legislation refer only to nationals of the Member States.

Gradually a number of discrete groups of non-EC nationals have acquired rights to enter and work in the EU through agreements made between the EU and third states.[130] EEA citizens, for example, have rights to enter and work in the EU almost on the same terms as EU nationals but they do not enjoy the rights to citizenship of the Union since *Article 18 EC* reserves this right to nationals of the Member States. The Community has developed a number of agreements under *Article 300 EC* (ex Article 228 EC), the most extensive being the Association Agreement with Turkey and the Co-operation Agreements with Algeria and Morocco.[131] The Court has ruled that some of the provisions of these international agreements are capable of direct effect.[132]

Two recent rulings have far-reaching consequences. First, in *Tetik v Land of Berlin*[133] the Court interpreted Article 6 of Decision 1/80 of the EEC/Turkey Association Agreement in parallel with the provisions of *Article 39 EC* (ex Article 48 EC) allowing a Turkish worker to remain in a Member State for a reasonable period to look for work after being legally employed in the Member State for at least four years. The second ruling is that of *Sürül*.[134] This was a preliminary ruling concerning the principle of non-discrimination on the grounds of nationality set out in Article 3(1) of Decision 3/80. In a number of cases concerning the Algerian and Moroccan Co-operation Agreements, the Court had ruled that the principle of

---

129 Böhning, W. *The Migration of Workers in Britain and the EC* (OUP/Institute for Race Relations, Oxford, 1972). See the discussion in Szyszczak, E., 'Race Discrimination: The Limits of Market Equality?' in Hepple, B. and Szyszczak, E, (eds) *Discrimination: The Limits of Law* (Mansell, London, 1992).

130 Peers, S., 'Towards Equality: Actual or Potential Rights of Third-Country Nationals' (1997) 33 *Common Market Law Review* 7; Cremona, M., 'Citizens of Third Countries: Movement and Employment of Migrant Workers Within the European Union' (1995/2) *Legal Issues of European Integration* 87; Hedemann-Robinson, M., 'Third-Country Nationals, European Union Citizenship and Free Movement of Persons: A Time For Bridges Rather Than Divisions' (1996) 16 *Yearbook of European Law* 321.

131 See Eicke, T., 'The Third-Country Agreements: The Right to Work and Reside in the First Generation Agreements' in Guild, E. (ed.) *The Legal Framework and Social Consequences of Free Movement of Persons in the European Union* (Kluwer, The Hague, 1999).

132 Case C-192/89 *Sevince v Staatssecretaris van Justitie* [1990] ECR I-3461; Case C-58/93 *Yousfi v Belgian State* [1994] ECR I-1353.

133 Case C-171/95 *Tetik v Land of Berlin* [1997] ECR I-329.

134 Case C-262/96 *Sema Sürül v Bundesanstaltfur Arbeit*, judgment of 4 May 1999. See Peers, S., 'Social Security For Turkish Nationals' (1999) 24 *European Law Review* 627.

equality applied notwithstanding the fact that a particular provision had not been implemented by the Co-operation Council. The Court agreed with the Commission that the:

> '... rule of equal treatment lays down a precise obligation of result and, by its nature, can be relied on by an individual before a national court as a basis for requesting it to disapply the discriminatory provisions of a member State under which the grant of a right is subject to a condition not imposed upon nationals.'[135]

The Court applied the same principle in *Sürül*, although it imposed a temporal application upon its ruling.

TCNs may also achieve immigration rights to enter and work in another Member State when they are legally resident in one of the Member States and their employer takes them as part of a labour force to fulfil a service contract under the free movement of services provisions of *Article 49 EC*. This happened in *Vander Elst*.[136]

3.11.1 The emergence of a legal regime to regulate third-country nationals

Conservative estimates suggest the number of TCNs legally resident in the EU is more than ten million.[137] Recent years have seen a greater interest in creating EC/EU competence to create a secure external frontier to control the flow of the TCNs into the EU and also to recognise some Community-law rights to allow TCNs free movement within the EU.[138] Although the SEA 1987 kept TCN immigration issues outside of the scope of Community competence, it signifies a turning point of the Member States working more closely at an intergovernmental level to co-ordinate immigration and refugee policy.[139]

A smaller group of Member States entered into the Schengen Agreement in 1985 and this created a 'fast-track' internal market for free movement of persons, divorced from the exercise of economic activities. At Maastricht the intergovernmental pillar of Justice and Home Affairs dealt with immigration issues of TCNs.[140] Most of the activity, while taking

---

[135] Para 63.
[136] *Supra* n.76.
[137] Communication on Immigration and Asylum Policies, COM (94) 23, Annex I, 22.
[138] There were earlier attempts to harmonise and combat illegal immigration, see the Social Action Programme, OJ 1976 C 277/2; Evans, A., 'Third-Country Nationals and the Treaty on European Union' (1994) 5 *European Journal of International Law* 199.
[139] See Chalmers, D., and Szyszczak, E. *European Law Two. Towards a European Polity?* (Ashgate, Aldershot, 1998), Chapter 3.
[140] Article K.1, TEU.

place in secret without democratic or judicial control,[141] has been in the form of Resolutions and Recommendations. For example, there has been a Resolution on the admission of TCNs to a Member State for employment.[142] The Resolution suggests that a TCN should be admitted only if it can be shown that the vacancy cannot be filled by an EC national. Prior authorisation for the employment must be given before the TCN enters the territory of the Member State. In a Resolution concerning the admission of TCNs for the purpose of pursuing activities as self-employed persons, Member States are only to admit TCNs if it can be shown that the activity is of economic benefit to the Member State concerned.[143] In a Resolution[144] on the admission of TCNs for study purposes, the Member States urge that in principle the right to reside should only be given for the purpose of study and a student should not be allowed to seek employment following study. Recommendations on illegal immigration[145] and Joint Actions on exchanges of information,[146] travel facilities for TCN school pupils resident in the EU,[147] transit visas,[148] uniform format for residence permits[149] and burden sharing of displaced persons[150] have also been passed, but the Member States appear unwilling to be bound by even soft law in this area.

At Maastricht, visa policy was brought within the remit of EC policy.[151] A Regulation on a common format for visas[152] was enacted as well as a Regulation to determine the third states whose nationals must be in possession of a visa when crossing the external frontiers of the Member States.[153]

---

141 See Meyring, B., 'Intergovernmentalism and Supranationality: Two Stereotypes for a Complex Reality' (1997) 22 *European Law Review* 221. For earlier discussions on Schengen, see Schutte, J., 'Schengen: Its Meaning for the Free Movement of Persons in Europe' (1991) 28 *Common Market Law Review* 549; O'Keeffe, D., 'The Schengen Convention: A Suitable Model for European Integration?' (1992) 12 *Yearbook of European Law* 185; Curtin, D. and Meijers, H., 'The Principle of Open Government in Schengen and the European Union: Democratic Regression?' (1995) 32 *Common Market Law Review* 391.

142 OJ 1996 C 274/3.

143 OJ 1996 C 274/7.

144 OJ 1996 C 274/10.

145 OJ 1996 C 5/1.

146 Decision 97/420/JHA, OJ 1997 L 178/6.

147 Decision 94/795/JHA, OJ 1994 L 327/1.

148 Decision 96/197/JHA, OJ 1996 L 63/8.

149 Decision 97/11/JHA, OJ 1997 L 7/1.

150 Decision 96/198/JHA, OJ 1996 L 63/10.

151 Article 100c(1), EC.

152 Regulation 1683/95/EC, OJ 1995 L 164/1.

153 Regulation 2317/95/EC, OJ 1995 L 234/1. This Regulation was declared illegal by the Court in Case C-392/95 *Parliament* v *Council* [1997] ECR I-3213 as the Council failed to reconsult the Parliament after introducing substantial alterations to the Regulation. As a result, a second Regulation had to be issued: Regulation 574/99 OJ 1997 C 180/18. The new Regulation reproduces the same text ignoring the position of the European Parliament.

The Commission has attempted to link TCN policy in with the completion of the Internal Market.[154] In 1995 it proposed the lifting of family members' visa requirements, a new Directive abolishing internal frontier checks on any individuals and a Directive on the travel rights of TCNs.[155] Until the Treaty of Amsterdam, however, the Member States were reluctant to expand EC competence.[156] Title IIIa of the Treaty of Amsterdam transfers immigration, asylum, external borders and judicial co-operation in civil matters into EC competence.[157]

A new category of 'denizens' has been created as a result of the failure of the EU and the Member States to accord full-blown citizenship rights to TCNs legally resident in the EU. The failure on the immigration rights front has now been tackled at the EU level by the use of a race discrimination action plan[158] to ameliorate the yawning gap created by the treatment of EU nationals and non-EU nationals under the free movement of persons programme.

---

[154] See Communication on Immigration and Asylum Policies COM (94) 23; White Paper on European Social Policy COM (94) 333.

[155] COM (95) 346, 347, 348.

[156] See Peers, S., 'The Visa Regulation: Free Movement Blocked Indefinitely' (1996) 21 *European Law Review* 150; Geddes, A., 'Immigrant and Ethnic Minorities and the EU's Democratic Deficit' (1995) 33 *Journal of Common Market Studies* 197; Hedmann-Robinson, M., 'Third-Country Nationals, European Union Citizenship and Free Movement of Persons: a Time for Bridges rather than Divisions' (1996) 16 *Yearbook of European Law* 321; Peers, S., 'Building Fortress Europe: The Development of EU Migration Law' (1999) 35 *Common Market Law Review* 1235. See also the essays in the section 'An Area of Freedom, Security and Justice' in O'Keeffe, D. and Twomey, P. (eds) *Legal Issues of the Amsterdam Treaty* (Hart, Oxford, 1999).

[157] See Action Plan of the Commission and the Council on how best to implement the provisions of the Treaty of Amsterdam on an Area of Freedom, Security and Justice, OJ 1998 C 19/1; *The Commission's Work Programme for 2000*, COM (2000) 155 final.

[158] COM (98) 183 final. See the discussion in Chapters 1 and 4.

CHAPTER 4

The equal treatment between women and men programme

The Treaty of Amsterdam provides the European Union with the first example of a relatively complete sex equality framework at the Community level – at least on paper.[1] The Court of Justice has elevated the principle of equal treatment between the sexes into one of the general principles of Community law.[2] This principle finds concrete application in a number of legal bases in the EC Treaty. The amended *Article 2 EC* adds the words 'equality between men and women' to the tasks of the Community. *Article 13 EC* provides a legal base to 'take appropriate action to combat discrimination' based on, *inter alia*, 'sex or sexual orientation'.[3] The new *Article 137 EC* allows the Council to act by qualified majority vote, using under *Article 138 EC* either the social partners or the co-decision procedure with the Parliament, to adopt measures relating to 'equality between men and women with regard to labour market opportunities and treatment at work'. *Article 141 EC* consolidates the Court's previous case law in the field of equal pay while *Article 141(3) EC* also provides a new legal base to develop legislation. Equal opportunities for men and women is the subject of the fourth pillar of the new Employment Guidelines adopted under the fast-tracked Employment Chapter of the Treaty of Amsterdam. *Article 129 EC* expressly states that the while measures may be taken to encourage co-operation between the Member States, such measures shall not include harmonisation of the laws and regulations of the Member States. From 1999 the concept of equal opportunities for men and women has been

---

[1] A vigorous analysis of this area of law can be found in Ellis, E. *EC Sex Equality Law* (Clarendon Press, Oxford, 1998).

[2] See Docksey, C., 'The Principle of Equality Between Women and Men as a Fundamental Right Under Community Law' (1991) 2 *Industrial Law Journal* 258; More, G., 'The Principle of Equal Treatment: From Market Unifier to Fundamental Right?' in Craig, P. and de Búrca, G. (eds) *The Evolution of EU Law* (OUP, Oxford, 1999).

[3] Other areas of competence are racial or ethnic origin, religion or belief and age.

mainstreamed through the other three pillars. In the Commission's Recommendations to the Member States on the implementation of the National Action Programmes, the Commission notes that very few Member States have addressed the question of mainstreaming in their employment policies.[4]

4.1 Equal pay

The original Treaty of Rome 1957 contained an equal pay for equal work clause in Article 119 EC (now amended, *Article 141 EC*). This was introduced for competition reasons at the insistence of France. France was the Member State with the most advanced equal pay laws and was afraid the other Member States might undercut French industry by exploiting female labour.[5] Given the reasons for Article 119 EC, it is rather strange that, until recently,[6] the Member States were unconcerned about the similar function played by third-country nationals in the EU labour markets. Despite its inclusion in the Treaty, the Member States ignored the obligations towards equal pay and even passed a Resolution in 1961 postponing the full implementation of Article 119 EC.[7]

The Court side-stepped the question of the application of Article 119 EC in two employment cases by determining the question of sex discrimination according to the general principles of Community law.[8] Life was brought to Article 119 EC by a series of test cases commenced in the Belgian courts by an airline hostess who was compelled to retire at the age of 40, whereas male cabin crew employees could work until the normal retirement age and thereby receive full pension rights. The first case[9] was unsuccessful since the Court ruled that a retirement pension established within the framework of a social security scheme laid down by legislation

---

[4] *Commission Recommendation for Council Recommendations on the Implementation of Member States' Employment Policies*, COM (99) 441.

[5] See Forman, J., 'The Equal Pay Principle Under Community Law: A Commentary on Article 119 EEC' (1982) 1 *Legal Issues of European Integration* 17; Szyszczak, E., 'Pay Inequalities and Equal Value Claims' (1985) 48 *Modern Law Review* 139; Barnard, C., 'The Economic Objectives of Article 119' in Hervey, T. and O'Keeffe, D. (eds) *Sex Equality Law in the European Union* (Wiley, Chichester, 1996). *Cf.* Hoskyns, C. *Integrating Gender* (Verso, London, 1996).

[6] In November 1999 the Commission presented the first proposal for a Directive addressing racial discrimination in the Community.

[7] Bulletin of the EC, Nos. 1, 7–9 (1962). In Case 43/75 *Defrenne* v *Sabena* (No. 2) [1996] ECR 455 the ECJ ruled that the Member States could not alter a binding Treaty obligation by means of a Resolution.

[8] Case 20/71 *Sabbatini* v *European Parliament* [1972] ECR 345; Case 32/71 *Chollet* v *European Commission* [1972] ECR 363.

[9] Case 80/70 *Defrenne* v *Belgian State* [1971] ECR 445.

did not fall within Article 119 EC, but fell within the old Article 117 EC, which did not create individual rights enforceable in the national courts.

4.1.1 The enduring significance of the second *Defrenne* case

The second *Defrenne*[10] case is one of the most significant and well-known cases in Community law. Earlier, in 1972, the heads of state or government had attempted to make the Common Market more palatable to the people of Europe by declaring that vigorous action in the social field was as important as the economic priorities of the process of European integration.[11] This provided the signal for the Court to take an ambitious approach, although part of its ruling in the second *Defrenne* judgment is hedged with caution and ambiguity. The Court ruled that Article 119 EC had both horizontal and vertical direct effect. As a result, the ensuing years have witnessed a dynamic between the national courts and the Court of Justice whereby men[12] and women have brought equal pay claims raising issues on the scope and substance of the equal pay principle and also procedural[13] and remedial issues.[14]

Because of the economic disruption which might ensue with women and men bringing back pay claims to 1 January 1958, the Court took the unusual step of giving a prospective ruling, stating that only applicants who had lodged equal pay claims before the date of the ruling on 8 April 1976 could rely upon Article 119 EC for periods of service before that date. The effects of this date are still being felt today. In *Magorrian*[15] the Court ruled that an English limitation period which only allowed for the back-dating of equal pay claims for a period of two years prior to the claim was invalid and that periods of service completed since 8 April 1976 must be taken into account when calculating entitlement to additional pension benefits. More recently, Advocate General Léger has given an Opinion

---

[10] Case 43/75 *Defrenne* v *Sabena (No. 2)* [1976] ECR 455.

[11] EC Bulletin 10/1972, para 6, p. 19.

[12] See Case C-218/98 *Oumar Dabo* v *Abdoulaye and Others* v *Regie Nationale des Usines Renault SA*, judgment of 16 September 1999 where the ECJ ruled that special treatment of women on maternity leave may be justified to compensate for disadvantages suffered by women as a result of being away from work.

[13] Attention has been focused by the Commission on the application of the equal treatment principle at the national level: McCrudden, C., 'The Effectiveness of European Equality Law: National Mechanisms for Enforcing Gender Equality Law in the Light of European Requirements' (1993) 13 *Oxford Journal of Legal Studies*, 320; Blum, J. *et al.*, *The Utilization of Sex Equality Litigation in the Member States of the European Community*, Brussels, Commission of the EC, V/782/96-EN, 1995.

[14] Szyszczak, E., 'Remedies in Sex Discrimination Cases' in Lonbay, J. and Biondi, A. (eds) *Remedies for Breach of EC Law* (Wiley, Chichester, 1997).

[15] Case C-246/96 *Magorrian and Cunningham* v *Eastern Health and Social Services Board, Department of Health and Social Services* [1997] ECR I-7153.

that the application of the two-year back-dating rule should not be applied to retroactive membership of an occupational pension scheme since the rule was contrary to the principle of effectiveness.[16] The two-year limitation on back pay rendered it virtually impossible or excessively difficult for part-time workers in the United Kingdom to exercise rights granted by Community law. The Advocate General recognised that the non-application of a back-dating rule would have financial consequences (in this case 60,000 actions had been be commenced by part-time workers in the employment tribunals of the United Kingdom) but this would be ameliorated by the fact that part-time workers would only be able to secure retroactive membership of occupational pension schemes if they first pay the contributions due in respect of all the periods of employment for which they seek recognition.

In the second *Defrenne* ruling the Court added another limitation to the direct effect of Article 119 EC by stating that its direct effect only related to 'direct and overt discrimination' which can be identified solely with the aid of criteria based on equal work and equal pay. What is described as 'indirect and disguised' discrimination, which needed further implementing measures at either Community or national level, could not fall within the direct effect of Article 119 EC. It took some time to fully appreciate this understanding of indirect discrimination since if indirect discrimination was excluded from the scope of Article 119 EC, the equal pay clause would be deprived of much of its potential. A better translation of the concept would be 'covert' discrimination which should be addressed by more sophisticated ways, at either the national or Community level.

A number of cases on part-time work have emerged from the United Kingdom and Germany where an ostensibly neutral rule favouring full-time work is challenged as a form of indirect discrimination since a higher proportion of part-time workers are female, and therefore it is argued that the rule has a disparate impact upon women.[17] The Court has clarified that this form of discrimination falls within the direct effect of *Article 141 EC* (ex Article 119 EC). The ECJ has accepted that where there is an opaque pay structure and statistical evidence reveals a difference in pay between male and female workers the burden of proof shifts to the

---

[16] Case C-78/98 *Preston and Others v Wolverhampton Healthcare NHS Trust and Others*, Opinion of 14 September 1999, judgment of 16 May 2000. See also Case C-326/96 *Levez v T.H. Jennings (Harlow Pools) Ltd* [1998] ECR I-7835 where the Court ruled that the two-year back-pay limitation could not apply where the equal-pay claim was delayed due to the provision of inaccurate or deliberately misleading information by the employer.

[17] See, for example, Case 170/84 *Bilka-Kaufhaus GmBH v Weber von Hartz* [1986] ECR 1607. *Cf.* the dismissal of the claim in Case C-249/97 *Gabriel Grüber v Silhouette International Schmied GmbH & Co KG*, judgment of 14 September 1999.

employer to explain the pay difference by factors unrelated to sex.[18] The Court of Justice has not given any precision to the nature of the statistical evidence to be adduced. In more recent cases, the ECJ has ruled that where 'significant statistics disclose an appreciable difference in pay between two jobs of equal value, one of which is carried out almost exclusively by women and the other predominantly by men ...'[19] a new form of discrimination, 'apparent discrimination', is disclosed and the onus is then upon the employer to explain the difference unrelated to factors based on sex.

In *R* v *Secretary of State for Employment, ex parte Seymour Smith and Perez*[20] the Court has given more precision to issues relating to proof in the concept of indirect discrimination. A national court must establish a set of criteria. First, it must establish whether the measure under scrutiny has a more unfavourable impact on women than men. This can be ascertained by comparing statistics on the respective proportions of men and women in the workforce who are able to satisfy the qualifying condition and those who are unable to do so, comparing the two proportions. The next question is to ask whether a considerably smaller proportion of women than men satisfy the condition. If the answer is in the affirmative, then this reveals apparent discrimination unless the disputed rule can be justified by objective factors unrelated to sex. It is for the national court to assess whether the statistics cover enough individuals, whether they illustrate purely fortuitous or short-term phenomena and whether in general they appear significant.[21] The Court was also asked at what time the assessment of the legality of the alleged discriminatory measure should be judged. The Court replied that the requirement of Community law must be complied with at all times: at the time of its adoption, the time it enters into force and at the time of the alleged discriminatory impact upon an individual.

Paradoxically, the Court has limited the scope of an indirect discrimination claim by introducing a defence or justification which may be raised by either private employers or Member States.[22] This defence is often referred to as the 'economic objective' test. An employer (or the state) must show that the discriminatory measure corresponds to a real need on the part of the employer/state, that the measures taken are appropriate with a view to

---

[18] Case 109/88 *Danfoss* [1989] ECR 3199.

[19] Case C-127/92 *Enderby* v *Frenchay Health Authority* [1993] ECR I-5535, 5573.

[20] Case C-167/97 [1999] ECR I-623.

[21] In this case the Court found that in 1985 when the legislation under scrutiny was introduced 77.4% of men and 68.9% of women fulfilled the qualifying condition. The Court concluded that, on the face of it, the statistics did not establish that a considerably smaller percentage of women than men were able to fulfil the qualifying requirement.

[22] See Hervey, T. *Justifications for Sex Discrimination in Employment* (Butterworths, London, 1993).

attaining the goals set out by the employer/state and that they are necessary to achieve those goals. This is an application of the Community principle of proportionality.[23] It is for the national court to determine if the discriminatory measures can be justified by objective factors unrelated to sex.[24] Where a Member State is alleging that its laws reflect broad social policy issues which it has a discretion to determine, it must not frustrate the implementation of a fundamental principle of Community law, such as the equal pay principle.

The Court's case law has now been consolidated in Article 2 of Council Directive 97/80/EC on the burden of proof in cases of discrimination based on sex.[25] Article 2(2) provides that:

> ... indirect discrimination shall exist where an apparently neutral provision, criterion or practice disadvantages a substantially higher proportion of the members of one sex unless that provision, criterion or practice is appropriate and necessary and can be justified by objective factors unrelated to sex.

In the second *Defrenne* case the Court adopted a teleological interpretation of Article 119 EC. It ruled that Article 119 EC fulfilled a two-fold function. On the one hand, it had an *economic* function to avoid the distortion of competition and, on the other hand, echoing the 1972 Declaration of the heads of state or government, it had a *social* function to fulfil the purposes of Article 117 EC and the Preamble to the Treaty of Rome to raise the standard of living in Europe. To this end, Article 119 EC required equalisation upwards: if discrimination was found, the lower wages should be raised to the higher level of those of the comparator.[26] The impetus from this ruling led to further cases being referred to the Court under *Article 234 EC* (ex Article 177 EC) and gave the Commission the confidence to commence *Article 226 EC* (ex Article 169 EC) actions against Member States who were lagging behind in applying the equal pay and equal treatment principle to be found in later Directives. The impact of direct effect was felt not only in strategic litigation, but also it provoked

---

[23] See generally, Tridimas, T. *The General Principles of EC Law* (OUP, Oxford, 1999).

[24] Case 171/88 *Rinner-Kühn* v *FWW Spezial-Gebaudereiningung GmBH & Co. KG* [1989] ECR 2743; Case C-100/95 *Kording* v *Senator für Finanze* [1997] ECR I-5289; Case C-1/95 *Gerster* v *Freistaat Bayern* [1997] ECR I-5253.

[25] OJ 1998 L 14/6. The Commission's original drafts had included social security issues within the Directive's remit but these were omitted by the Member States. It is interesting to note that this area of case law was not included in the Court's consolidation of equal-pay issues in *Article 141 EC*.

[26] Although this has not always been the case – see Case C-408/92 *Smith* v *Avdel* [1994] ECR I-4435 where the Court sanctioned a levelling down of a pension entitlement. In the field of social security, Member States have been able to give effect to the principle of equality by taking away social security benefits given to men on the ground that the public expenditure system cannot afford to level up social security entitlements.

the visibility of equal treatment and non-discrimination at the national level. [27]

The Community enacted a plinth of supporting secondary legislation in the field of equal pay[28] (introducing in Article 1 of the Equal Pay Directive the concept of equal pay for work of equal value[29]), equal treatment,[30] equal treatment in state[31] and occupational social security[32] as well as a plethora of soft law measures.[33] There is also a little known Directive, often dubbed 'the farmer's wife Directive', which aims to give equal treatment to self-employed people.[34] It is aimed at spouses who work in a family business. The review of this Directive is often mentioned, but, to date, no concrete revisions have emerged.[35] Taken with the subsequent interpretative rulings given by the Court, this plinth of secondary legislation has led to what Sciarra[36] describes as a form of proceduralised law which takes advantage of the multiplicity of actors involved as well as the differentiated legal instruments to be adopted in order to secure equal treatment between the sexes in the labour market.

Finally, in the second *Defrenne* case, the Court ruled that it was the duty of the national courts to scrutinise discrimination which arises directly from legislative provisions or collective labour agreements as well as the usual public and private employment contractual issues. This led to cases such as the *Rinner Kühn*[37] ruling. Here part-time workers were excluded from an occupational sick pay scheme which was based upon a scheme established by the German government. The Court ruled that the employer and the German state must show a 'necessary' aim was being pursued which could justify the exclusion of part-time employees from an occupational social security scheme. The German government's generalised statements on the position of part-time work were considered to be too vague to satisfy the objective justification demanded by Community law.

---

[27] Sciarra, S., 'European Social Policy and Labour Law – Challenges and Perspectives', *Collected Courses of the Academy of European Law*, Vol. IV, Book 1, 301 (1995).

[28] Council Directive 75/117/EEC, OJ 1975 L 45/19.

[29] See Case C-236/98 *Jämställdhetsombudsmannen Lena Svenaenus v Örebrolänslandsting*, pending.

[30] Council Directive 76/207/EEC, OJ 1976 L 39/40.

[31] Council Directive 79/7/EEC, OJ 1979 L 6/24.

[32] Council Directive 86/378/EEC, OJ 1986 L 225/40, amended by Council Directive 96/97/EC OJ 1997 L 46/20.

[33] See Nielsen and Szyszczak, *op. cit.*, Ch. 2, p. 204; Report from the Commission to the Council, the Economic and Social Committee and the Committee of the Regions, *Equal Opportunities for Women and Men in the European Union, 1999*, COM (2000) 123 final.

[34] Council Directive 86/613/EEC, OJ 1986 L 359/5.

[35] See, for example, The Fourth Medium-Term Action Programme on Equal Opportunities for Women and Men (1996–2000) COM (95) 381 final.

[36] *Supra* n. 27.

[37] Case 171/88 [1989] ECR 2743.

The ruling in the second *Defrenne* case has also created problems for Member States with institutionalised collective bargaining. Allowing employees to challenge the content of collective bargaining alters the balance of power between the social partners and interferes with the autonomy of the social partners. Nevertheless, it allows for independent scrutiny of institutionalised aspects of discrimination in collective bargaining. In *Nimz* v *Freie und Hansestadt Hamburg*[38] the Court applied Article 119 EC to a collective agreement under which employees with at least three-quarters of normal full-time work were treated more favourably than employees working between one-half and three-quarters of normal working hours. The Court viewed the problem of the autonomy of the social partners solely from the perspective of the supremacy of Community law.

In *Bötel*[39] and *Lewark*[40] the Court addressed the problem of providing compensation for part-time workers attending staff training courses. It was argued that such training schemes, necessary to participate fully in promotion and decision-making structures such as Staff Councils, often required attendance at work-related courses over the number of hours normally worked by part-time employees, yet they were only paid according to hours they would normally work. The Court ruled that it was contrary to Article 119 EC and Council Directive 75/117/EEC to limit such compensation on the basis of individual work schedules. In *Lewark* the Court accepted that the concern to protect the independence of members of a Staff Council may reflect a legitimate aim of a Member State's social policy in order to justify the discrimination. These cases have attracted a number of criticisms. The political problem is that members of the Staff Council receive no money or salary or other advantages for their work done on the Council. This was considered to be an important tool to secure the independence of members of the Staff Council. However, as the Court recognised, if part-time workers were not compensated for the time spent attending training courses they would be deterred from participating in Staff Council functions.[41]

In *Danfoss*[42] a claim was brought by a trade union on behalf of a group of female workers who earned on average 7% less than a comparable

---

[38] Case C-184/89[1991] ECR I-297.
[39] Case C-360/90 [1992] ECR I-3589.
[40] Case C-457/93 [1996] ECR I-243. See also Case C-278/93 *Freers and Speckmann* v *Deutsche Budespost* [1996] ECR I-1165.
[41] Cf. Ellis, E., *supra* n. 1, at p. 132 who questions the logic of the Court's ruling arguing that if the sums in question are pay for the purposes of *Article 141 EC* then discrimination in relation to them ought not to be justified by arguments which rely on the fact that they are not pay.
[42] Case C-109/88 [1989] ECR 3199.

group of male workers. The two groups of workers earned the same basic wage but the employer supplemented the basic rate according to a number of criteria which, it was alleged, created indirect discrimination against female workers. It was not transparent as to how and when these criteria applied. The Court ruled that in order for there to be transparency in the wage-determination process, and in order to meet the obligation of providing an effective remedy contained in Article 6 of Council Directive 75/117/EEC, a partial reversal of the burden of proof should take place. The onus was upon the employer to explain the wage determination process. This case, which used statistical evidence to show a *prima facie* case of discrimination, was built upon in *Enderby*[43] where the Court refused to accept that a different history of collective bargaining could explain away wage differentials in segregated employment. More recently, the Court has declined to rule on how far it will scrutinise different historical reasons for the classification of jobs. In a dispute over the classification of psychotherapists' pay, the Court ruled that where medical doctors were being paid more than psychologists for carrying out psychotherapeutic tasks, the two groups were not in a comparable situation since medical doctors may be asked to perform a wider range of medical duties.[44]

Together with the concept of indirect discrimination, the *Danfoss* and *Enderby* rulings motivated the Community to adopt a proposal for a Directive on the burden of proof in equal pay and equal treatment claims.[45]

In *Krüger*[46] a female employee who was engaged in what is described as 'minor employment'[47] after the birth of her child was refused payment of a Christmas bonus which was payable under the German collective agreement on allowances. The employer argued that Krüger was not entitled to the bonus since she was not covered by the general collective agreement for public-sector employees (the BAT). In two cases brought under the state social security Directive, 79/7/EEC, the Court of Justice had accepted the German state's justification for exempting employees who were in 'minor employment' from the scope of the obligation to make social security contributions.[48] Although it was alleged that this created indirect discrimi-

---

[43] Case C-127/92 [1993] ECR I-5535.

[44] Case C-309/97 *Angestellten betriebsrat der Wiener Gebietskrankenkasse and Wiener Gebietskrankenkasse,* judgment of 11 May 1999.

[45] Council Directive 97/80/EC, OJ 1998 L 14/6, amended and extended to the United Kingdom by Council Directive 98/52/EC, OJ 1998 L 14/205.

[46] Case C-281/97 *Andrea Krüger v Kreiskrankenhaus Ebersberg,* judgment of 9 September 1999.

[47] Minor employment is defined as a normal working week of less than 15 hours and normal pay not exceeding one seventh of the average monthly salary of workers.

[48] Case 317/93 *Nolte v Landesversicherungsanstalt Hanover* [1995] ECR I-4625; Case C-444/93 *Megner and Scheffel v Innungskrankenkasse Rheinhessen-Pflaz* [1995] ECR I-4741.

nation against female employees, the German government argued that it was justified on objective grounds to meet the demand for minor employment. The Court in *Krüger* distinguished the *Nolte* and *Megner* cases arguing that *Krüger* concerned exclusion from the benefits of a collective agreement, whereas the former cases concerned the discretionary power of a Member State to determine its national social security and employment policy.

The *Krüger* ruling reveals that the institutional dynamics of equal treatment are complex, and sometimes contradictory. In *Barber* v *GRE*[49] a non-contributory 'contracted-out'[50] pension scheme and a statutory redundancy scheme were held to fall within the scope of Article 119 EC. The UK government had tried to argue that the statutory redundancy payment fell within Article 118 EC, but the Court ruled that the severance payments facilitated the adjustment to new circumstances as a result of the termination of employment which provides a worker with a source of income during the period in which a worker is seeking new employment. The Court reiterated the point made in the second *Defrenne* case that Article 119 EC applies to discrimination which arises from legislative provisions and which affects a worker's immediate or future pay by reason of the existence of an employment relationship. Statutory or *ex gratia* payments were not excluded from Article 119 EC, even if they reflected considerations of social policy. In *Barber* the Court ruled that the principle of equal pay must be ensured in respect of each element of remuneration in order to ensure transparency of the pay system.

In the same way that the direct effect of Article 119 EC came as a shock, not only to the Member States, but also private employers, in 1976, the inclusion of occupational pension benefits came as an even bigger surprise in 1990. The Community had enacted two Directives on equal treatment in state[51] and occupational social security.[52] Both Directives had long transitional periods and were hedged with exclusions and *lacunae*. In cutting across this secondary legislation, the Court recognised that the Member States and private parties – not just employers but insurance companies – were reasonably entitled to think that Article 119 EC did not apply to occupational pensions and severance payments paid out under statutory schemes. Since there was the need to avoid upsetting retroactively the financial balance of many contracted-out schemes, the Court followed the precedent set in the second *Defrenne* ruling by setting a temporal limita-

---

49 Case 262/88 [1990] ECR 1889.
50 This is where the employer could substitute the state-earnings-related part of statutory pensions with his/her own pension scheme.
51 Council Directive 79/7/EEC, OJ 1979 L6/24.
52 Council Directive 86/378/EEC, OJ 1986 L 225/40.

tion on the ruling. Only claims brought after the date of the ruling (17 May 1990), except where an action had been initiated before the ruling, could rely upon raising the principle of equal treatment in occupational social security schemes.[53]

Even this use of a temporal ruling did not prevent an avalanche of equal treatment claims. Despite the ruling in the second *Defrenne* case, that the Member States could not, by political declaration, alter their obligations under Article 119 EC, the Member States attached a Protocol (Protocol 2) to the TEU 1992 'explaining' the scope of the *Barber* ruling, which a perhaps more timid court than the one in 1976 decided to follow in the *Ten Oever*[54] case. Here the issue was whether equal treatment applied to employer contributions into a pension scheme as well as benefits accrued within the scheme. The Court accepted in *Ten Oever* that the principles of *Barber* applied to benefits payable in respect of periods of service after 17 May 1990.

In an earlier ruling, *Bilka-Kaufhaus*,[55] the Court had ruled that Article 119 EC applied to *access* to occupational pension schemes. This created a number of problems where part-time workers or married women had been denied access to occupational pension schemes. The Court has ruled that there was no temporal limitation to the *Bilka-Kaufhaus* ruling and therefore access to occupational pension schemes and periods of service must be acknowledged from 8 April 1976, the date of the direct effect of Article 119 EC from the second *Defrenne* case. For many part-time female workers this right may be illusory since the Court has ruled they must pay the employee contribution to the pension scheme in order to qualify for the full benefits.[56]

In one of the post-*Barber* cases the Court ruled that the *trustees* of a pension scheme are under a duty to do everything within the scope of their powers to ensure compliance with the equal treatment principle.[57] If securing the principle of equality is beyond the powers of the trustees, then employers and trustees are under a duty to use all the means available

---

[53] See Case C-147/95 *Dimosia Epicheirisi Ilektrismou (Dei) v Erthimios Evrenopoulos* [1997] ECR I-2057. Here the applicant, a widower, had commenced proceedings in the Greek courts on 12 June 1989, arguing that the denial of a survivor's pension to a widower, when such a pension was available to a widow, was contrary to Article 119 EC. The Court ruled that survivor's benefits fell within Article 119 EC and should be available to male and female beneficiaries on the same terms. See also C-50/99 *Podesta*, pending.

[54] Case C-109/91 [1993] ECR I-4879.

[55] Case 170/84 [1986] ECR 1607.

[56] Case C-435/93 *Dietz v Stichting Thuiszorg Rotterdam* [1996] ECR I-5223; Case C-246/96 *Maggorian* [1997] ECR I-7153; See also Case C-78/98 *Preston and Others v Wolverhampton Healthcare NHS Trust and Others*, pending, Opinion of 14 September 1999.

[57] Case C-200/91 *Coloroll* [1994] ECR I-4389.

under domestic law, for example recourse to the courts, particularly where the involvement of the courts is necessary to amend the provisions of a pension or trust deed.

4.2 The Equal Treatment Directive

4.2.1 Scope of the equal treatment principle

The *Defrenne* litigation provided the impetus for further legislation in the field of equal treatment beyond equal pay. Based upon *Article 308 EC* (ex Article 235 EC), Council Directive 76/207/EEC, the Equal Treatment Directive (ETD),[58] has the potential to be a far-reaching device to extend the principle of equal treatment as regards access to employment, vocational training, promotion and working conditions. The principle of equal treatment goes beyond a lot of national measures, embracing the concept of direct and indirect discrimination,[59] a toleration of positive discrimination,[60] and covers marital or family status discrimination. The most expansive interpretation of the concept of sex discrimination in the Directive is the ruling by the Court of Justice in *P* v *S*.[61]

There are derogations where sex is a determining fact in a job[62] and where there are special provisions protecting women during pregnancy and maternity.[63] In *Johnston* v *RUC*,[64] the Court ruled that any derogation from the equal treatment principle should be interpreted strictly and justified according to the principle of proportionality. The case concerned a challenge to the practice of not allowing full-time female officers in a reserve police force to receive firearms training or to carry firearms. The Chief Constable was concerned that it would increase the risk of assassination and would be a departure from the ideal of an unarmed police force. The Court argued that women should not be excluded from one particular occupation on the ground that public opinion demanded that women be

---

[58] OJ 1976 L 39/40.

[59] Now defined in Article 2(2) of Council Directive 97/80/EC, OJ 1998 L 14/6.

[60] Article 2(4) Equal Treatment Directive 76/207/EEC and the new *Article 141 EC* introducing the SPA into the Treaty, but compare the Court's mixed response in Case C-450/93 *Kalanke* v *Freie Hansestadt Bremen* [1995] ECR I-3051, Case C-409/95 *Marschall* [1997] ECR I-6363. There is a difference in wording from Article 6(4) SPA and the new *Article 141(4)* with the latter relating more closely to the Court's interpretation of Article 2(4) of the Equal Treatment Directive. Compare, however, the *Declaration to Article 141 EC* which contradicts the wording of *Article 141(4) EC*.

[61] Case C-13/94 *P* v *S and Cornwall County Council* [1996] ECR I-2143.

[62] Article 2(3). See also Council Directive 92/85/EEC, OJ 1992 L 348/1.

[63] Article 2(2).

[64] Case 222/84 [1986] ECR 1651.

given greater protection than men against risks which affect both sexes and which were distinct from women's specific needs of protection.

Recent cases have challenged the exclusion of women from the armed forces. The Court has accepted that in certain circumstances a Member State may exclude women from certain roles; in *Sirdar*, for example, women were not allowed to join the marines since this was a special category used for rapid deployment as assault troops.[65] The Court ruled that any derogation from the equal treatment principle must be strictly defined and be applied in accordance with the principle of proportionality. In *Kreil v Federal Republic of Germany*[66] the Court followed Advocate General Pergola's Opinion that a blanket exclusion of women from the combat units of the armed forces in Germany is contrary to the ETD. Where a Member State has exercised a derogation under the Directive, it is under a duty under Article 9 of the ETD to review the justification for a derogation in the light of changing social conditions. There are also some exclusions, for example social security matters, which are left outside of the scope of the Directive and provided for in later Directives.

4.2.2 Procedural rights as human rights

The Directive has strong procedural aspects. Member States are under a duty to amend any laws, regulations or administrative provisions which are contrary to the Directive and to make provision for the amendment or nullification of discriminatory provisions in collective agreements, rules of undertakings and professional associations.[67] There has been some fruitful litigation under Article 6 of the Directive which, together with Articles 7 and 8, imposes a duty upon Member States to ensure that employees have access to the judicial process to assert their rights under the Directive and that employees are made aware of their rights. From this obligation, the Court has developed a notion of 'effective' remedies. In *Von Colson*[68] the Court ruled that the full implementation of Article 6 entailed that sanctions chosen for the breach of the Directive must be such as to guarantee real and effective judicial protection and have a deterrent effect upon the employer. In *Johnston* v *Chief Constable of the RUC*[69] the principle of access to effective judicial protection was elevated into a general principle of Community law with the Court referring to Articles 6 and 13 ECHR and the Joint Declaration of the respect for fundamental human rights adopted by the Community Institutions in 1977.

---

[65] Case C-273/97, judgment of 26 October 1999.
[66] Case C-285/98, judgment of 11 January 2000; Opinion of 26 October 1999.
[67] Article 3. See Case 165/82 *Commission* v *United Kingdom* [1983] ECR 3431.
[68] Case 14/83 [1984] ECR 1891.
[69] Case 222/84 [1986] ECR 1651.

In *Dekker*[70] the Court implied that when sanctions are at issue there is a duty upon national courts to set aside national provisions which are incompatible with the Directive. This idea is implemented in *Marshall (No. 2)*[71] where a woman challenged the level of compensation available at the national level for discrimination occurring as a result of differences in retirement age between men and women.[72] The different retirement ages reflected the differences between the statutory pension age for men and women which were excluded from the scope of the statutory social security Directive[73] and equalisation of state pension ages was deferred in the occupational social security Directive.[74] Nevertheless, the Court drew a distinction between state pension ages and the occupational retirement age, ruling that the latter fell within the scope of Article 5, ETD. When Ms Marshall was finally awarded compensation, she faced a statutory limit on the amount of compensation, which could be awarded. She argued that this limitation plus the fact that interest could not be granted on the award denied her an effective remedy within the meaning of Article 6, ETD. In a more recent ruling, the Court has ruled that national laws may impose a ceiling upon the amount of compensation available, provided that the remedy offered was real and effective.[75]

4.2.3 Working conditions

Article 5 of the Directive relates to discrimination in working conditions. This provision generated most of the early litigation around the Directive. The Court has been asked to rule on the scope of Articles 5 and 6 of the ETD in relation to discrimination which occurred *after* the employment relationship had ended.[76] Coote brought a claim of sex discrimination against her employer. The claim was settled and the employment relationship ended by mutual agreement. Coote found it difficult to obtain a new job which she alleged was due to her former employer failing to provide a reference. Under English law her claim fell outside the scope of the Sex Discrimination Act 1975 and the United Kingdom government also submitted that any measures taken after the employment relationship had

---

70 Case C-177/88 [1990] ECR I-3941.
71 Case C-271/91[1993] ECR I-4367.
72 Case 152/84 *Marshall v Southampton and South West Hampshire Area Health Authority* [1986] ECR 723.
73 Council Directive 79/7/EEC, OJ 1979 L 6/24.
74 Council Directive 86/378/EEC, OJ 1986 L 225/40, now amended by Council Directive 96/97/EC OJ 1997 L 46/20.
75 Case C-180/95 *Nils Draehmpaehl v Urania Immobilien Service ohg* [1997] ECR I-2195.
76 Case C-185/97 *Coote v Granada Hospitality Ltd* [1998] ECR I-5199.

ended fell outside of the scope of the Directive.[77] The Court reiterated its case law on Article 6 of the Directive ruling that Article 6 'is an essential factor for attaining the fundamental objective of equal treatment for men and women' which, as the Court has repeatedly held, is one of the fundamental human rights whose observance the Court has a duty to ensure. The Court pointed out that the principle of effective judicial control, which is also recognised as a fundamental human right in Community law, would be deprived of an essential part of its effectiveness if it did not cover the situation in this case since employees would be deterred from bringing sex discrimination claims if they knew that an employer could engage in such reprisals without any redress for the employee from the legal system. The Court ruled that it was not the intention of the drafters of the Directive to limit retaliatory measures to dismissal (mentioned in Article 7). Article 6 provided an overriding duty to provide effective judicial protection for victims of sex discrimination even after the employment relationship had ended.

The protective laws of the Member States preventing women from working at night have also posed problems for the application of the ETD. A number of Member States had legislation implementing obligations under the ILO Convention No. 189 of 1948 which prohibited night work by women. A new non-discriminatory ILO Convention No. 171 was passed in 1992. The ECJ has ruled that Article 5 ETD precludes a Member State from maintaining divergent systems of derogations from the ban on night working.[78] In *Commission* v *France*[79] the Court ruled that it was not evident, except in cases of pregnancy and maternity, that the risks incurred by women working at night were different from those incurred by men. If it was the case that the risk of assault was greater at night than by day suitable measures could be adopted to handle this risk without jeopardising the fundamental principles of equal treatment.[80]

---

[77] The UK government pointed to Article 7 of the Directive which requires the Member States to take the necessary measures to protect employees against dismissal by the employer as a reaction to any legal proceedings aimed at enforcing compliance with the equal treatment principle.

[78] Case 158/91 *Levy* [1993] ECR I-4287.

[79] Case 312/86 [1988] ECR 3559. See Kilpatrick, C., 'Production and Circulation of EC Night Work Jurisprudence' (1996) 25 *Industrial Law Journal* 159; Sciarra, S., 'Dynamic Integration of National and Community Sources: The Case of Night Work for Women' in Hervey, T. and O'Keeffe, D. (eds) *Sex Equality Law in the European Union* (Wiley, Chichester, 1996).

[80] See also Case C-207/96 *Commission* v *Italy* [1997] ECR I-6869. A further infringement action was taken against France: Case C-197/96 *Commission* v *France* [1997] ECR I-1489. Neither Member State has complied with the ECJ rulings and in 1998 a further reasoned opinion was sent to France and a letter to Italy under the infringement procedure.

4.2.4 Troublesome cases

Pregnancy

Article 2(3) ETD allows for special protection to be afforded to women in relation to pregnancy and maternity. The Court has not been responsive to claims for paternity leave brought under this derogation.[81] In contrast, the Court has built upon Articles 2(1) and 3(1) of the ETD to afford protection for women who are discriminated against on the grounds of pregnancy. In *Dekker*[82] the Court ruled that discrimination against a woman because she was pregnant amounted to direct discrimination without the need to make comparisons with how a man would be treated in a comparable situation. An employer cannot rely upon exemptions or exclusions or justifications which might be available under national law. The *Dekker* ruling has generated an interest in forcing the law to recognise and accommodate the most crucial of differences between men and women at work.

The Court added a touch of ambiguity in *Webb* v *EMO Cargo*[83] and *Habermann-Beltermann* v *Arbeiterwohlfahrt*[84] where there is the suggestion that if the employee is working on a temporary or fixed term basis there may be a justification for such discrimination. This idea is problematic since it is arguable that direct discrimination should not be open to justification. Justification is usually associated with indirect discrimination and any justification should not be related to the sex of the worker. Direct discrimination automatically establishes a direct link between the sex of the worker and the discrimination.

One question which has troubled the Court is the question of how long pregnancy-discrimination protection lasts in relation to alleged discriminatory acts of employers. The question is now settled by Article 10 of Council Directive 92/85/EC,[85] which provides for protection against dismissal from the beginning of pregnancy until the end of the period of maternity leave. Article 8 of the Directive places an obligation upon the Member States to provide a continuous period of maternity leave of at least 14 weeks. This can be allocated before or after confinement but at least two weeks of the leave must be allocated for a minimum period of two weeks before, or after, the birth of the baby. Thus, after the birth of a baby, the protection of pregnancy and maternity only lasts for the length of maternity leave established by each state.[86] Once this is exhausted, the

---

[81] Case 184/83 *Hofmann* v *Barmer Ersatzkasse* [1984] ECR 3047.
[82] Case C-177/88 [1990] ECR I-3941. See also Case 207/98 *Mahlburg*, judgment of 3 February 2000.
[83] Case C-32/93 [1994] ECR I-3567.
[84] Case C-421/92 [1994] ECR I-1657.
[85] OJ 1992 L 348/1. See Case C-394/96 *Brown* v *Rentokil* [1998] ECR I-4185.
[86] Case C-179/88 *Hertz* v *Dansk Abejdsgiverforening* [1990] ECR I-394; Case C-400/95 *Larsson* [1997] ECR I-3979.

special status is lost and the national laws of the Member States will be able to compare the treatment of the woman with that of a man in comparable circumstances (usually a sick man who is unable to work).

The ETD is still important for acts of discrimination against pregnant women which fall short of dismissal. In *Thibault*[87] a woman was denied the right to assessment of her performance which might allow for the possibility of career advancement since she had been on sick leave and then maternity leave. The Court was asked if this was a breach of Articles 1, 2(1), 5(1) and, if relevant, Article 2(4) of the ETD. The Court ruled that Article 2(3) of the Directive cannot be interpreted in a way that would lead to unfavourable treatment against women. The Court ruled that 'the result pursued by the Directive is substantive, not formal equality'.[88] Article 5(1) of the Directive precludes a national provision of contractual origin which provides in neutral terms that an employee who has been present in post for six months should obtain a staff report from his/her superiors but which in practical terms constitutes sex discrimination when it allows an employer to count maternity leave as a period of absence due to sickness.

Positive action

Article 2(4) of the ETD permits derogations from the concept of formal equality where Member States have introduced measures in order to promote equal opportunity between men and women in the form of positive action. Positive action is also favoured by the Commission.[89] The Court has ruled that any measures taken by the Member States must be specific, addressing concrete situations where women are underrepresented at a workplace.[90] In the controversial ruling of *Kalanke*[91] the Court rejected the use of a 'soft form' of positive action, a tie-break policy where there were two suitably qualified candidates for a job and there was underrepresentation of one sex. Then the candidate from the underrepresented sex automatically was awarded the job. The Court was obliged to rethink its position in the *Marschall*[92] ruling, arguing that the difficulty with the positive action programme in *Kalanke* was that it was automatic and offered no scope for the individual circumstances of the disappointed applicant to be taken into account. Where a positive action programme did allow for individual factors to be taken into account then such a scheme could be accepted as complying with the equal treatment principle.

---

87 Case C-136/95 *CNAVTS* v *Thibault* [1998] ECR I-2011.
88 Para 31.
89 See Szyszczak, E., 'Positive Action After *Kalanke*' (1996) 59 *Modern Law Review* 876.
90 Case 312/86 *Commission* v *France* [1988] ECR 6315.
91 Case C-450/93 *Kalanke* v *Frei Hansestadt Bremen* [1995] ECR I-3051.
92 Case C-409/95 *Marschall* v *Land Nordrhein-Westfalen* [1997] ECR I-6363.

The cases focus upon the concept of individual rights and the desire not to make individual employees suffer for historical or institutional factors which have led to imbalances in the workplace. Two cases pending address even more challenging questions on the scope of equal treatment. In *Badeck*[93] a reference has been made as to the legality of the positive action policy of the state of Hesse in Germany. Here a female quota of at least 50% must be instituted in public offices where women are underrepresented and there must be guarantees that redundancies do not decrease the balance of male–female office holders. The law also allows for quotas in vocational training and also states that the proportion of female staff in universities must reflect the proportion of female graduates from each Faculty. Even more challenging is a reference from Sweden[94] where a special fund has been established to increase the number of female professors. The board of nomination at Gothenburg University had recommended that a man be appointed to a vacant chair, but this was overridden by the principal of the university who appointed a woman to the post. Fredman[95] has argued that the Court in *Marschall* has not offered an intellectually coherent analysis of the problems posed by positive action. The emphasis placed on the discretionary proviso in *Marschall* does not equip EC law to deal with the more problematic issues raised in *Badeck* and *Anderson and Abrahamsson*. In Advocate General Saggio's Opinion in *Badeck*,[96] he recognises the inadequacies of the current Community law in dealing with the complex question of positive discrimination. He finds the German quota system compatible with the Directive in so far as it permits the employer to select the employee with the most suitable profile for the job. The same Advocate General delivered the Opinion in *Abrahamsson*.[97] Here he has come to the opposite conclusion in relation to the Swedish law. He argues that the preference given to the female candidate does not consider the professional qualifications of the competitors and there is no opportunity for a saving clause as in *Marschall* for the particular circumstances of the disappointed applicant to be considered. The Advocate General did not accept the proposition that the positive discrimination programme had only limited circumstances which might render it compatible with the Directive.

---

[93] Case C-158/97 (judgment given on 28 March 2000).
[94] Case C-407/98 *Anderson and Abrahamsson v Fogelqvist*, pending.
[95] Fredman, S., 'After *Kalanke* and *Marschall*: Affirming Affirmative Action' (1998) 1 *The Cambridge Yearbook of European Legal Studies* 199.
[96] 10 June 1999.
[97] 16 November 1999.

4.3 Social security issues

There are two Directives handling equal treatment in social security: one covers state social security schemes,[98] the other covers occupational social security schemes.[99] It was envisaged that a third Directive would be enacted to bridge the two Directives and fill in some of the *lacunae* evident in the two Directives, but this Directive has not materialised.[100]

In contrast to the more expansive attitude taken towards the effectiveness of Community law in equal pay and treatment issues generally, the Court has taken a more cautious and tougher stance in the state social security arena. There has been an inherent tension between the social and economic objectives of the Community and the perceived need on the part of the Member States to restrain public expenditure. Community law has had to grapple with new forms of family labour market participation[101] as well as the different forms of social security that are emerging in the Member States, in particular the way the Member States use the public and private mix of insurance schemes to cover different and emergent risks.[102]

4.3.1 State social security

Council Directive 79/7/EEC, covering state social security schemes, has generated a lot of litigation. The Directive contained a six-year transitional (implementing) period but during this time the Member States were not able, and not always willing, to adjust fiscal structures or adapt outdated notions of social security, often based upon a 'male breadwinner, head of household' family structure. In contrast, the Court has taken some bold initiatives. The Court has, for example, brought a carer's allowance within the scope of the Directive where a person gives up work to look after a

---

[98] Council Directive 79/7/EEC, OJ 1979 L 6/24.

[99] Council Directive 86/378/EEC, OJ 1986 L 225/40, amended by Council Directive 96/97/EC OJ 1997 L 46/20.

[100] Draft Directive completing the implementation of the principle of equal treatment in statutory and occupational social security schemes COM (87) 494 final. It remains on the Commission agenda: Communication From the Commission Social Action Programme 1998–2000 COM (98) 259 final.

[101] Department of Social Welfare, *Report of Conference Proceedings on Beyond Equal Treatment: Social Security in a Changing Europe, Dublin 10–12 October 1996* (Dublin, 1997).

[102] See the Commission's Social Action Programme, *supra*, n. 100; EC Commission, *A Concerted Strategy for Modernising Social Protection* COM (99) 347 final; *Towards a Europe For All Ages – Promoting Prosperity and Intergenerational Solidarity* COM (1999) 221 final.

person caught by one of the risks covered in the Directive.[103] This has proved to be an exceptional case in the light of subsequent case law.[104] The Court has also included within the personal scope of the Directive workers in 'minor employment' who were working less than 15 hours per week and attracting a salary of less than one-seventh of the monthly salary.[105] It has also been prepared to include persons seeking work within the scope of the Directive.[106]

The material scope of the Directive is set out in Article 3(1). This provides that the principle of equal treatment shall apply in statutory social security schemes which provide protection against sickness, invalidity, old-age, accidents at work and occupational diseases and unemployment. Sohrab[107] has argued that these are 'masculine' risks favoured by traditional notions of social insurance. There is a need to update these risks so that they reflect women's participation in the paid labour market, differences in family structure, as well as the changing nature of social insurance. The Court has not been prepared to extend the list of risks covered by the Directive to cover a housing benefit[108] available to people on a low income or vocational training benefits[109] or a child-rearing allowance intended to secure the maintenance of the family during child-rearing years.[110]

Article 4 of the Directive defines the scope of the equal treatment principle, embracing direct and indirect discrimination. Article 4 has direct effect in the national courts. While many of the claims brought under Article 4 have been successful in tackling discrimination against married women, the

---

[103] Case 150/85 *Drake v Chief Adjudication Officer* [1986] ECR 1995. *Cf.* Case C-77/95 *Züchner v Handelskrankenkasse (Ersatzkasse) Bremen* [1996] ECR I-5689. More recently the Court has included a 'winter fuel payment' within the risks associated with old-age and outlawed the use of different ages applicable to men and women for eligibility for the payment based on differences in the state retirement age: Case C-382/98 *The Queen v Secretary of State for Social Security, ex parte John Henry Taylor,* judgment of 16 December 1999.

[104] See, for example, Cases C-48, C-106/88 and C-107/88 *Achterberg-te Riele and Others v Sociale Versekeringsbank Amsterdam* [1989] ECR 1963. Three women had not worked in the paid labour market for a number of years prior to retirement. One had given up paid work voluntarily, one lost her job but did not look for alternative employment and a third had never engaged in paid work. The Court ruled that all three did not belong to the 'working population' for the purposes of the Directive.

[105] Case C-444/93 *Megner and Scheffel* [1995] ECR I-4741.

[106] Case C-280/94 *Van Damme* [1996] ECR I-179.

[107] Sohrab, J. *Sexing the Benefit* (Dartmouth, Brookfield, 1996).

[108] Case C-243/90 *R v Secretary of State for Social Security, ex parte Florence Smithson* [1992] ECR 1995.

[109] Joined Cases C-63/91 and C-64/91 *Jackson and Cresswell v Chief Adjudication Officer* [1992] ECR I-4737.

[110] Joined Cases C-245/94 and C-312/94 *Ingrid Hoever and Iris Zachow v Land Nordrhein-Westfalen* [1996] ECR I-4895.

Directive has not had much success in encouraging the Member States to move towards individualisation of social security schemes protecting against loss of employment based on risk.

In contrast to the ETD, the Court has taken a more timid approach to the issue of justifying indirect discrimination and the issue of remedies. This is in part a recognition of the Member States' competence to determine the nature and scope of social security schemes and presumably to protect the state, and the taxpayer, against a multiplicity of back-dated claims. As was pointed out earlier, social security issues are excluded from the scope of the burden of proof Directive.[111] In *Megner and Scheffel*[112] the Court ruled that the Member States have a broad margin of discretion to pursue their employment and social security aims. Here it was seen as a legitimate aim to foster minor and short-term employment, and the methods chosen were unrelated to sex. In *Laperre*[113] conditions relating to age and previous employment for the grant of certain income support benefits were also justifiable on social policy grounds. The Court has retreated from its bold position in *Emmott*[114] where it ruled that national time limits cannot begin to run until a Member State has fully and correctly transposed the obligations contained in the Directive. In an attempt to argue by analogy with the interpretation of Article 6 of the ETD in *Marshall (No. 2)*[115] that a Member State was obliged to pay interest on arrears of social security benefits not paid in contravention of Council Directive 79/7/EEC, the Court stated emphatically that arrears of social security benefits in no way constitute reparation for loss of damage sustained and the reasoning of the Court in *Marshall (No. 2)* cannot be applied.[116]

The Court did suggest that a *Francovich* action might be available where an individual has suffered harm as a result of non-implementation or the improper transposition of a Directive into national law. In *Emmott*,[117]

---

[111] Council Directive 97/80, OJ 1998 L 14/6.

[112] Case C-444/93 *Megner and Scheffel* v *Innungskrankenkasse Vorderpflaz, now Innungskrankenkasse Rheinhessen-Pfalz* [1995] ECR I-4741.

[113] Case C-8/94 *Laperre* v *Bestuurscommissie Beroepszaken in de Provincie Zuid-Holland* [1996] ECR I-273.

[114] Case C-338/91 *Steenhorst-Neerings* v *Betsuur van de Bedrijfsverening voor Detailhandel, Ambachten en Huisvrouwen* [1993] ECR I-5475; C-410/92 *Johnson* v *Chief Adjudication Officer (No. 2)* [1994] ECR I-5483; Case C-114-5/95 *Texaco A/S* v *Havn* [1997] ECR I-4263.

[115] Case C-271/91 [1993] ECR I-4741.

[116] Case C-66/95 *The Queen* v *Secretary of State for Social Security, ex parte Sutton* [1997] ECR I-2163.

[117] Case C-208/90 *Emmott* v *Minister for Social Welfare and the Attorney General* [1991] ECR I-4269.

Cotter[118] *and Marshall (No. 2)*[119] the Court has consistently stressed the importance of effective remedies in sex discrimination law. A corollary of this is the provision of adequate remedies in national law.

4.3.2 Occupational social security

The *Barber* ruling, bringing occupational pension schemes within the scope of Article 119 EC, created havoc for the original occupational social security Directive 86/378/EEC,[120] and in the light of the Court's case law, this Directive has now been amended by Council Directive 96/97/EC.[121] This Directive defines occupational social schemes and Article 7 excludes a number of schemes from the scope of Community law.[122] The Directive applies to the working population, including the self-employed; people whose economic activity is interrupted by illness, maternity, accident, involuntary unemployment; people seeking employment; the retired; disabled workers; and dependants claiming under national law or practice. Article 1(3) of Council Directive 96/97/EC codifies the Court's case law by providing a list of provisions caught by the Directive. The Member States had until 1 July 1998 to adjust occupational social security schemes to meet the principle of equal treatment as set out in Community law, although any rights and obligations relating to periods of membership of occupational schemes, prior to revision, will continue. Once again, Member States are allowed to defer the implementation of the equal treatment principle in a number of areas: the determination of the pensionable age and the implications for other benefits, survivors' benefits and actuarial factors.[123] A new Article 9a allows men and women to claim a flexible pension age under the same conditions. A new Annex to the Directive gives examples of elements which may be unequal in respect of funded defined-benefit schemes.[124]

---

[118] Case C-377/89 *Cotter and McDermott* v *Minister for Social Welfare (No. 2)* [1991] ECR I-1155.

[119] Case C-271/91 *Marshall* v *Southampton and South-West Hampshire Area Health Authority* [1986] ECR I-723.

[120] OJ 1986 L 225/40.

[121] OJ 1997 L 46/20.

[122] These include individual contracts for self-employed workers; schemes for self-employed workers having only one member; insurance contracts for salaried workers where the employer is not a party to the contract; optional provision of occupational schemes offered to participants individually to guarantee them additional or a choice of benefits; schemes where benefits are financed by contributions paid by workers on a voluntary basis. Employers may also offer supplementary pensions to equalise the amount of pension paid to both sexes (Article 1(1)).

[123] Article 1(5). See Cases C-377/96 to C-384/96 *De Vriendt and Others* v *Rijksdienst voor Pensioenen and Others* [1998] ECR I-2105.

[124] *Inter alia*: conversion into a capital sum of part of a periodic pension; transfer of pension rights; a reversionary pension payable to a dependant in return for the surrender of part of a pension; a reduced pension on voluntary early retirement.

Article 2 clarifies the temporal limitations of *Barber*. The equal treatment principle covers all benefits derived from periods of employment after 17 May 1990 and such measures shall apply retroactively to 17 May 1990, but for any workers who have raised equality claims prior to 17 May 1990, the implementing measures must cover all benefits relating to periods of employment from that date. However, Article (2) allows for national time limits to apply, provided that they are not less favourable than those applying to similar actions under domestic law and do not render the exercise of Community rights impossible in practice.

The Commission has initiated infringement actions against a number of Member States for non-notification of the Directive or for failing to implement the Directive properly.[125]

4.4 Soft law and the principle of equal treatment

What is remarkable about the field of equal treatment between the sexes is that alongside the hard law framework there is also a considerable amount of 'soft law' measures dealing with equality. This is a form of subsidiarity: of setting Community goals but allowing the Member States a discretion to implement such goals through national practices. This is important given the differences between the Member States as to how much legislation on equal opportunity/treatment issues falls within the remit of Community law and the fact that equal treatment affects the public/private divide. The Community has used Action Programmes to develop a framework for equal opportunities policies.[126] Although the use of soft law can entrench the differences between the Member States, it has some positive dimensions.[127] In particular, the four equal opportunities Action Programmes have created the framework for a wide range of equal opportunity initiatives, some being financed from Community sources. This creates a ripple effect throughout the EU whereby the effect of priorities recognised at the Community level penetrate into the national sphere.

Soft law has some binding force since it may be used as a teleological aid

---

[125] *Fifteenth Annual Report on the Control of the Application of Community Law 1997* COM (98) 317 final. *Sixteenth Annual Report of the Application of Community Law 1998* COM (1999) 301 final; Case C-354/98 *Commission v French Republic*, judgment of 8 July 1999.

[126] The current programme will expire on 31 December 2000. At the informal meeting of Equality Ministers in Berlin, 14–15 June 1999, support was given for a Fifth Action Programme. See also Resolution of the European Parliament EP 279.323 of 4 May 1999. These proposals were endorsed at the Labour and Social Affairs Council Meeting of 22 October 1999.

[127] See Beveridge, F. and Nott, S., 'A Hard Look at Soft Law' in Craig, P. and Harlow, C. (eds) *Lawmaking in the European Union* (Kluwer, The Hague, 1998).

by national courts[128] and the Court of Justice. Beveridge and Nott have argued that it can have an empowering effect.[129] It encourages an exchange of dialogue and 'best practice' between the Member States and between the Member States and the institutions. This can iron out differences between the Member States but may not always lead to legislation at the Community level. An example of this law-making process is seen in the treatment of sexual harassment. After a research project investigating the extent, perception and reaction to sexual harassment in the Community,[130] and the Commission and the Parliament proposing that a Directive on sexual harassment should be adopted,[131] the Member States in the Council of Ministers were only prepared to agree to a Resolution.[132] The Resolution was followed up by a Commission Recommendation and a Code of Conduct.[133] After the Social Policy Agreement was accepted, the Commission initiated consultations with the social partners under Article 3(2) of the SPA (now *Article 138 EC*). The social partners agreed that a legally-binding measure in this area was desirable. During the second stage of the negotiations the social dialogue broke down when the employers' representatives, UNICE, refused to make a concrete commitment to a legally-binding measure. ETUC, the employees' representatives, also called upon the Commission not to take legislative action in this area. For the time being, the matter has been dropped since in a speech to the European Parliament on 21 January 1998 the then Commissioner for Social Policy, Padraig Flynn, stated that the Member States did not want to pursue the matter.

In contrast, initiatives in the area of parental leave culminated in the adoption of a collective agreement between the social partners and a Directive in the area.[134] The issue of how Community law and policy might be used to allow men and women to reconcile their occupational and family obligations is one which permeates the Commission's Action Programmes, although it is not always an issue which occupies the mind of

---

[128] Case C-322/88 *Grimaldi v Fonds des Maladies Professionnelles* [1989] ECR 4407.

[129] *Supra* n. 127.

[130] M. Rubenstein, *The Dignity of Women at Work: A Report on the Problem of Sexual Harassment in the Member States of the European Communities* (October 1987). See also Elman, R. (ed.) *Sexual Politics and the European Union* (Providence, Berghahn Books, 1996); EC Commission, *Sexual Harassment in the Workplace in the European Union* (OOPEC, Luxembourg, 1998).

[131] OJ 1986 C 176/79.

[132] OJ 1990 C 157/2.

[133] Commission Recommendation 92/131/EEC OJ 1992 L 49/1. EC Commission, *How to Combat Sexual Harassment at Work: A Guide to Implementing the Code of Practice* (OOPEC, 1993).

[134] Council Directive 96/34/EC, OJ 1996 L 145/9.

the Court of Justice. After a Council Recommendation on childcare,[135] the social partners were able to move forward under the SPA and draw up the first Community-wide collective agreement on parental leave.[136]

A new area of action is that of home-working.[137] A Recommendation[138] has been adopted on the ratification of ILO Convention No. 177 on Home-working. The Member States are invited to ratify the ILO Convention and to inform the Commission of the steps taken pursuant to the Convention.

The Commission has also used soft law to attempt a co-ordinated, multi-disciplinary approach to women's human rights in addition to the market-based activities of the EU.[139] A particular focus is gender-based violence. One initiative, with the acronym DAPHNE, recognises the role of non-governmental organisations and networks.[140] Projects monitoring violence against female domestic workers, migrant women and women with disabilities have been initiated. An observatory, similar to the race observatory, RAXEN (see p. 104), has been established to monitor violence against women.

4.5 Widening the equal treatment principle

Hepple[141] has argued that we need a fundamental re-think of Article 119 EC (*Article 141 EC*) in the light of the changing structure and composition of labour markets in Europe. As well as embracing the idea of a human-rights base to equality, he argues for an appreciation of the role of positive action measures (now recognised in *Article 141(4) EC*) to tackle the collective or group nature of social disadvantage and discrimination. Part of this new strategy should be to extend the equal treatment principle to cover the disadvantage suffered by other groups such as ethnic minorities, people with disabilities and older workers. The means to do this is now possible using the legal base of the new *Article 13 EC* of the Treaty of Amsterdam.

---

135 Recommendation 92/241/EEC, OJ 1992 L 123/16.
136 Council Directive 96/34/EC, OJ 1996 L 145/4.
137 See the Commission's Medium Term Social Action Programme (1995–1997) COM (95) 134.
138 OJ 1998 L 165/32.
139 For an overview of the Commission's policy, see EC Commission, *Equal Opportunities For Women and Men in the European Union 1998*, OOPEC, Luxembourg, 1999.
140 See *Communication from the Commission to the European Parliament on the Common Position of the Council on the Proposal for a European Parliament and Council Decision adopting a programme of Community action (the Daphne Programme) (2000–2003) on preventive measures to fight violence against children, young persons and women* (98/0192 (COD)).
141 'The Principle of Equal Treatment in Article 119 EC and the Possibilities for Reform' in O'Leary, S. and Dashwood, A. (eds) *The Principle of Equal Treatment in EC Law* (Sweet and Maxwell, London, 1997).

On 25 November 1999 the Commission adopted a proposal for a Directive Establishing a General Framework for Equal Treatment in Employment and Occupation.[142] This draft introduces the principle of equal treatment as regards access to employment and occupation, including promotion, vocational training, employment conditions and membership of certain organisations for all persons 'irrespective of racial or ethnic origin, religion or belief, disability, age or sexual orientation'. There are justifications which may be raised on the grounds of a genuine occupational qualification. There is also scope for the Member States to use positive action programmes, to improve upon the minimum requirements laid down in the proposed Directive and to use the social partners to negotiate specific agreements. The Directive has strong proposals for enforcement, the reversal of the burden of proof in indirect discrimination cases and sanctions as well remedies for victimisation.

Despite its limitations, the sex equality programme of the Community is regarded with envy by other disadvantaged groups who, at the national level, are seeking to use law to gain recognition of their rights. The new *Article 13 EC* introduced by the Treaty of Amsterdam will allow the Community to enact further legislation in the non-discrimination field beyond issues of nationality and sex discrimination.[143] In some areas, such as sexual orientation,[144] neither the Community nor the Court has been receptive to widening the existing base of Community law to cover such claims. In other areas, such as disability, the Community has adopted a number of Resolutions and Decisions as well as using macro-projects using Community structural funds to develop policies.[145] Article 1 of the proposed Directive covers disability discrimination. Soft law is also in evidence in addressing issues relating to older people.[146] Arguably, many of the proposals relating to pension arrangements and social exclusion

---

[142] COM (1999) 565.

[143] Szyszczak, E., 'Building A European Constitutional Order: Prospects For A General Non-Discrimination Standard' in Dashwood, A. and O'Leary, S. (eds) *The Principle of Equal Treatment in E.C. Law* (Sweet and Maxwell, London, 1997); Bell, M. and Waddington, L., 'The 1996 Intergovernmental Conference and the Prospects of a non-Discrimination Treaty Article' (1996) 25 *Industrial Law Journal* 320.

[144] Case C-249/96 *Grant v SW Trains* [1998] ECR I-621. See also Case T-264/97 *D v Council* [1999] ECR II-11 (appeal pending).

[145] See Nielsen and Szyszczak, *op. cit.* pp. 212–13; Waddington, L. *Disability, Employment and the European Community* (London, Blackstone, 1995); Thornton, P. and Lunt, N. *Employment Policies for Disabled People in Eighteen Countries: A Review* (Social Policy Research Unit, University of York, 1997).

[146] See paras 24 and 25 of the Community Charter of Fundamental Social Rights of Workers 1989; Council Decision 91/49/EEC, OJ 1991 L 28/29; Council Decision 92/440/EEC, OJ 1992 L 245/43; Council Resolution on the Employment of Older Workers, OJ 1995 C 228/1.

address the needs of the ageing society. It is interesting to note the lack of attention paid to older workers in the human rights discourse of the EU.[147] There has been a Council Recommendation on the retirement age.[148] The year of 1999 was declared the International Year of Older Persons and, as part of its preparatory measures in respect of *Article 13 EC,* the Commission has supported a number of actions in favour of older people.[149]

Under the draft proposal for a Directive Establishing a General Framework for Equal Treatment in Employment and Occupation, age discrimination is covered in Article 1. However, Article 5 establishes a set of justifications to alleged discrimination based on age where they are reasonably justified by a legitimate aim and are appropriate and necessary to the achievement of that aim. The circumstances covered are: the prohibition on access to employment or the provision of special working conditions to ensure the protection of young people and older workers; the fixing of a minimum age as a condition of eligibility for retirement or invalidity benefits; the fixing of different ages for employees or groups or categories of employees for the entitlement to retirement or invalidity benefits on grounds of physical or mental occupational requirements; the fixing of a maximum age for recruitment which is based on training requirements for the post or the need for a reasonable period of employment before retirement; the establishment of requirements concerning the length of professional experience; and the establishment of age limits which are appropriate and necessary to pursue legitimate labour market objectives.

One of the most problematic areas is finding a legal base to tackle race discrimination.[150] Again, resort has been made to soft law, often with the European Parliament leading the way with new initiatives.[151] Symbolic action has been taken; for example, the Council declared 1997 the Year

---

[147] Note the omission in Alston, P. (eds) *The EU and Human Rights* (OUP, Oxford, 1999).

[148] Council Recommendation of 10 December 1982 on the principles of a Community policy with regard to retirement age, OJ 1982 L 357/27. Report from the Commission to the Council on the application of the Council Recommendation of 10 December 1982 on the principles of Community policy with regard to retirement age, COM (86) 365 final.

[149] European Commission, *Forum Special Active Ageing. Promoting a European Society For All Ages,* OOPEC, Luxembourg, 1999.

[150] Szyszczak, E., 'Race Discrimination: The Limits of Market Equality?' in Hepple, B. and Szyszczak, E. (eds) *Discrimination the Limits of Law* (Cassell, London, 1992); Curtin, D. and Geurts, M., 'Race Discrimination and the European Union Anno 1996: From Rhetoric to Legal Remedy?' (1996) 14 *Netherlands Quarterly of Human Rights* 147; Guild, E., 'EC Law and the Means to Combat Racism and Xenophobia' in Dashwood, A. and O'Leary, S. (eds) *op. cit.* A summary of Community action can be found in 'Racism and Xenophobia' at http://europa.eu.int/comm/dg05/fundamri/racism/intro-en.htm

[151] See Nielsen and Szyszczak, *op. cit.* p. 214.

Against Racism[152] and proposed a Racism Monitoring Centre.[153] A key turning point in developing a coherent EC policy towards race discrimination and racism was the publication by the Commission of a Communication on racism, xenophobia and anti-Semitism.[154] This document charted the EC policy in the past and provided an agenda for future action.[155] One of the first pieces of action was the designation of 1997 as the 'European Year Against Racism'.[156] A number of events, conferences and sporting activities were held and the Commission concluded that the European Year Against Racism '... served to confirm the role of the European Institutions in the fight against racism'.[157] The Consultative Commission on Racism and Xenophobia proposed the establishment of a monitoring centre and this was set up in Vienna.[158] The purpose of this Centre is to study the trends and extent of racism, xenophobia and anti-Semitism in the EU. The Centre will co-ordinate a European Racism and Xenophobia Network, called 'RAXEN', and will also co-ordinate its work with the activities of the Council of Europe. The Commission has also adopted a proposal which extends the Community co-ordination of social security schemes set out in Regulation 1408/71 to TCNs legally resident in the EU.[159]

In the Communication from the Commission for an Action Plan Against Racism[160] is the promise of a proposal for legislation to combat racial discrimination. The rest of the Action Plan utilises the multi-layered approach seen elsewhere in the development of EU social policy and labour law. The focus is upon mainstreaming, developing and exchanging information and strengthening information and communication networks.

Until recently the concrete idea of a directly effective principle of non-discrimination on the ground of race/racism seemed beyond the Community legislator's grasp.[161] At the time of writing, the Commission, while still

---

[152] Report from the Commission on the Implementation of the European Year Against Racism, COM (99) 268 final.

[153] OJ 1995 OJ C 166/32.

[154] OJ 1986 C 158/1.

[155] Further information can be found at: http://europa.eu.int/comm/dg05/fundamri/racism/intro-en.htm

[156] Resolution of the Council and the Representatives of the Governments of the Member States Meeting within the Council of 23 July 1996 concerning the European Year Against Racism (1997) OJ 1996 C 237/1.

[157] Communication from the Commission, an Action Plan Against Racism, COM (1998) 183 final, 5.

[158] Regulation 1035/97 OJ 1997 L 151 7. The Regulation uses Article 284 EC (ex Article 213 EC) and Article 308 EC (ex Article 235 EC) as its legal base.

[159] COM (97) final.

[160] Supra n. 157.

[161] See Gearty, C., 'The Internal and External 'Other' in the Union Legal Order: Racism, Religious Intolerance and Xenophobia in Europe' in Alston, P. (ed.) The EU and Human Rights (OUP, Oxford, 1999).

uncertain about the scope of a wider anti-discrimination package, has adopted two proposals presented at the Council Meeting of 29 November 1999. [162]

The proposed Directive on equal treatment irrespective of racial or ethnic origin defines direct and indirect discrimination in Article 2. Direct discrimination is to mean 'where one person is treated less favourably than another is, has been or would be treated on grounds of racial or ethnic origin'. Indirect discrimination is said to occur 'where an apparently neutral provision, criterion or practice is liable to adversely affect a person or a group of persons of a particular racial or ethnic origin, unless that provision, criterion or practice is objectively justified by a legitimate aim which is unrelated to the racial or ethnic origin of a person or a group of persons and the means of achieving that aim are appropriate and necessary'. This definition must be read in conjunction with the rules on the burden of proof set out in Article 8. The language of the Directive is reminiscent of the language used in the United Kingdom's race relations legislation where the concepts have given rise to much litigation over definitions. There is also provision for a 'Genuine Occupational Defence' in Article 4. In the Explanatory Memorandum the Commission suggests that this definition should be consistent with the definitions of indirect discrimination established in equal treatment and free movement law.

The proposed Directive also addresses racial harassment[163] and victimisation. The proposed Directive covers a wide range of situations: access to employed and self-employed activities and working conditions; membership of organisations; social protection and social security; social advantages; education, including grants and scholarships; and access to the supply of goods and services. Article 5 is likely to cause controversy in the light of the Court of Justice's case law. It allows Member States to authorise legislative or administrative measures which are necessary to prevent and correct situations of inequality, that is, positive action. The proposal is also strong on access to justice and effective remedies. Article 11 encourages the use of the social dialogue in this area.

It may be that if the EU is able to secure the external frontiers of the EU there will be greater acceptance on the part of the Member States to allow the Community competence to secure the civil liberties as well as the eco-

---

[162] 'Brussels Seeks Tougher Rules on Discrimination', *Financial Times*, 3 November 1999. COM (1999) 565; COM (1999) 566; COM (1999) 567.

[163] In the Explanatory Memorandum the harassment is explained as 'Such conduct may take different forms, ranging from spoken words and gestures to the production, display or circulation of written words, pictures or other material and, to be caught by the directive, must be of a serious nature, creating a generally disturbing or hostile working environment'.

nomic rights of third-country nationals who are legally resident within the EU.[164] Part of such a raft of rights would inevitably have to handle race discrimination.

4.6 Conclusion

The Equal Treatment Programme has been criticised for its narrow focus upon the market-oriented activities of women, particularly in the highly industrial or professional sectors.[165] At times there seems to be a lack of motivation upon the Court to tackle head on the difficulties women face of reconciling child-bearing, child-rearing and other domestic obligations with paid work in the labour market. Many of these hard issues are dealt with in soft law and the use of the structural funds. The dynamic that created a core of 'hard' legislation has now been lost. Many of the new initiatives are watered down versions of the Commission's original proposals. These initiatives are important, however, since they begin to address the specificity of issues affecting the differences between men and women, for example the protection afforded to pregnancy. It may be that in the face of legislative stalling the newly worded Article 119 EC (*Article 141 EC*) will remain the lynchpin around which economic rights of men and women in the labour market will revolve. But as O'Leary and Mancini[166] point out, the Court has only limited legal tools when asked to deal with complex societal reasons for men and women's different and unequal status in society.

The Equal Treatment Programme stands as a model for the new *Article*

---

[164] See, for example, the Commission's Fourth Medium Term Action Programme on Equal Opportunities for Women and Men (1996–2000), COM (95) 381 final, where one of its principal objectives is deemed to be promoting the active exercise of citizenship rights by women who are nationals, *or resident in*, the EU. *Cf. Proposal for a Council Decision establishing a Community action programme to combat discrimination (2001–2006)*, COM (99) 567 final.

[165] The criticisms are raised, *inter alia*, by Hoskyns, C. *Integrating Gender* (Verso, London, 1996); Fredman, S., 'European Community Discrimination Law: a Critique' (1992) 21 *Industrial Law Journal* 119; Fenwick, H. and Hervey, T., 'Sex Equality Law in the Single Market: New Directions for the European Court of Justice' (1995) 32 *Common Market Law Review* 443; Hervey, T. and Shaw, J., 'Women, Work and Care: Women's Dual Role and Double Burden in EC Sex Equality Law' (1988) 8 *Journal of European Social Policy* 43; Nielson, J., 'Equal Opportunities for Women in the European Union: Success or Failure?' (1998) 8 *Journal of European Social Policy* 64; Roseberry, L. *The Limits of Employment Discrimination Law in the United States and European Community* (DJØF, Copenhagen, 1999). See also the collection of essays in Hervey, T. and O'Keeffe, D. (eds) *Sex Equality Law in the European Union* (Wiley, Chichester, 1996).

[166] O'Leary, S. and Mancini, F., 'The New Frontiers of Sex Equality Law in the European Union' (1999) 24 *European Law Review* 331. See also Arnull, A. *The European Union and Its Court of Justice* (Oxford, OUP, 1999), Ch. 13.

13 EC in showing the dynamic that can be created through the interaction of directly effective rights in the national courts and the use of *Article 234 EC*. Despite the criticisms, EC labour law has created a discourse about substantive and procedural rights to equality in the workplace and changed a number of perceptions at the national level about the role of women and men in the labour market.

CHAPTER 5

Employment protection

Employment protection was viewed originally as one of the core objectives of EC labour law as set out in the Social Action Programme 1974.[1] Yet, only three Directives emerged from this programme, dealing with collective redundancies,[2] employment protection on the transfer of an undertaking[3] and insolvency.[4] These three areas formed the fragile core of EC labour law in the area of employment protection. The Charter of Fundamental Rights of Workers 1989 is referred to in the Preamble to a number of employment-rights Directives, but the rights to employment protection were built upon only marginally after 1989.

Mückenberger and Deakin[5] have put forward an argument for viewing the Community's involvement with employment protection issues as part of a 'floor of rights' strategy. The strategy can be seen as a form of re-regulation within EC labour law whereby differences between the Member States are co-ordinated to allow for more efficient working of the Internal Market. The reasons for the introduction of employment protection rights tend to be regarded as primarily economic. If we disassociate our thinking about employment rights from traditional national perspectives of providing a *coherent* set of individual rights and take a broad perspective of the areas of EC labour law which provide employment protection for both individual and collective interests, we can discern a number of core employment protection rights emerging at the EC level. Two areas – health and safety and the equal treatment programme – form relatively coherent programmes and have developed Community policies towards providing employment protection rights. This chapter will group together the *ad hoc* measures of EC labour law which, it might be argued, add to the 'floor of rights' protection of individual and collective interests in the labour market.

---

[1] *Bulletin of the EC*, Supplement 2/74, OJ 1974 C 13/1.
[2] Council Directive 75/129/EEC, OJ 1975 L 48/29.
[3] Council Directive 77/187/EEC, OJ 1977 61/26.
[4] Council Directive 80/987/EEC, OJ 1980 L 283/23.
[5] 'From Deregulation to a European Floor of Rights: Labour Law, Flexibilisation and the European Single Market' (1989) 3 *Zeitschrift für ausländisches und internationales Arbeit- und Sozialrecht* 57.

5.1 Collective redundancies

Looking first at redundancies, the underlying reason motivating Community intervention was the disparity of regulation of redundancy situations across the Community.[6] The original Directive was amended in 1992,[7] but both Directives were repealed by Council Directive 98/59/EC.[8] Blanpain[9] argues that the motivation for the original Directive is one of a 'social dumping perspective'. The Directive was influenced by the behaviour of a Dutch/German multinational, AKZO, which wanted to restructure. Some 5,000 jobs would be lost. AKZO compared the costs of dismissing workers in the various Member States and decided to dismiss workers in the Member States where the costs were lowest. The Commission identified three areas where it was necessary to harmonise the Member States' approach: compulsory consultation with workers' representatives over impending redundancies (collective dismissals); compulsory notification of impending redundancies to public authorities; and powers on the part of public authorities to postpone or prohibit dismissals in certain circumstances. The last goal was contentious and in the final version of the Collective Redundancies Directive it was changed to an optional provision.[10]

The purpose or aims of the original Directive were very narrow.[11] The Court, taking a teleological approach from the wording of the Preamble to Council Directive 75/129/EEC, stated that the purpose of the Directive was to ensure two objectives, first, '... that greater protection should be afforded to workers in the event of collective redundancies while taking into account the need for balanced economic and social development within the Community'. Second, to promote 'approximation ... while the improvement (in living and working conditions) is being maintained within the meaning of Article 117 of the Treaty'.[12] The real effect of the Directive was to ensure

---

6   *Bulletin of the EC*, 9/72; Freedland, M., 'Employment Protection: Redundancy Procedures and the EEC' (1976) 5 *Industrial Law Journal* 24.

7   Council Directive 92/56/EC, OJ 1992 L 245/3.

8   OJ 1998 L 225/16.

9   Blanpain, R. *Labour Law and Industrial Relations of the European Community* (Kluwer, Deventer, 1991).

10 Article   1(2)(d),   of   Council   Directive   75/117/EEC,   Case   284/83   *Dansk Metalarbejdarforbund and Specialarbejderforbundee i Danmark v H Nielsen & Søn, Masinjabrik A/S* in liquidation [1985] ECR 553, amended by Council Directive 92/56/EEC, OJ 1992 L 245/3. For comment, see Bourn, C., 'Amending the Collective Dismissals Directive: A Case of Rearranging the Deckchairs' (1993) *International Journal of Comparative Labour Law and Industrial Relations* 227; Dolding, L., 'Collective Redundancies and Community Law' (1992) 21 *Industrial Law Journal* 310.

11 The Directive does not apply to redundancies which occur as a result of the termination of an undertaking's operations in consequence of a judicial decision: Case C-250/97 *Dansk Metalarbejderforbund, acting on behalf of John Lauge and Others* [1998] ECR I-8737.

12 Case 215/83 *Commission v Belgium* [1985] ECR 1039, para 2.

that large-scale redundancies are subject to proper consultation with the relevant trade unions or worker representatives and that the competent public authority[13] is notified prior to dismissal. Freedland argues the Directive can be viewed as an employment *policy* measure:

> ... an attempt to create a more controlled approach to economic dismissals than had previously existed. In this conception, the 1975 Directive is at least as much concerned with the influence of the state over collective dismissals as with the rights of the particular workers concerned.[14]

National provisions may be more favourable, and Article 5 of the new Directive allows Member States to promote or permit the application of collective agreements more favourable to workers, in terms of worker participation/industrial democracy. The Directive does not allow workers' representatives a say in whether there are other ways of accommodating work shortages.[15]

The 1989 Social Charter added to the scope of the Collective Redundancies Directive by guaranteeing the right of every worker to adequate social protection (Article 10) and reinforcing in Articles 17 and 18 rights to information, consultation and participation of workers, with Article 18(iii) referring specifically to collective redundancies. Part 3 of the Action Programme to implement the 1989 Social Charter addressed the loophole contained in Article 1(2)(d) of the original Directive excluding a redundancy situation determined by a judicial decision from the scope of the Directive. The development of the Common Market also brought about transfrontier restructuring activities and the Directive failed to address the situation where decisions on collective redundancies were taken by a decision-making centre or an undertaking located in another Member State.[16] It was to this end the original 1975 Directive was amended by Council Directive 92/56/EEC.[17] At the same time, the minimum requirements for the content of information and consultation were specified and enlarged, but a clause which would have created an effective sanction by making dismissals null and void if the Directive was not observed was not included in the original version of the Directive.

---

[13] The reason for notification to the competent authority is to allow for the shock of large-scale lay-offs to be planned and absorbed, for example allowing for extra staff in unemployment social security offices, social services, job centres, etc.

[14] Freedland, M., 'Employment Policy' in Davies, P. *et. al.* (eds) *European Community Labour Law Principles and Perspectives Liber Amicorum Lord Wedderburn* (Clarendon Press, Oxford, 1996), p. 289.

[15] Case 284/83 *Nielsen* [1985] ECR 553, para. 10. See Szyszczak, E. *Partial Unemployment* (Mansell, London, 1990), Ch. 6.

[16] See now Article 2(4) of Council Directive 92/56/EEC; Case C-449/93 *Rockfon A/S v Specialarbejderfrobundet i Danmark* [1995] ECR I-4291.

[17] OJ 1992 L 245/3.

The Directive, as amended, leaves the Member States to choose between a number of criteria, set out in Article 1(1), as to what kind of redundancy situations the Directive should apply. There are also exclusions to the Directive, namely redundancies in fixed-term/specific-task contracts;[18] redundancies affecting workers employed by public administrative bodies or establishments governed by public law; and redundancy affecting crews of sea-going vessels.

In *Dansk Metalarbejderforbund*[19] the Court stated that the sole objective of the Collective Redundancies Directive was '... to provide for consultation with the trade unions and for notification of the competent public authority prior to such dismissals'.[20] Thus, the consultation provisions are seen as the central raft of employment protection rights. Article 2(1) sets out certain requirements as to the nature of consultations, with the view that they should at least cover ways and means of avoiding collective redundancies or of reducing the number of workers affected and mitigating the consequences (Article 2(2)).

In an infringement action against the UK,[21] the Court of Justice was asked to judge whether the requirements of worker representative consultations were met in UK law. In both the Redundancy and Transfer of Undertakings Directives, the requirement is that the 'laws or practice of the Member State' are followed. The UK government opted for consultation procedures with trade unions recognised for the purposes of collective bargaining. Thus, if no union was recognised by the employer there would be no consultation process. During the 1980s and 1990s the Conservative governments made a number of inroads into trade union rights which resulted in widespread loss of trade union membership and de-recognition of unions by employers. When faced with the question as to how far Community law may make inroads into national autonomy in choosing the form of worker consultation, the Court of Justice was circumspect. It stated that Community law required the consultation of representatives elected by the whole workforce. This allows new *ad hoc* forms of worker representatives to emerge for the purposes of complying with Community law, occupying an uncertain place alongside other forms of established worker representatives.[22]

---

18 The Directive does apply where such redundancies take place prior to the date of expiry/completion of the contract.
19 *Supra* n. 10.
20 *Ibid.*, para 10.
21 Case C-383/92 *Commission* v *United Kingdom* [1994] ECR I-2479.
22 See Davies, P., 'A Challenge to Single Channel' (1994) 23 *Industrial Law Journal* 272; Hall, M., 'Beyond Recognition? Employee Representation and EU Law' (1996) 25 *Industrial Law Journal* 15.

Of particular importance in the consultation process is Article 2(3), which establishes a basic list of information which the employer must give to workers' representatives so that they are able to make constructive proposals.

Finally, the Directive outlines the content and scope of the obligations to notify collective redundancies[23] to the competent public authorities. Such notification must be in writing[24] and contain all the relevant information set out in Article 2. The workers' representatives are to receive a copy of the notification and may send in their comments to the public authority. Any redundancy cannot take place until 30 days have elapsed from the notification.

The Directive, even as revised, provides a limited amount of employment protection. Indeed, it excludes some vulnerable workers,[25] thus denying the safety net of legislative rights to workers who are often excluded at the national level and under collective bargaining. The Directive could be said to provide a set of procedural employment protection rights rather than individual substantive rights.

5.2 The Transfer of Undertakings Directive

The original Transfer of Undertakings Directive[26] aimed to safeguard the rights of workers where the employer changes identity. Bercusson[27] describes this Directive as sitting uneasily 'on the cusp between the EU's policy on labour in the enterprise and the free labour market policy of the common market origins of the EU'. In contrast, Benson argues that the

---

[23] Article 5 of the Directive allows the Member States to apply/introduce laws, regulations, administrative provisions which are more favourable to workers. The Court will scrutinise variations to the Directive to assess their adequacy: Case 91/81 *Commission* v *Italy* [1982] ECR 2133; Case 131/84 *Commission* v *Italy (No. 2)* [1985] ECR 3531; Case 215/83 *Commission* v *Belgium* [1985] ECR 1039.

[24] Article 3.

[25] Fixed-term contracts, specific-task contracts, workers employed by public administrative bodies or by establishments governed by public law, and contracts relating to the crews of sea-going vessels are excluded: Article 1(2) (a)–(c). Note the new Council Directive 1999/70/EC of 28 June 1999 concerning the Framework Agreement on Fixed-Term Work concluded by ETUC, UNICE and CEEP, OJ 1999 175/43, applies the principle of non-discrimination to fixed-term contracts and encourages the Member States to prevent abuse of employment protection laws by allowing the successive use of fixed-term contracts.

[26] Council Directive 77/187/EEC, OJ 1977 L 61.26. See Hepple, B., 'Community Measures For The Protection of Workers Against Dismissal' (1997) 14 *Common Market Law Review* 14; De Groot, C., 'The Council Directive on the Safeguarding of Employees' Rights in the Event of Transfers of Undertakings: An Overview of the Case Law' (1993) 30 *Common Market Law Review* 331.

[27] Bercusson, B. *European Labour Law* (Butterworths, London, 1996) p. 234.

Directive is one of the few pieces of Community legislation which 'deal unashamedly with social matters'.[28] The idea is to allow the worker to continue working under the same terms and conditions for the new employer and to protect the worker from dismissal as a result of the transfer of the business.[29] The Directive was modelled upon French law, but has created difficulties for a number of Member States which have different ways of dealing with changes of employer and the ownership of an undertaking. These disparities led to a watering down of the Commission's original proposals so that the protections afforded to employees were much weaker than what was anticipated.

As a result of new forms of restructuring, such as the privatisation of services, issues have arisen as to how far the 'costs' of maintaining a workforce on a transfer should be borne by the transferee. As a result of the Court's case law, the Directive has become one of the most controversial pieces of EC labour law. The Commission[30] declared its intention to produce a Memorandum explaining the case law of the Court and this was issued in March 1997.[31] A proposal[32] to amend the Directive, first mentioned in the Action Programme[33] to introduce the 1989 Social Charter was adopted on 29 June 1998.[34] The amendment works by way of inserting new Articles 1–7b into the old Directive. Member States have until 17 July 2001 to implement the changes.[35]

The Directive is limited. For example, it is not intended to create a 'floor of rights' or uniform level of employment protection throughout the Community on the basis of common criteria.[36] Yet, the Directive has attracted a controversial status as a champion of employees' rights.[37] The new amending Directive gives the Member States even greater latitude in the way certain aims are to be met. Despite this limitation, the Court has ruled that the Transfer of Undertakings Directive is mandatory on every

---

[28] Benson, E., 'The Employment Protection Directives' in Gold, M. (ed.) *The Social Dimension: Employment Policy in the European Community* (London, Macmillan, 1993).

[29] Case 19/83 *Knud Wendelboe mfl v LJ Music* [1985] ECR 457.

[30] Medium-Term Social Action Programme (1995–1997) COM (95) 134 final, para 11.3.2.

[31] COM (97) 85.

[32] COM (94) 300.

[33] COM (89) 568.

[34] Council Directive 98/50/EC. For a discussion on the political backgroud to the amendment, see Hunt, J., ' Success At Last? The Amendment to the Acquired Rights Directive' (1999) 24 *European Law Review* 215.

[35] Article 2, Council Directive 98/50/EC.

[36] Case 105/84 *Foreningen af Arbejdsledere i Danmark v A/S Danmols Inventar* [1985] ECR 2639.

[37] More, G., 'The Concept of 'undertaking' in the Acquired Rights Directive: The Court of Justice Under Pressure (Again)' (1995) 15 *Yearbook of European Law* 135.

point.[38] An employer cannot derogate from one provision on the argument that, on the whole, the contract of employment is favourable to the employee. Article 7 allows the Member States to introduce more favourable provisions for workers.

In *Daddy's Dance Hall*[39] the Court ruled that the protection provided by the Directive was a matter of public policy, thereby applying independently of the will of the parties. It followed, therefore, that employees' contracts were transferred independently of the employees' consent to the transfer. Later cases have cast doubt upon this assumption. In *Katsikas*[40] an employee of a restaurant owned by Konstantinidis refused to work for the person to whom Konstantinidis had sublet the restaurant. As a consequence, Katsikas was dismissed by Konstantinidis. The Court ruled that unless the Member States take the option not to apply Article 3(1), the transferor is automatically released from his or her obligations as an employer and this legal consequence is not conditional upon the consent of the employees concerned.

In a second case, *Skreb and Schroll*,[41] a part of a business was transferred and the two employees concerned refused to accept the transfer of their employment relationship to the new employer. The employees argued that German law and the jurisprudence of the German courts did not compel the employees to accept the automatic transfer of their contracts of employment. In Advocate General van Gerven's Opinion in *Katsikas* these provisions fell within the scope of Article 7 of the Directive. The Court agreed with the German implementation of the Directive. It argued that the Directive did not impose an obligation upon employees to continue their relationship with the new employer. To rule otherwise would undermine the fundamental rights of employees' freedom to choose their employer. Employees cannot *waive* their rights under the Directive.

One of the questions referred to the Court in *Skreb and Schroll*[42] concerned whether a worker can object to the transfer of his/her contract of employment/employment relationship. This question was addressed in *Europièces*.[43] In July 1993 Europièces went into voluntary liquidation and a liquidator was appointed. The liquidator informed the employee, Sanders, that he was dismissed with 22 months' notice on 27 July 1993.

[38] Case 324/86 *Foreningen af Arbejdsledere i Danmark v Daddy's Dance Hall A/S* [1988] ECR 739.

[39] Case 324/86 [1988] ECR 739.

[40] Case C-132/91 [1992] ECR I-6577.

[41] Cases C-138/91 and C-139/91 [1993] ECR I-6577.

[42] *Ibid.*

[43] Case C-399/96 *Europièces SA and Wilfred Sanders, Automotive Industries Holding Company SA* [1998] ECR I-6965.

On 13 August 1993 the liquidator informed Sanders that Europièces had transferred part of its stock and equipment to another company (Automotive Industries). As from 24 August 1993, Sanders would have to carry out his activities on behalf of the liquidation under the direct orders of the liquidator's representative. The liquidator also indicated that draft contracts of employment had been submitted by Automotive Industries to some members of staff including Sanders who had refused the offer. Sanders alleged that his contract of employment had been the subject of a unilateral breach, or at the very least, had been terminated. The Court ruled that the Directive's protections became redundant where a person voluntarily decides not to continue the employment relationship with the new employer after the transfer. The Court noted that the liquidator had indicated that it was not the intention to change Sanders' duties unilaterally but that the circumstances and legal requirements made it necessary to allocate tasks to him. It was for the national court to examine the reasons why the employee refused the contract of employment offered to him and to determine whether the contract involved a substantial change in working conditions to his detriment.

The Directive applies to the transfer of any type of undertaking, business or part of a business (with the exception of sea-going vessels) and covers persons with a contract of employment or persons in an employment relationship as defined by the law of employment in the Member State at the time of the transfer.[44] This approach is in stark contrast to the Community definition given to a 'worker' for the purposes of the fundamental free movement provision of *Article 39 EC* (ex Article 48 EC) discussed in Chapter 3.

The Court of Justice has given a broad application to the Directive to cover a wide range of restructuring tactics such as outsourcing, competitive tendering, market testing, facilities management as well as third-party administration. The original Directive stated that it applied to a transfer which takes place as a result of a legal transfer or merger. The Directive did not apply to transfers taking effect in the context of insolvency proceedings, though Member States could extend the scope of the Directive to cover such situations on their own initiative. The mere fact that the transferor has suspended payment of debts is not sufficient to exclude the scope of the Directive. The Court has accepted that the Directive can apply where a state of crisis has been recognised[45] and where there is a suspension of payments by the transferor. The Directive also applies to a transfer

---

[44] Case 105/84 *A/S Danmols Inventar* [1985] ECR 2639. The Directive does not apply where an employee of his/her own free will does not occupy an employee post with the transferee: Case 19/83 *Wendelbo* [1985] ECR 457.

[45] Case 472/93 *Spano* [1995] ECR I-4321.

as a result of a repudiation of a contract,[46] even though in this situation there is no direct contractual link between the transferor and the transferee.

The crucial element of recognising when the Directive applies is that there must be a transfer of the undertaking,[47] or part of the undertaking, to another employer.[48] Thus, the Directive does not apply when the majority of shares in a limited company is acquired by another company (a share takeover). The decisive criterion for deciding if there is a transfer of an undertaking for the purposes of the Directive is the question 'does the entity retain its economic identity?' as indicated, *inter alia,* by the fact that its operation is actually continued or resumed. In *Spijkers*[49] the Court ruled that a national court must consider all the facts characterising the transaction in question. These include, *inter alia*: the type of undertaking or business; whether or not the tangible assets (such as buildings and moveable property) are transferred; the value of intangible assets at the time of the transfer; whether or not the majority of its employees are taken over by the new employer; whether or not its customers are transferred; the degree of similarity between the activities carried on before and after the transfer; and the period, if any, for which those activities were suspended.

In *Schmidt*[50] the Court was asked to rule on whether the cleaning operations of a branch of an undertaking can be treated as part of a business where the work was performed by one employee before being transferred by contract to an outside undertaking. The Court applied its earlier ruling of *Rask* to confirm that even where the activity transferred is merely an ancillary activity not necessarily connected with the objects of the undertaking this does not preclude the Directive from applying. In *Süzen*[51] the question arose as to whether a person who had entrusted the cleaning of his premises to an undertaking and then terminated the contract and entered into a new contract to perform similar work with a second undertaking without any transfer of tangible or intangible business assets from one undertaking to the other fell within the scope of the Directive.

---

[46] Case 287/86 *Ny Mølle Kro* [1987] ECR 5465; Case C-29/91 *Sophie Redmond Stichting* [1992] ECR I-3189; Case C-209/91 *Rask* [1992] ECR I-5755.

[47] Case 287/86 *Ny Mølle Kro, supra* n. 46. This includes the situation where a lessee is in breach of a lease agreement and the owner rescinds the agreement and takes over the running of the undertaking or leases the business to a new lessee: Case 324/86 *Daddy's Dance Hall* [1988] ECR 739.

[48] Case 186/83 *Botzen* [1985] ECR 519; Case C-29/91 *Sophie Redmond Stichting, supra* n. 46.

[49] Case 24/85 *Spijkers v Benedik* [1986] ECR 1119.

[50] Case C-392/92 *Christel Schmidt v Spar-und Leihkasse der Früheren Ämter Bordesholm, Kiel und Cronshagen* [1994] ECR 1311.

[51] Case C-13/95 *Ayse Süzen v Zehnacker Gebäudereinigung GmbH Krankenhausservice* [1997] ECR I-1259. See Bourn, C., 'When Does the Transfer of a Service Contract Constitute the Transfer of an Undertaking?' (1998) 23 *European Law Review* 59.

Repeating the criteria from *Spijkers,* the Court ruled that the mere fact that the service provided by the old and new awardees of a contract is similar does not support the conclusion that an economic entity has been transferred. The Court also ruled that an entity cannot be reduced to the activity entrusted to it. Its economic identity emerges from other factors, for example its workforce, its management staff, the way in which work is organised, its operating methods and operational resources. Thus, the mere loss of a service contract to a competitor cannot by itself indicate the existence of a transfer within the meaning of the Directive. The undertaking previously entrusted with the contract does not cease to exist and the business cannot be regarded as being 'transferred' to the new contractor.

In *Vidal*[52] the Court ruled that the Directive applied to a situation where an undertaking decided to terminate the contract it had with another undertaking to provide cleaning services and instead carried out the cleaning work itself when the operation was accompanied by the transfer of an economic entity between the two undertakings. The Court defined the term 'economic entity' as an organised grouping of persons and assets enabling an economic activity which pursues a specific object to be exercised. The mere fact that the work carried out first by the cleaning undertaking and then by the undertaking owning the premises is similar does not justify the conclusion that a transfer of such an entity has occurred. In *Hidalgo*[53] a public body had contracted out its home-help services and premises surveillance services. On the termination of the original contract, a second undertaking was entrusted with the service provision. The Court ruled that the Directive would only apply to this second generation contract if there is a transfer of an economic entity. The Directive does not apply merely because the tasks being carried out are similar.

Thus, a rigorous application of the 'economic entity' test has resulted in some controversial rulings in the privatisation and contracting out arena.[54]

---

[52] Joined Cases C-127/96, C-229/96 and C-74/97 *Francisco Hernández Vidal SA* v *Prudencia Gómez Pérez and Others* [1998] ECR I-8179.

[53] Joined Cases C-173/96 and C-247/96 *Francisca Sánchez Hidalgo and Others* v *Associación de Servicios Aser and Others* [1998] ECR I-8237.

[54] See More, G., 'The Acquired Rights Directive: Frustrating or Facilitating Labour Market Flexibility' in Shaw, J. and More, G. (eds) *New Legal Dynamics of European Union* (Clarendon Press, Oxford, 1995); Hunt, J., 'The Court of Justice as a Policy Actor: the Case of the Acquired Rights Directive' (1998) *Legal Studies* 336; de Groot, C., 'The Council Directive on the Safeguarding of Employees' Rights in the Event of Transfers of Undertakings: An Overview of Recent Case Law' (1998) 35 *Common Market Law Review* 707; Engels, C. and Salas, L., 'Cause and Consequence, What's the Difference in Respect of the EC Transfer Directive?' in Engles, C. and Weiss, M. (eds) *Labour Law and Industrial Relations at the Turn of the Century. Liber Amicorum in Honor of Professor Roger Blanpain* (Kluwer, The Hague, 1998); Bourn, C. (ed.) *The Transfer of Undertakings in the Public Sector* (Ashgate, Aldershot, 2000).

This was one of the main reasons why Member States, particularly the UK government, pressed for a revision of the Directive.

In *Dassy and Sovam*[55] the Court ruled that the Directive could apply where an undertaking was being wound up, either voluntarily or by court proceedings and administration. Dassy had been employed by Sovam since 1974. On 15 May 1991 the Commercial Court made an order putting Sovam into liquidation and appointed a liquidator. The liquidator dismissed Dassy on 5 June 1991 and on 27 June 1991 transferred the assets of Sovam to Dethier under an agreement approved of by the Commercial Court on 10 July 1991. Dassy brought an action before the Labour Court for Sovam and Dethier to be held jointly and severally liable to pay compensation in lieu of notice, paid holiday leave and end-of-year bonuses. The liquidation was taking place for the benefit of the company and for creditors. While the objectives of a winding up by the court may sometimes be similar to insolvency proceedings, and may sometimes precede an insolvency, this is not always the case and the Court argued that the determining factor is the *purpose* of the procedure in question. In this particular case, the liquidator, though appointed by the court, is an organ of the company which sells the assets under the supervision of the general meeting. There was no special procedure for establishing liabilities under the supervision of the court and, as a rule, the creditors can enforce debts against the company and obtain judgment against the company. This is in direct contrast to an insolvency situation where the administrator, where he/she represents the creditors, is a third party *vis-á-vis* the company and realises the assets under the supervision of the court and the liabilities of the company are established in accordance with a special procedure and individual enforcement actions prohibited. Thus, the differences between an insolvency and a winding up by a court are different so as not to rule out the application of the Transfer of Undertakings Directive in the latter situation. In the winding up procedure, an undertaking continues to trade and continuity of the business is assured when the undertaking is transferred. There was, therefore, no justification for depriving employees of their rights under the Directive.

Europièces SA[56] addressed the question of whether the Directive applied to a company in voluntary liquidation which transfers all or part of its assets to another company from which the worker then takes his orders which the company in liquidation states are to be carried out. The Court ruled that under the original Directive the Directive did not apply to the

---

[55] Case C-319/94 *Jules Dethier Équipement SA* v *Jules Dassy and Sovam SPRL*, in liquidation, [1998] ECR I-1061.
[56] Case C-399/96 [1998] ECR I-6965.

transfer of an undertaking, business or part of a business in the course of insolvency proceedings. The Court referred to its earlier ruling in *Dassy and Sovam*,[57] that the Directive applies in the event of a transfer of an undertaking which is being wound up by the court if the undertaking continues to trade. It was noted that where the undertaking continues to trade while it is being wound up by the court, continuity of the business is assured when the undertaking is transferred. There is thus no justification for depriving employees of the rights guaranteed by the Directive. Voluntary liquidation is essentially similar to winding up by the court except for the fact that it falls to the shareholders in general meeting and not to the court to take the decision to wind up the company, appoint the liquidators and determine their powers. Thus, in some procedural respects, voluntary liquidation has even less in common with insolvency than winding up by the court. The Court made the point that the reasons which led the Court to its conclusions in *Dassy and Sovam* are all the more pertinent where the undertaking transferred is being wound up voluntarily.

In *Dassy and Sovam* the Cour du Travail Liège[58] also asked the Court whether, on the proper construction of Article 4(1), only the *transferee* may dismiss employees for economic, technical or organisation reasons, or whether the *transferor* may do so as well. The Court ruled that Article 4(1) protects the rights of employees against dismissal whose sole justification is the transfer, both *vis-à-vis* the transferor as well as *vis-à-vis* the transferee. In as much as Article 4(1) precludes dismissals from taking place solely by reason of the transfer, it does not restrict the power of the transferor any more than that of the transferee to effect dismissals for the reasons permitted in the Directive.

Following *Bork*,[59] employees who are dismissed before the undertaking is transferred, contrary to Article 4(1), are regarded as still employed by the undertaking on the date of the transfer. The rules protecting employees against dismissal are mandatory and cannot be derogated from.

The Court has ruled also that the Directive does *not* apply to the situation where building works, with a view to completion, are transferred by an undertaking to another undertaking, by merely making available to the new contractor certain workers and materials.[60] There must be a stable economic entity whose activity is not limited to performing one specific works contract.

---

[57] *Supra* n. 55.
[58] *Ibid.*
[59] Case 101/87 [1988] ECR 3057.
[60] Case C-48/94 *Ledernes Hovedorganisation, acting on behalf of Ole Rygård v Dansk Arbejdsgiverforening, acting on behalf of Strø Mølle Akustik A/S* [1995] ECR I-2745.

The crucial aim of the Directive is to safeguard employee rights, and this aim is outlined in Article 3. Since employee rights are automatically transferred from the transferor to the transferee, an employee cannot object to the release of the transferor's obligations.[61] The transferee must continue to observe the terms of a collective agreement, even in respect of workers who were not employed by the undertaking at the time of the transfer.[62] While the transfer of the undertaking shall not *in itself* constitute a ground for dismissal by either the transferor or the transferee,[63] Article 4(1) allows for dismissals to be made on the grounds of 'economic, technical or organisation reasons entailing changes in the workforce'.

Another aspect of the Directive is employee information/consultation in decisions taken during the transfer. Although the Directive was not intended to bring about harmonisation of employee representation, its effects are far-reaching since it is necessary for a Member State to have some kind of employee representation in order to comply with the Directive. The Court pointed out in *Commission* v *UK*[64] that national rules which, by not providing for a system for the designation of employees' representatives in an undertaking where an employer refuses to recognise such representatives, allow an employer to frustrate the protection provided for employees by Article 6(1) and (2) of Directive 77/187/EEC, must be regarded as contrary to the provisions of that Directive.

The Directive preserves the rights of employee representatives on the transfer of the undertaking. The transferor and transferee must supply information to the employee representatives relating to the reasons for the transfer, the legal, economic and social implications of the transfer for the employees and any measures envisaged in relation to the employees.[65] This information must be given by the transferor in good time before the transfer is carried out. The transferee must give information on the conditions of work and employment in good time and before the employees are directly affected by the transfer.

Where the transferor or the transferee envisages measures in relation to the employees, there is a duty to consult with the employee representatives

---

[61] Cases 144 and 145/87 *Harry Berg and Johannes Theodorus Maria Busschers* v *IVO Martin Besselsen* [1988] ECR 2559; Joined Cases C-132/91 and C-139/91 *Grigorios Katsikas et al* v *Angelo Konstantinidis et al* [1992] ECR I-6577.

[62] Case 287/86 *Landsorganisationen i Danmark for Tjiernerforbundet i Danmark* v *My Mølle Kro* [1987] ECR 5465.

[63] If the contract of employment or the employment relationship is terminated because the transfer of the undertaking involves a substantial change in working conditions to the detriment of the employee, the employer is then regarded as creating a 'constructive dismissal'.

[64] Case C-382/92 [1994] ECR I-2435.

[65] Article 6.

with a view to seeking agreement on such measures.[66] Such consultation must take place in good time before the transfer of the undertaking. The consultation obligation is more limited than the duty to provide information. The obligation to consult only arises where the transferor and transferee envisage measures in relation to the employees, for example a reduction in the size of the workforce.[67] A Member State must provide penalties for a failure to meet the consultation requirements of the Directive.[68]

5.2.1 The new Directive

Hunt[69] remarks that one of the most notable aspects of Council Directive 98/50/EC[70] is the flexibility it offers the Member States. Such flexibility was necessary to secure the adoption of the revised Directive, for example in Article 3(1) on the joint and several liability of the transferor and transferee, and in Article 4a on the application of the Directive to insolvency situations. In Article 3(4)(a) on the inclusion of old-age, invalidity and survivors' benefits, the Member States are given the option of whether or not to apply the Directive. Hunt notes the change from prescriptive methods to allowing the Member States wider range of options. In Article 4a(2)(b) a new provision allows the social partners to agree to derogations from the Directive in the economic interests of the undertaking concerned. This provision is part of a strategy to allow flexibility in restructuring processes and reflects tendencies we see in the Commission's social policy strategy generally[71] and more specifically in the newer Directives/Agreements being negotiated under the Social Policy Protocol and Agreement now incorporated into the Treaty of Amsterdam in *Article 138 EC*.

Article 1(1) of the Directive is intended to codify the Court's case law. Recital 4 of the Directive states that the Directive does not provide a new definition of what kind of transfers are included in the scope of the Directive. Hunt[72] asserts the opposite. She argues that the Directive introduces new requirements that the entity in question must be an 'organised

---

[66] Where employees have recourse to an arbitration board the Member States may limit the obligation to consult to situations which entail serious disadvantages for a considerable number of employees.

[67] The Court has interpreted the similar provision in the collective redundancies Directive 75/129/EEC as not creating an obligation with regard to results. While Member States have a choice as to penalties, they must be analogous to those applicable to infringements under national law and be 'effective, proportionate and dissuasive'.

[68] Case C-382/92 *Commission* v *UK* [1994] ECR I-2435.

[69] Hunt, J., 'Success at Last? The Amendment of the Acquired Rights Directive' (1999) 24 *European Law Review* 215.

[70] OJ 1998 L 201/88.

[71] *Commission Communication on the Social Action Programme 1998–2000* COM (98) 259.

[72] *Supra* n. 69 at 227.

grouping of resources' and have the 'objective of pursuing an economic activity'. These were criteria identified in the *Süzen* case but, Hunt argues, were not regarded 'as representing conditions of general applicability to transfer cases'.[73] The inclusion of these words suggests that new hurdles have been created to make the Transfers Directive bite and in the interim the uncertainty and confusion surrounding the scope of the new Directive could lead to confusion and litigation.

5.3 Insolvency

Differences in insolvency protection of workers' rights may affect the operation of the Common/Internal Market and, for this reason, Council Directive 80/987/EEC[74] was enacted using Article 100 EC (now *Article 94 EC*) as its legal base. The Directive does not apply to insolvency situations which occurred before the end of the transitional period.[75] The Directive defines the kind of insolvency situations it covers but allows the crucial definitions of 'employer', 'employee', 'pay' and rights to entitlement to be determined by national law. A number of employees are excluded from the scope of the Directive and these are listed in the Annex to the Directive.[76]

The Directive obliges the Member States to take the necessary measures to ensure that guarantee institutions guarantee the payment of an employee's outstanding claims resulting from contracts of employment or employment relationships relating to pay for the period prior to a given date. The Member States are given a choice over the definition of the 'given date'. It may be either the date of the onset of the employer's insolvency, the date of the notice of dismissal or the date on which the contract of employment/employment relationship ended. Different rules apply to the different 'given dates' chosen.[77]

Article 5 stipulates that the Member States must establish detailed rules for the organisation, financing and operation of the guarantee institutions. These must comply with three principles:

---

[73] *Ibid.*, but *cf.* the *Vidal and Hidalgo* cases, *supra* nn. 52 and 53.

[74] OJ 1980 L 283/23, as amended by Council Directive 87/164/EEC OJ 1987 L 66/11.

[75] Joined Cases C-140/91, 141/91 and C-278/91 *Suffritti, Friori Giacometti, Dal Pane and Baletti* v *Instituto Nazionale della Previdenza Sociale* [1992] ECR I-6337.

[76] Case C-53/88 *Commission* v *Hellenic Republic* [1990] ECR I-3917; Case C-479/93 *Andrea Francovich* v *Italian Republic* [1995] ECR I-3843.

[77] In Case C-125/97 *Regeling* v *Bestuur van de Bedrijfsvereniging voor de Metaalnijverheid* [1998] ECR I-4493 the Court ruled that an employee could not claim for the full loss of earnings and other payments due before the reference period and also could not ask for payments from the guarantee insitution where the actual payments made during the reference period were more than the obligations set out in the Directive.

1 the assets of the institutions must be independent of the employer's operating capital and be inaccessible to proceedings for insolvency;
2 employers shall contribute to the financing of the guarantee institution unless it is covered fully by the public authorities;
3 the guarantee institutions' liabilities shall not depend on whether or not obligations to contribute to financing have been fulfilled.

In an infringement action against Italy[78] the Commission's allegation that the obligations contained in Articles 3 and 5 of the Directive had not been met was countered by the Italian government claiming that the national provisions in force gave equivalent, if not greater, protection. The Court upheld the Commission's complaint but Italy did nothing to adapt its laws to take account of the Court's ruling. As a result, a group of employees who were not able to claim sums of money owing to them on account of an insolvency, brought a claim for compensation against the Italian state.[79] The claim was novel in both Italian law and Community law. In an historic ruling the Court stated that while the obligations to create guarantee institutions did not give rise to direct effect, it was possible for an individual who had suffered loss as a result of a Member State's failure to implement the provisions of a Directive to sue the Member State for compensation in the national courts.

The first *Francovich* and *Bonifaci* action was followed up by claims in the Italian courts by applicants employed by insolvent firms for compensation from the Italian state for its failure to implement Council Directive 80/987/EEC.[80] The Italian government introduced a legislative decree on 27 January 1992 which sought to transpose the Directive into Italian law and also dealt with the losses suffered by employees as a result of the belated transposition of the Directive into Italian law. The new Italian law introduced a one-year time limit in which claims for reparation could be brought. The Italian National Security Institute considered that certain claims being brought for reparation fell outside the period of protection envisaged in the Italian law. In the 1992 law, the Italian government chose to designate the date prior to which the outstanding claims would be calculated as the date of the onset of the employer's insolvency. This is one of the options allowed in the Directive (Article 4). The Italian law extended the minimum reference period of six months to 12 months and laid down

---

[78] Case 22/87 *Commission v Italy* [1989] ECR 143.
[79] Joined Cases C-6/90 and C-9/90 *Francovich and Bonifaci v Italian State* [1991] ECR I-5357.
[80] Joined Cases C-94/95 *Daniela Bonifaci and Others and Wanda Berto and Others v INPS* [1997] ECR I-4006; Case C-373/95 *Federico Maso and Others, Graziana Gazzetta and Others v INPS* [1997] ECR I-4062; Case C-261/95 *Palmisani v INPS* [1997] ECR I-4062.

that this date would be the date on which the judgment to open proceed-ings to satisfy collectively the claims of the creditors was taken. This deprived the applicants in *Bonifaci and Berto* of their rights under the Directive since their periods of employment did not fall within the refer-ence period. The Court noted that the employees had suffered as a result of the length of time taken between the request to open the proceedings and the decision to open proceedings. Citing the *Francovich and Bonifaci* case, the Court ruled that the onset of the employer's insolvency could not be held subject to the conditions set out in Article 2(1). The Court concluded that the term 'onset of the employer's insolvency' must be interpreted as the date of the request to open proceedings if the social purposes of the Directive are to be fulfilled. There was a need to settle precisely the refer-ence periods but this should not preclude a Member State from introducing more favourable provisions for employees which is acknowl-edged in Article 9 of the Directive.

In relation to state liability, the Court stated that reparation for breach of Community law should be commensurate with the loss or damage sus-tained so as to ensure effective protection.[81] The national courts have the role of deciding upon state liability applying the rules of national law. The Court went on to point out that the Italian state was already liable to pay damages to individuals due to the failure to transpose the Directive on time as set out in the first *Francovich* ruling.

In *Maso and Gazzetta* the Court was asked to rule on whether limita-tions could be imposed on the amount of compensation to be paid. The Court repeated its views expressed in the *Bonifaci and Berto* case that any compensation must be commensurate with the damage sustained in order to provide effective protection for employees. Provided the Directive was properly transposed, the Member States could apply the rules limiting the liability of the guarantee institution which were set out in the 1992 law. The Court reminded the national court that it was under an obligation to ensure that adequate reparation was provided for the beneficiaries. The limitation imposed in the Italian law prohibited the aggregation of the reparation to be provided under the Directive with a job seeker's allowance which supported the employee for three months after the termination of the employment relationship. The Court ruled that such a prohibition did not fall within the scope of the provisions of the Directive. This allowed the Member States to set a ceiling to the liability in order to avoid paying sums going beyond the social objective of the Directive or to take measures to avoid abuses. Thus, the Court ruled that the prohibition on the aggrega-

---

[81] See Joined Cases C-46 and 48/93 *Brasserie du Pêcheur and Factortame* [1996] ECR I-1029.

tion of the amounts guaranteed by the Directive with the job seeker's allowance was not justifiable.

The third issue in *Maso and Gazzetta* concerned the words 'the last three months of the employment relationship'. The applicants argued that this should be interpreted as the three months preceding the termination of the employment relationship and the national court asked whether this should be the last three calendar months. The Court gives contradictory answers to the question. In paragraphs 55–59 the Court states that the period of time represents a period of time between the day of the month corresponding to the event referred to in Article 4(2) of the Directive and the same day in the third preceding month. However, in paragraphs 60–64 of the judgment the Court states that 'the term must be interpreted as meaning three calendar months'.

In the *Palmisani* case the Court addressed the issue of the one-year limitation period. The Court reasserted the principle of the effective protection of rights of the individual arising from Community law. As we have seen in relation to the equal treatment between the sexes principle, effective protection means the principle of effectiveness of remedies and protection equivalent to domestic remedies. The Court ruled that the principle of effectiveness was not breached solely by the application of a reasonable limitation period. An objective justification for a limitation period may be the application of the principle of legal certainty. When looking at which national remedy to compare the limitation with the Court rejected the idea of using actions related to social security benefits. The claim of the applicants here was for compensation for breach of Community law by a Member State. However, where the national court was unable to make an appropriate comparison, the application of a one-year time limit to bring the claims was acceptable.

In reviewing these cases, Odman[82] argues that, while the Court refrains from establishing a set of rules for the national courts to follow, it does rule upon the appropriateness of the measure in the light of the aim and scope of the Insolvency Directive. The Court allows for general retroactive application of belated implementation measures as a remedy provided that the damage of the individual is fully compensated, but the Court refrains from stating expressly what may be included as loss and the extent of damages that may be claimed.

The issue of whether ceilings for the guarantee payment may be relied upon when the Commission has not been officially notified under Article 4(3) of the Directive was raised in *AGS Assedic Pas-de-Calais* v *François*

---

[82] Ayse Odman, N. (1998) 35 *Common Market Law Review* 1395.

Dumon and Maître Froment.[83] France had set different ceilings on the amount of guarantee payments but had not notified the Commission of these ceilings in accordance with Article 4(3) of the Directive. Article 11(1) of the Directive provides that the Member States must inform the Commission of the laws used to comply with the Directive. Under Article 11(2) they are further required to communicate to the Commission the texts of the laws, regulations and administrative provisions which they adopt in the area governed by the Directive. The French government had sent two reports to the Commission in 1984 and 1986 setting out in detail the methods for setting the general salary guarantee ceiling. The French laws had been in operation since 1976 and so the French government merely communicated the tables of equivalence between the Community law provisions and the French provisions. The Commission submitted that the French legislation had indeed been the model for preparing the Insolvency Directive and that it had been in a position to take note of the methods setting the ceiling as early as 1979. Therefore, the Commission considered that it had received the information from the French government in accordance with Article 4(3) of the Directive. The Court of Justice ruled that the obligation to notify the Commission under Article 4(3) of the Directive:

> ... does not imply that the duty to inform the Commission gives rise to a Community procedure for monitoring the methods chosen by the member State, or that member States' exercise of the option to set a ceiling is subject to the express or implied agreement of the Commission.[84]

The Court then went on to rule that the obligation contained in Article 4(3) is simply to inform the Commission whether the Member States have exercised the option. Neither the wording of Article 4(3) nor the purpose of the provision suggests that non-compliance with the obligation would render the exercise of the option to set ceilings unlawful.

The Court had been asked to rule on whether Article 4 of the Directive gave rise to direct effect but felt that there was no need to rule on this question. In relation to Article 11(2) of the Directive, the Court ruled that the provision concerned relations between the Member States and the Commission '... and confers no right upon individuals which could be infringed' where a Member State had failed to make the notification.

With the idea of the free movement of persons as a fundamental tenet of the Internal Market, it may occur that an employee resides in one Member State but is employed by an employer situated in another Member State. In the event of an insolvency, the question arises as to which guarantee insti-

---

[83] Case C-235/95 [1998] ECR I-4531.
[84] Para 29.

tution should meet the insolvency claim. This issue arose in *Mosbaek*.[85] Mosbæk resided and worked in Denmark for an English company, Colorgen. Colorgen was neither established nor registered in Denmark but rented an office in Denmark for Mosbæk to carry out her activities. In July 1994 Colorgen was declared insolvent and its employees were dismissed. Under Article 3 of the Directive Mosbæk applied to the Danish Guarantee Fund and to Colorgen's English receiver for outstanding payments of salary, commission and expenses. Rather surprisingly, given the free-movement principle, the Insolvency Directive is silent on which guarantee institution should meet a claim in this kind of situation. The Court ruled that in accordance with Article 2(1) of the Directive it must be the guarantee institution *either* in the Member State where it had been decided to open proceedings for the collective satisfaction of creditors' claims *or* in the Member State where it had been established that the employer's undertaking or business had been definitively closed down. It was noted that in practice the opening of proceedings to satisfy creditors' claims collectively was usually the state in which the employer was established.

Another problem which arises is the interrelationship of insolvency rights with other statutory social security schemes. Article 6 of the Directive prevents the duplication of claims by allowing the Member States to exclude the obligations contained in Articles 3, 4 and 5 from applying to contributions due under national social security or supplementary/inter-company pension schemes outside the national statutory social security schemes. Article 7 obliges the Member States to take the necessary measures to ensure that non-payment of compulsory contributions due from the employer before the insolvency to insurance institutions under national statutory social security schemes does not affect adversely an employee's benefit entitlement in respect of these insurance institutions in as much as the employee's contributions were deducted at source (i.e. from wages). This is the only condition Member States can attach to an employee's entitlement to benefits. Article 8 imposes an obligation upon the Member States to ensure the protection of employees who have left the employment at the onset of the insolvency. Such rights include immediate or prospective entitlement to old-age benefits (including survivors' benefits) under supplementary company/inter-company pension schemes outside national schemes.

---

[85] Case C-117/96 *Danmarks Aktive Handelsrejsende, acting on behalf of Mosbaek* v *Lønmodtagernes Garantifond* [1997] ECR I-5017.

5.4 Information on the contract of employment

Council Directive 91/533/EEC on an employer's obligation to inform employees of the conditions applicable to the contract or employment relationship was adopted on 14 October 1991.[86] It has attracted little attention to date.[87] While the 1989 Social Charter is the inspiration for the Directive, the source of the Directive emanates from British rules.[88] The Directive may arouse interest in future since it embraces the notion of employment relationships which may allow workers, including those who may be defined as 'self-employed', to be brought within its ambit.[89]

The impetus for the Directive came from two factors. The first was the growth in different *types* of employment relationship.[90] The Member States have reacted in different ways to this development and have attempted to regulate the new forms of employment relationships for different reasons. Such regulation is considered necessary, firstly to inform employees of their rights under national labour law and secondly, to provide greater transparency on the labour market. The second factor relates to the development of free movement of labour. According to Article 9 of the Rome Convention on the Law Applicable to Contractual Obligations a contract of employment is valid *as regards form* if it fulfils either the law of the *lex loci contractus* or of the *lex causa*. In order to assess whether or not such conditions are met in employment relationships straddling one or more of the Member States, it is necessary to have harmonisation of the formal requirements of labour contracts. There was a sharp divide between continental European Member States which utilised legislation to regulate employment contracts/relationships and the Anglo-Saxon tradition of less reliance on legislation but acceptance of collective agreements, which were not legally binding, to regulate employment conditions. In the United Kingdom and Ireland there was a duty imposed upon the employer to provide the employee with written particulars of the principal terms of the

---

[86] OJ 1991 L 288/32.
[87] Clark, J. and Hall, M., 'The Cinderella Directive? Employee Rights to Information about Conditions Applicable to Their Contract or Employment Relationship' (1992) 21 *Industrial Law Journal* 106.
[88] See the Commission's Explanatory Memorandum attached to the draft Directive: COM (90) 563 final; Nielsen, R., 'The Contract of Employment in the Member States of the European Communities and in Community Law' (1990) 33 *German Yearbook of International Law* 258.
[89] See the discussion by Bercusson, B. *European Labour Law* (Butterworths, London, 1996), Ch. 29.
[90] For a general survey, see Kravaritou-Manitakis, Y. *New Forms of Work. Labour Law and Social Security Aspects in the European Community* (Luxembourg, OOPEC; Dublin, European Foundation for The Improvement of Living and Working Conditions, 1988).

employment contract which constitutes *prima facie* proof of the terms of the contract. This fact provided a bridge between the Continental and Anglo-Saxon approaches which enabled a Directive at European level to be enacted. The Directive is based upon Article 100 EC (now *Article 94 EC*) and implements Article 9 of the 1989 Social Charter which provides:

> The conditions of employment of every worker of the European Community shall be stipulated in laws, a collective agreement or a contract of employment; according to arrangements applying in each country.

The resulting Directive allows the Member States to exclude a limited group of employment relationships from the scope of the Directive.[91] The idea behind such exclusions is to allow the Member States to maintain some flexibility within national labour markets.

The purpose of the Directive, according to its Preamble, is to ensure that the conditions of employment of every worker of the Community is stipulated in legislation, a collective agreement or a contract of employment according to the arrangements of each Member State. It is now a Community law obligation that every employee covered by the Directive must be provided with a document containing information on the essential elements of his/her contract of employment/employment relationship.[92] A number of cases were referred to the Court of Justice asking for an interpretation of the purpose of the Directive.[93] The German courts wanted to know if the purpose of the Directive was to modify, in the employee's favour, the burden of proof in enforcing contractual obligations. Since it was alleged that the German government had not implemented the Directive completely by the end of the transitional period, the Court also asked if the provisions of the Directive became directly applicable in German law at the end of the transitional period for implementation and could, therefore, be used against the German state, acting as an employer in private law. The German court also asked for clarification of the nature and scope of the information to be provided to the employee under Article 2 of the Directive. The

---

[91] The exclusions cover employees with an employment relationship with a total duration not exceeding one month, and/or with a working week not exceeding eight hours; or an employment relationship of a casual and/or specific nature, provided, however, that the non-application of the Directive is justified by objective considerations.

[92] According to Article 2 of the Directive, the employer must notify an employee of the essential aspects of the contract/employment relationship which are listed in this Article. Article 3 provides that this obligation is met by either a written contract, a letter of appointment or other documents provided they are signed by the employer.

[93] Case C-253/96 *Helmut Kampelmann* v *Landschaftsverband Westfalen-Lippe*; Case C-254/96 *Wilfried Tilsch* v *Landschaftsverband Westfalen-Lippe*; Case C-255/96 *Dieter Klingelhöfer* v *Landschaftsverband Westfalen-Lippe*; Case C-256/96 *Henrich Schmidt* v *Landeschaftsverband Westfalen-Lippe*; Case C-257/96 *Stadtwerke Witten GmbH* v *Andreas Schade*; Case C-258/96 *Klans Haseley* v *Stadtwerke Altena GmbH* [1997] ECR I-6907.

Directive does not affect the Member States' right to introduce provisions which are more favourable to employees. In its ruling the Court of Justice referred to Article 6 of the Directive which preserves national law and practice concerning proof as regards the existence and content of a contract or employment relationship. The Court also placed strong emphasis on the objectives of the Directive and the Community concept of effectiveness:

> The national courts must therefore apply and interpret their national rules on the burden of proof in the light of the purpose of the Directive, giving the notification ... such evidential weight as to allow it to serve as factual proof of the essential aspects of the contract of employment ... enjoying such presumption as to its correctness as would attach, in domestic law, to any similar document drawn up by the employer and communicated to the employee.[94]

This presumption could be rebutted by the employer bringing evidence to show that the information in the notification was either inherently incorrect or had been shown to be so in fact.[95] In relation to notifications under Article 9(2) of the Directive, the Court stated that notification amounts to a presumptive contract which is capable of being rebutted by the employer.

The Court ruled that Article 2(2)(c) has vertical direct effect. It was not open to an employer in every case to confine the information conveyed to a mere job designation. Thus, while the Court did not find the German legislation to be in breach of Community law, it directed the national courts to interpret the German legislation to give effect to the Directive's objectives.

Taking cognisance of the free movement of labour principle in Community law special provisions are included to cover employees working in Member States (or third states) other than the Member State whose law or practice governs the contract or employment relationship. In addition to the information set out in Article 2, a posted worker must be given the relevant information connected with the posting[96] and this information must be given before the posting.

A number of protections are built into the Directive; for example, where there is a change to the main terms of the contract/employment relationship the change must be communicated to the employee in writing. Article 5 states that any changes (including those relating to the contract/employment relationship or a posted worker) must be in a written document and

---

[94] Para 33.

[95] Para 34.

[96] Certain minimum information must be presented covering the duration of the employment abroad; the currency to be used for the payment of remuneration; where appropriate, the benefits in case or in kind which apply to the employment abroad; and, where appropriate, the conditions governing the employee's repatriation.

given to the employee at the earliest opportunity and not later than one month after the date of application of any change. A written document is not necessary where the changes take place as a result of new laws, regulations, administrative, statutory provisions or collective agreements cited in the initial documents. The Member States must guarantee that employees can claim the rights conferred on them by the Directive and Member States must introduce the means by which all employees can pursue their claims under the Directive by judicial process, after possible recourse to other competent authorities.

5.5 Atypical work

During the 1980s the Commission focused attention upon achieving greater protection for what was described as 'atypical work': work which was either temporary, part-time, self-employed, home-work, tele-working, or net-working.[97] The labour market across Europe has changed dramatically over the last two decades, in response to changes in capital ownership as well as the need to compete in the global market with the flexible and deregulated or unregulated labour markets found in the Far East and the United States. The EC interest in atypical work has been motivated by a number of factors.[98] At one level there is a regulatory interest in securing a level playing field to avoid distortions in the labour markets of Europe and distortions in investment/location of firms/factories. At a different level there is another regulatory interest: addressing European unemployment. Many of the Commission's proposals in the 1980s were aimed at providing protection for atypical work to make it more attractive in order to encourage workers to move from full-time/over-time working to part-time work, thus making the labour market more flexible. One side-effect of the interest in atypical work was that initially it was work undertaken predominantly by female workers who found it accommodated their double burden of juggling the need to undertake paid work outside the home with their unpaid domestic caring responsibilities within the home. The responsive attitude taken by the Court of Justice in recognising that unequal treatment of part-time work as compared with the more favourable working conditions of full-time workers could amount to indirect discrimi-

---

[97] Cordóva, E., 'From Full-time Wage Employment to Atypical Employment: A Major Shift in the Evolution of Labour Relations?' (1986) 125 *International Labour Review* 641; Blanpain, R. and Biagi, M. (eds) Non-Standard Work and Industrial Relations (1999) 5 *Bulletin of Comparative Labour Relations*.

[98] See Szyszczak, E. *Partial Unemployment* (Cassell, London, 1990); Disney, R. and Szyszczak, E., 'Protective Legislation and Part-Time Employment in Britain' (1984) 22 *British Journal of Industrial Relations* 78.

nation against female workers motivated an interest in securing the regulation of atypical work at the Community level by interest/pressure groups involved in women's rights.[99]

After failing to introduce measures during the 1980s, due to the need for unanimity voting under the then available legal bases of Articles 100 and 235 EC (now *Articles 94* and *308 EC*), the Commission seized the new opportunity offered by the SEA and the Charter of Fundamental Social Rights of Workers 1989 Action Plan[100] and adopted three proposals based upon Article 100 EC (now *Article 94 EC*) on part-time work,[101] Article 100A EC (now *Article 95 EC*) on part-time and temporary work[102] and Article 118A EC (now as amended, *Article 137 EC*) on temporary work.[103] The last proposal was the first to be adopted by the Council of Ministers on 25 June 1991, as Council Directive 91/383/EEC.[104]

5.5.1 The Temporary Work Directive 1991

Council Directive 91/383/EEC completed the protection afforded to temporary workers in the health and safety programme built up from the Framework Directive 1989.[105] The Directive covers temporary work when the contract is made directly with the employer and also when the temporary worker is supplied through an agency. The Directive aims to reduce the disparity in treatment between temporary and permanent workers by ensuring that both sets of workers receive the same treatment in terms of health and safety at work conditions.

The contract between a user company and an agency must specify the nature of the task to be performed, the occupational qualifications required, the place of work, the hours of work, the particular features of the position to be filled and whether the job is within the category of major health and safety risks as defined by the national legislation. Under Article 3 of the Directive, the temporary worker must be informed of these facts and of any risks inherent in the tasks and receive appropriate training if necessary. Where there are special occupational qualifications, skills or special medical supervision involved Article 5 provides that this must also be notified to the worker and special training given. Except for exceptional circumstances, temporary workers cannot be used for work requiring special medical supervision over a long period of time. Where there are special

---

[99] See the discussion in Chapter 4.
[100] COM (89) 568 final.
[101] COM (90) 228 final.
[102] COM (90) 228 final, amended COM (90) 533 final.
[103] COM (90) 228 final, amended COM (90) 533 final.
[104] OJ 1991 L 206/19.
[105] OJ 1989 L 183/1.

circumstances, then the Member State must ensure that the temporary worker receives medical supervision after the expiry of the temporary contract. Article 4 provides that without prejudice to the liability of the temporary employment agency Member States must ensure that user undertakings and/or establishments are responsible for the duration of a temporary work assignment and for the heath and safety and hygiene conditions covering the work involved.

5.5.2 The Part Time Work Directive 1997

The proposal based upon Article 100A EC (now *Article 95 EC*) did not progress very far in the legislative process. Little happened after November 1990 and in the Belgian Presidency of the Council (in the second half of 1993) it was merged with the proposal based upon Article 100 EC (now *Article 94 EC*). The proposal was withdrawn by the Commission since a Directive has now been enacted under the Social Policy Agreement.

In 1995 the Commission decided to speed up progress in the area of atypical work by invoking the SPA procedure (i.e. excluding the United Kingdom from the decision-making process). In a new proposal, based upon Article 4(2) of the SPA, the social partners' consultation resulted in formal negotiations over an agreement described as 'flexibility of working time and security for workers'.[106] A framework agreement between the social partners was drawn up on 6 June 1997 and the social partners asked the Commission to submit it to the Council of Ministers. On 23 July 1997 the Commission adopted a draft Directive aimed at transposing into Community law the social partners' framework agreement. The Council of Ministers adopted the Directive on 15 December 1997 but with some alterations. The final version did not include the principle of non-discrimination which had been included by the Commission.[107]

The Preamble to Council Directive 97/81/EC runs into 26 recitals. We discover in this Preamble the wide range of factors which motivated the adoption of the Directive, ranging from human rights to job creation to reducing unemployment. Article 2 of the Directive gave the Member States until 20 January 2000 to implement the Directive/Framework Agreement. Article 2 states that the Directive may be implemented through laws, regulations, administrative provisions or necessary measures taken by the social partners. If the latter route is chosen Member States have an extra year in which to implement the Directive to take account of implementation by a collective agreement. An extra year is also granted where there

---

[106] COM (97) 392.
[107] Council Directive 97/81/EC of 15 December 1997 concerning the Framework Agreement on Part-Time Work Concluded by UNICE, CEEP and the ETUC, OJ 1998 L 14/9.

are 'special difficulties'. In both instances the Commission must be informed. This sort of provision is found in the new Directives and creates gaps in judicial control and protection. It would seem that the Commission has a wide discretion to agree to such variations with little possibility of interest groups gaining *locus standi* to challenge the discretion.

The *purpose* of the Directive/Framework Agreement is defined, firstly, as removing discrimination against part-time work. Secondly, it is defined as facilitating the development of part-time work on a voluntary basis, thus contributing to the flexible organisation of working time in a way which is responsive to the needs of employers and workers.

The *scope* of the Directive Agreement covers part-time workers who have an employment contract *or* an employment relationship which is defined by the law/collective agreement/practice in force in each Member State. It is possible for the Member States and/or the social partners to exclude casual workers from the scope of the Agreement, but any exclusion must be in consultation with the social partners (following national law/practice/ collective agreements). The exclusion must be reviewed periodically to establish if the objective reasons raised for the exclusion remain valid.

Clause 3 of the Agreement provides some definitions. A 'part-time worker' is defined as 'an employee whose normal hours of work, calcu-lated on a weekly basis or on an average over a period of employment up to one year are less than the normal hours of work of a comparable full-time worker'. Thus, we have to know what is meant by a 'comparable full-time worker', who is defined in Clause 3(2) as 'a full-time worker in the same establishment having the same type of employment contract or relationship, who is engaged in the same or a similar work/occupation, due regard being given to other considerations which may include seniority and qualifications/skills'. Reading this clause invokes the haunted spectre of the volume and complexity of the litigation which has arisen over similar ideas contained in equal pay legislation discussed in Chapter 4. Clause 3(2) also states that where there is no 'comparable full-time worker' in the same establishment, the appropriate comparison is by reference to the applicable collective agreement. Where there is no collective agreement, then the com-parison should be drawn in accordance with national law, collective agreements or practice.

The Agreement defines the principle of non-discrimination as:

in respect of employment conditions part-time workers shall not be treated in a less favourable manner than comparable full-time workers, solely because they work part-time, unless different treatment is justified on objective grounds.

where appropriate, the principle of *pro rata temporis* shall apply.

The Member States and/or the social partners will implement the non-discrimination principle, having regard to European legislation, national law/collective agreements/practice. If it can be justified, the non-discrimination principle may be modified by the requirement that access to particular employment conditions is subject to qualifying periods/hours or an earnings qualification/threshold. However, any qualifications to the non-discrimination principle must be reviewed periodically in the light of the non-discrimination principle. The introduction of the possibility of a qualifying threshold by means of the subsidiarity principle avoids the earlier barriers that were raised to the acceptance of a Part Time Work Directive when there were differences of opinion as to whether there was the need for a threshold, and if so, where it should be set.[108] In the context of state social security schemes the Court of Justice has allowed Germany to set qualifying thresholds and to justify these thresholds against a claim that they created indirect discrimination against women. In *Megner and Scheffel*[109] the German government claimed that it was necessary to create a qualifying threshold excluding workers who worked less than 15 hours per week and earning less than one-seventh of the average monthly salary from the contributory unemployment benefits scheme. The German government argued that to include such forms of what it described as 'minor employment' would drive low paid work into the informal labour market. In *Megner and Scheffel* the Court did not scrutinise the aims or the means chosen to implement the aims closely but concluded that the social and employment policy aim relied upon by the German government was objectively unrelated to any discrimination on the grounds of sex and that, in exercising its competence, the national legislature was reasonably entitled to consider that the legislation in question was necessary in order to achieve that aim.

In the *Krüger*[110] case the Court of Justice ruled that the principle of equality in relation to equal pay applied to employees excluded from a collective agreement even where the justification for their exclusion from the social security scheme had been upheld by the Court in *Megner and Scheffel*.

The House of Lords refused to accept the British government's justification to a claim of indirect discrimination of an eight or 16 hours per week threshold to exclude part-time workers from the raft of employment protection rights set up from the 1970s.[111] An *Article 234 EC* (ex Article 177

---

[108] See Disney and Szyszczak, *supra* n. 98.
[109] Case C-444/93 [1995] ECR I-4741.
[110] Case C-281/97 *Andrea Krüger v Kreiskrankenhaus Ebersberg*, judgment of 9 September 1999.
[111] *R v Secretary of State for Employment, ex parte EOC* [1994] 2 WLR 409.

EC) reference was not sought in this case but a reference was made in a subsequent case, *Seymour-Smith and Perez*.[112] This related to the two-year qualifying conditions for employment protection rights in the United Kingdom.[113] The case is discussed in Chapter 4. The answers to these questions may prove pertinent to the implementation of Council Directive 97/81/EC.

One of the aims of Council Directive 97/81/EC is to create opportunities for part-time work. To this end Clause 5 of the agreement charges the Member States, in consultation with the social partners, to identify and review legal and administrative obstacles which may limit opportunities for part-time work and, where appropriate, eliminate them. The social partners are charged to do the same within their sphere of competence. Transfers to part-time work are regarded as voluntary and a worker's refusal to transfer from full-time to part-time work (or vice versa) should not in itself constitute a valid reason for terminating employment, but this general rule is subject to qualification in that a termination may be possible where it is in accordance with national law, collective agreements and practice or for other reasons 'such as may arise from the operational requirements of the establishment concerned'. This clause seems hedged with flexibility. One of the ways of reducing unemployment is to consider various ways of sharing out the available work through job-sharing, transfer to part-time work, etc.[114] If such policies are official strategies, outlined say in the NAP created under the new European Employment Strategy introduced by the Treaty of Amsterdam, then Clause 5(2) will presumably provide employers and the Member States with an adequate defence to such terminations. Clause 5(3) states that employers should *as far as possible* give consideration to:

(a) requests by workers to transfer from full-time to part-time work that becomes available in the establishment;
(b) requests by workers to transfer from part-time to full-time work or to increase their working time should the opportunity arise;
(c) the provision of timely information on the availability of part-time and full-time positions in the establishment in order to facilitate transfers from full-time to part-time or vice versa;
(d) measures to facilitate access to part-time work at all levels of the enterprise, including skilled and managerial positions, and where appropriate, to facilitate access by part-time workers to vocational

---

[112] Case C-167/97 R v *Secretary of State For Employment, ex parte Nicole Seymour Smith and Laura Perez* [1999] ECR I-623.
[113] Another case is pending, Case C-414/96 *Kehrl*.
[114] See Szyszczak, *supra* n. 98.

training to enhance career opportunities and occupational mobility;

(e) the provision of appropriate information to existing bodies representing workers about part-time working in the enterprise.

In many respects, this clause is exhortatory rather than creating firm legally binding obligations to facilitate flexible adaptation of working patterns. The looseness of the arrangements is demonstrated further in Clause 6 which reveals the 'minimum harmonisation' nature of the Directive/Agreement. Clause 6 allows the Member States and/or the social partners to maintain or introduce more favourable provisions and the Directive/Agreement may not provide valid grounds for reducing the general level of protection afforded to workers in the field of the Agreement. Equally, the Member States and/or the social partners may develop different legislative, regulatory or contractual provisions in the light of changing circumstances provided the principle of non-discrimination outlined in Clause 4.1 is complied with. The right of the social partners to conclude at the appropriate level (including the European level) agreements which adapt or complement the Part Time Work Agreement according to the specific needs of the social partners concerned is also recognised.

This Directive/Agreement reflects the responses to 'atypical' work which have emerged across the EU. The responses have resulted in a fragmented approach falling between the need on the one hand to extend some of the ideas of employment protection previously associated with the standard, full-time, permanent 'typical' employment contract model in order to make part-time work an attractive proposition and to meet the claims of indirect discrimination voiced by female workers, and on the other hand, to recognise that the growth in part-time work is a market response to the need for flexibility in labour markets.

This approach has been put on the agenda by the Commission in its Green Paper, *Partnership for a New Organisation of Work,* issued on 5 January 1997. The Part Time Work Agreement is but the first of a series of measures the Commission would like to see implemented to bring about the 'flexible, open-ended process of organisational development, a process that offers new opportunities for learning, innovation, improvement and thereby increased productivity'.[115] The Commission embraces the role of the social partners as well as setting the restructuring of labour market policy within the context of public policy, life-long education and training and restructuring of tax and social security systems. Although this kind of Directive does begin to extend traditional principles of labour law to newer forms of work which in the past have appeared vulnerable, it is also

---

[115] Green Paper: *Partnership For A New Organisation of Work*, 5 January 1997, para 18.

a much weaker form of Directive. Many of its provisions are not sufficiently clear, precise and legally perfect enough to give rise to direct effect
and the Directive reveals the new compromise between alignment of individual labour law rights through a 'minimum harmonisation' process and
the use of EC law to direct macro-economic policies.

5.5.3 Fixed-term work

Following the agreement on part-time work, the Council adopted a
Directive on 28 June 1999 implementing the social partners' agreement on
fixed-term work.[116] The Directive had a short transitional period. Member
States had to implement its provisions by 10 July 1999 and had a
maximum of one more year to take account of special difficulties or implementation by a collective agreement. In the Recitals to the Directive we see
references to the Community Charter of the Fundamental Social Rights of
Workers 1989 but also to the Essen Priorities discussed in Chapter 1.
Recital 5 states: 'The conclusions of the Essen Council stressed the need to
take measures with a view to increasing the employment-intensiveness of
growth, in particular by a more flexible organisation of work, in a way
which fulfils both the wishes of employees and the requirements of competition.' The Preamble also refers to the Council Resolution of 9 February
1999 on the 1999 Employment Guidelines which invited the social partners at all appropriate levels to negotiate agreements to modernise the
organisation of work, including flexible working arrangements, with the
aim of making undertakings productive and competitive, and achieving
the required balance between flexibility and security.

In the Preamble to the annexed agreement there is again mention of the
role of the social partners adopting this kind of legislation and the place
of his particular Agreement in the development of the European
Employment Strategy. Clause 8(4) allows the social partners to conclude at
the appropriate level (including a European Agreement) further agreements
adapting or complementing the Fixed Term Work Agreement in ways
which take note of the specific needs of the social partners concerned.

The Agreement applies to workers who have an employment contract or
employment relationship as defined in law, collective agreements or practice in each Member State. A 'fixed-term worker' is given more precision in
Clause 3 as 'a person having an employment contract or relationship
entered into directly between an employer and a worker where the end of

---

[116] Council Directive 1999/70/EC of 28 June 1999 concerning the framework agreement on
fixed-term work concluded by ETUC, UNICE and CEEP, OJ 1999 L 175/43. See the
Special Issue devoted to the impact of this Directive: (1999) 15 *The International Journal
of Comparative Labour Law and Industrial Relations*.

the employment contract or relationship is determined by objective conditions such as reaching a specific date, completing a specific task or the occurrence of a specific event'. Workers who are placed by a temporary work agency are not covered by the Agreement, but it is noted in the Preamble that the social partners intend to consider the need for a similar Agreement covering such workers. The Member States may exclude initial vocational training relationships and apprenticeship schemes and employment contracts and relationships which have been concluded within the framework of a specific public or publicly supported training, integration and vocational retraining programme. Such exclusions can only take place after consultation with the social partners.

The agreement uses the principle of non-discrimination as its basis for giving rights to fixed-term contract workers. A comparison is to be made with the treatment of a 'comparable permanent worker'. This concept is defined as 'a worker with an employment contract or relationship of indefinite duration, in the same establishment, engaged in the same or similar work/occupation, due regard being given to qualifications/skills'.[117] Where, however, there is no comparable worker available, the comparison can be made by reference to the applicable collective agreement, or, where there is no applicable collective agreement, in accordance with national law, collective agreements or practice.

Clause 4 sets out the definition of the principle of non-discrimination. Firstly, in respect of employment conditions, fixed-term workers shall not be treated in a less favourable manner than comparable permanent workers solely because they have a fixed-term contract or relationship unless different treatment is justified on objective grounds. There is no guidance as to what are objective grounds. In Chapter 4 we saw similar ideas in relation to defences to indirect discrimination where the objective grounds must not be related to or based upon sex discrimination. The fixed-term Agreement moves beyond discrimination based upon sex. Clause 4 also provides for the principle of *pro rata temporis* where this appropriate. The implementation of these principles is left for the Member States after consulting the social partners and having regard to Community law, national law, collective agreements and practice. There is specific mention of periods of service qualifications for employment rights. These shall be the same for fixed-term and permanent workers except where differences are justified on objective grounds.

The second aim of the Agreement is to prevent abuse arising by the successive use of fixed-term employment contracts. Again, after consulting the social partners and bearing mind national provisions, the Member States

---

[117] Clause 2(2).

are under a duty to introduce legal measures where none exist to prevent abuse occurring. Any measures taken must take into account the needs of specific sectors or categories of workers and must address one or more of the following issues: objective reasons justifying the renewal of such contracts or relationships; the maximum total duration of successive fixed-term employment contracts or relationships; and the number of renewals of such contracts or relationships.

5.6 Young people at work

Council Directive 94/33/EC[118] protects young people at work. Member States are to take the necessary measures to prohibit work by children and to set a minimum working age which is not to be lower than the age of 15 years or, if higher, the minimum school leaving age. The Directive applies to any young person under the age of 18 who has an employment contract or an employment relationship defined by the law in force in a Member State. The Member States are to ensure that work carried out by young people is strictly regulated and that employers guarantee to young people conditions of work which suit their age. In particular, protection against economic exploitation and against health and safety risks are singled out. The latter are defined widely, embracing physical, mental, moral, social development or any risks likely to jeopardise a young person's education.

5.7 Pregnancy and maternity protection

Article 2(3) of Council Directive 76/207/EEC[119] allows the Member States to create special protection for women in relation to pregnancy and maternity. In relation to equal-pay issues, we have also seen the Court of Justice recognising the special nature of maternity rights, but in *Gillespie*[120] the Court ruled that the amount of occupational maternity pay could not be set so low as to undermine the purpose of maternity leave, namely the protection of women before and after giving birth. As the case law of Chapter 4 reveals, an anti-discrimination approach cannot give a full set of rights to protect the special nature of pregnancy.[121] To this end the Community has

---

[118] OJ 1994 L 216/12.

[119] OJ 1976 L 39/40.

[120] Case C-342/93 [1996] ECR I-475. In Case C-333/97 *Susanne Lewen v Lotha Denda*, judgment of 21 October 1999, the Court ruled that a refusal to pay a Christmas bonus to a woman on child-rearing leave can be seen as discrimination if the bonus is regarded as pay for work performance in the past, but where the bonus is paid as incentive for future performance of work, a woman is on special leave and cannot be compared to the situation of people who are at work.

[121] See Szyszczak, E., 'Community Law on Pregnancy and Maternity' in O'Keeffe, D. and Hervey, T. (eds) *Sex Equality Law in the European Union* (Wiley, Chichester, 1996).

adopted a Directive dealing with aspects of maternity and pregnancy rights in the context of the health and safety programme.[122] Council Directive 92/85/EC provides for a period of maternity leave of at least 14 weeks with pay or an allowance equivalent to what the woman would receive if she were off work sick. Article 9 provides for time off work to attend antenatal appointments if these have to take place during working hours. Articles 3, 4, 5 and 6 focus upon the health and safety aspects which might affect pregnant women and women who have recently given birth. The Directive also provides for restrictions on night work[123] and exposure to a number of dangerous agents or work processes which are listed in the Annex. Dangerous chemical substances are also identified by reference to what are regarded as comparatively lax standards set out in a 1967 Directive of the Community.[124]

Article 10 of the Directive consolidates the Court's case law under the Equal Treatment Directive, 76/207/EEC, by prohibiting dismissals on the grounds of maternity in the period from the beginning of the pregnancy and the period of maternity leave set by the Member State after giving birth. The Directive does not provide protection for other acts of discrimination falling short of dismissal, for example promotion opportunities, and therefore the Equal Treatment Directive is still relevant to provide protection for pregnancy and maternity discrimination.

5.8 Data protection

In 1995 the Community adopted a Directive on the protection of data.[125] The Directive reflects the growing interest at the national level of protecting personal data and reconciling the protection of such data with rights to privacy recognised at the constitutional level in some Member States and in international human rights documents, such as the ECHR.[126] The Directive sets out a number of general rules which are to apply to the processing of personal data: there is the rule that data can only be processed for explicit purposes specified in advance;[127] a duty to provide the data

---

[122] Council Directive 92/85/EC, OJ 1992 L 348/1.
[123] Article 7.
[124] Directive 67/548/EEC.
[125] Directive 95/46/EC of the European Parliament and of the Council of 24 October 1995 on the protection of individuals with regard to the processing of personal data and on the free movement of such data, OJ 1995 L 281/31. See Simitis, S., 'From the Market to the Polis: The EU Directive on the Protection of Personal Data' (1995) 80 *Iowa Law Review* 467.
[126] *Cf.* Pearce, G. and Platten, N., 'Achieving Personal Data Protection in the European Union' (1998) 36 *Journal of Common Market Studies* 529.
[127] Article 6(1)(b).

subjects with a series of information permitting the assessment of the scope and the implications of the processing of the specific data,[128] and the right of access to data processed.[129] In Recital 68 to the Directive the Commission recognises the necessity for sectoral Directives and already there has been a Directive in the telecommunications sector.[130] The Commission has already acknowledged intervention is necessary in the sphere of labour law.[131] Simitis[132] has argued that there are compelling reasons why the Community should adopt a sectoral Directive addressing data protection in the employment context. Employers' and third parties' use of personal data needs to be controlled, given its growing importance in personnel policy, from hiring decisions to efforts to monitor individual conduct, rationalise personnel policy and maximise work productivity.

5.9 Regulation of working time

The 1989 Social Charter recognised the need to address issues of working time regulation from both the social and economic perspective. In 1979 a Resolution had been adopted on the adaptation of working time as part of the Commuity's attempts to introduce flexibility in working arrangements.[133] After the SEA 1987 it was possible to resurrect some of these ideas as health and safety issues, using the qualified majority voting base of the old Article 118A EC. The wide divergence of approaches towards the regulation of working time[134] created the impression that any Community measures could only be loosely formed or would be part of measures leading towards harmonisation of working time regulation. The United Kingdom government challenged the use of Article 118 A EC as the legal base for such a measure and abstained from the vote in the Council.

Council Directive 93/104/EC[135] is a detailed health and safety type Directive. The Directive adopts a benchmark of a maximum working week

---

[128] Articles 10 and 11.

[129] Article 12.

[130] Directive 97/66 of the European Parliament and of the Council of 15 December 1997, OJ 1997 L 24/1.

[131] *Communication from the Commission on the Social and Labour Market Dimension of the Information Society*, COM(97) 390 final.

[132] Simitis, S., 'Reconsidering the Premises of Labour Law: Prolegomena to an EU Regulation on the Protection of Employees' Personal Data' (1999) 5 *European Law Journal* 45.

[133] OJ 1980 C-2. Szyszczak, E. *Partial Unemployment* (Cassell, London, 1992), Ch. 6.

[134] EC Commission, *Comparative Study on Rules Governing Working Conditions in the Member States – a Synopsis*, SEC (89) 1137, 30 June 1989; Bercusson, B. *Working Time in Britain: Towards a European Model, Part I: The European Union Directive* (Institute of Employment Rights, London, 1994).

[135] OJ 1993 L 307/18.

of 48 hours in Article 6. The Directive also prescribes daily rest periods of at least 11 hours every 24 hours and a maximum of eight hours for night work. Article 5 added a qualification to these rules by stating that the minimum period of rest should in principle include a Sunday. There is some flexibility in the Directive; for example, reference periods are set out over which time the minimum and maximum periods of working time are to be calculated. The role of the social partners is also acknowledged in using collective agreements to set certain standards, for example in relation to the calculation and duration of rest periods. In Article 17 there is the possibility of derogations from the Directive, and Article 18 provides for delayed implementation of the Directive.

The United Kingdom contested the validity of the Directive. In *UK v Council*[136] the Court found in favour of the United Kingdom in that the Council had failed to explain why Sunday, as a weekly rest day, is more closely connected with the health and safety of workers than any other day of the week, but the Court did not annul the whole Directive. It ruled that the second sentence of Article 5 could be annulled since it was severable from other provisions of the Directive. The Court also ruled that the principal objective of the Directive was the protection of health and safety of workers and that the old Article 118A EC was the correct legal base for the Directive. It also ruled that the principle of subsidiarity had not been breached.[137]

The Commission is committed to extending the scope of the regulation of working time.[138] Two proposals were put forward on 18 November 1999. The first proposal covered working time in the maritime sector and doctors in training. The second proposal covered the road-haulage sector. At the time of writing, only an Agreement has been reached with the social partners in the maritime sector and adopted as a Council Directive.[139]

---

[136] Case C-84/94 [1996] ECR I-5755.

[137] Fitzpatrick, B., ' Straining the Definition of Health and Safety?' (1997) 26 *Industrial Law Journal* 115.

[138] COM (98) 259 final.

[139] Council Directive 1999/63/EC of 21 June 1999 concerning the agreement on the organisation of working time of seafarers concluded by the European Community Shipowners' Association (ECSA) and the Federation of Transport Workers' Unions in the European Union (FST), OJ 1999 L 167/33. The proposal covering the road haulage sector (COM (98) 662) is waiting for a Common Position to be reached in the Council.

CHAPTER 6

The interaction of EC labour law with other EC policies

So far we have explored the opportunities offered for the development of EC labour law from the fragmented legal base of the EC Treaty. Labour law issues may also arise in other areas of EC policy and may conflict with those policies. This raises the question as to the value attached to labour law when it comes into conflict with other values of the Internal Market programme, particularly in cases before the Court of Justice.

6.1 EC labour law and the Internal Market

The case law revolves around balancing the alleged incompatibility of national rules governing labour regulation with the Internal Market programme, in particular the four economic freedoms and competition policy. Maduro argues that the expansion of market rules into areas of national law is not, as implied by formal reasoning, a neutral policy. It involves choices between conflicting values.[1] A balancing policy is carried out by the Court, and by national courts, when they are asked to consider the validity of national labour law provisions against the norms of the Internal Market and the perceived constitutional rights protected in the European Economic Constitution. Maduro argues that the balance between economic freedoms and social rights in the European Economic Constitution has largely been defined by the balance between market integration and *national* social rights. If we are beginning to recognise an employment strategy as one of the aims of the EU, and labour law as a discrete area of EC law, a different discourse emerges: a discourse balancing the competing values of EC labour law and Internal Market law.[2]

---

[1] Poiares Maduro, M., *We. The Court* (Hart, Oxford, 1998) p. 24. See also Poiares Maduro, M., 'Striking the elusive balance between economic freedom and social rights in the EU' in Alston, P. (ed.) *The EU and Human Rights* (OUP, Oxford, 1999).

[2] There are indications that the Court is willing to recognise competing interests within the EU and not merely apply the imperatives of the Internal Market as dominant values: Case C-341/95 *Gianni Bettati v Safety Hi-Tech Srl* [1998] ECR I-4355.

There are two ways in which the Court handles an allegation that national labour laws or practices are contrary to the principles of the Internal Market. It can decide whether or not the national law falls within the scope of one of the four freedoms. If the rule is not caught, then the national law cannot be challenged using the principles of Community law. The other method is for the Court to decide that the national law does fall within the scope of the four freedoms and then decide whether or not a Member State can justify the law according to Community law criteria. There has been a tendency on the part of the Court to follow the latter approach; bringing many aspects of 'trading rules' within the scope of Community law scrutiny and then leaving it for the national courts to decide if the rules can be justified. This process is described by Maduro as promoting deregulation of the market at the national level.[3] Maduro argues that the Court has approached this task through a methodology of 'majoritarian activism'. This is explained as where a certain social regulation is shared by a majority of Member States it has normally been upheld by the Court even if it restricts trade. But the fundamental rights character granted to the free movement provisions and the wide definition of their scope in order to extend European supervision over national regulation, thereby lending support to the 'constitutionalization' of Community law, have led to a 'spill-over' of market integration rules into virtually all areas of national law. As a consequence, many national social rights and policies have been challenged under the free movement provisions.

In Chapter 3 we looked at the far-reaching effects of the *Bosman* case[4] where the Court reaffirmed that the right to free movement was a fundamental right in the Community and held up for scrutiny rules which were not discriminatory but nevertheless acted as barriers or disincentives to the free movement of persons. A number of national provisions relating to labour law and other aspects of national regulation such as professional education and qualifications and taxation systems may now be challenged as proving to be a disincentive to the right to free movement of labour. Another example is *Kalliope Schoning-Kougebetopoulou* v *Freie und Hansestadt Hamburg*[5] where a discriminatory clause in a collective agreement applicable to the public sector in Germany was held to be incompatible with *Article 39 EC* where a Greek doctor's previous experience in Greece was not taken into account for promotion purposes in his

---

[3] *Supra* n. 1.
[4] Case C-415/93 *Union Royal Belge des Sociétés de Football Association ASBL* v *Bosman* [1995] ECR I-4921. On the question of horizontal application of the Internal Market provisions, see Baquero Cruz, J., 'Free Movement and Private Autonomy' (1999) 24 *European Law Review* 603.
[5] Case C-15/96 [1998] ECR I-47.

post in Germany. Similarly, in *Bobadilla*[6] the provisions of a collective agreement were held up to scrutiny against the free movement principle. The Court has also ruled that national labour law provisions which prevent economic operators from pursuing their activities as self-employed persons in another Member State may be contrary to the free movement of services provisions of the EC Treaty.[7] What we see in the Court's case law is a fundamental belief in the market citizenship right to choose where to work and to buy services in the Internal Market.

The free movement of goods is another area where the fundamental freedoms of the EU may be in conflict with national provisions regulating the labour market. There has been a tendency for individual litigators to use the rules and values of the Internal Market to challenge a wide range of national provisions which are allegedly in conflict with the free movement principle. In *Dassonville*[8] and *Cassis de Dijon*[9] the Court drew a wide range of national measures into the scope of scrutiny. The Court of Justice has been asked to balance these conflicting values.[10] In the *Sunday Trading* cases the Court accepted that shop opening hours 'reflect certain political and economic choices in so far as their purpose is to ensure that working and non-working hours are so arranged as to accord with national or regional socio-cultural characteristics'.[11] After the ruling in *Keck*[12] the scope for challenging such forms of labour market regulation has been narrowed down[13] and the Court has also shown a more generous sensitivity to national policy objectives and a willingness to leave the balancing of national values against the values of the Internal Market in the hands of national courts.[14]

There is one major area of potential conflict between labour law and Internal Market law within Community policy itself. This is the conflict between the health and safety programme and the free movement provisions. The Community's advanced health and safety programme under the old Article 118A EC (now as amended, *Article 137 EC*) and Article

---

6 Case C-234/97, judgment of 8 July 1999.
7 Case C-398/95 *SETT* v *Ypourgos Ergasias* [1997] ECR I-3091.
8 Case 8/74 [1974] ECR 837.
9 Case C-120/78 [1979] ECR 649.
10 See Davies, P., 'Market Integration and Social Policy in the Court of Justice' (1995) 24 *Industrial Law Journal* 49.
11 Case 145/88 *Torfaen Borough Council* v *B&Q plc* [1989] ECR 765, para 14. See also Case 312/89 *Conforama* [1991] ECR I-997; Case C-332/89 *Marchandise* [1991] ECR I-1027; Case C-169/91 *Stoke-on Trent* [1992] ECR I-6457.
12 Joined Cases C-267 and 268/91 *Keck and Mithouard* [1993] ECR I-6097.
13 Joined Cases C-401/92 and C-402/92 *'Tankstation Heukske and Boermans* [1994] ECR I-2199; Joined Cases C-69/93 and C-258/93 *Punto Casa and PPV* [1994] ECR I-2355.
14 See Poiares Maduro, M., 'The Saga of Article 30 EC Treaty: To Be Continued' (1998) 5 *Maastricht Journal* 298.

100A(1) EC (now *Article 95 EC*) aimed to improve the living and working conditions of workers and their families, while the industrial policy pursued under Article 100A EC aimed at abolishing trade barriers in order to enable machinery, technical equipment, chemical substances etc. to be marketed across the Internal Market. This makes the working environment an area of potential and actual conflict between a trend towards raising standards of protection for workers and a trend towards deregulation. Article 100(A)(4) (now *Article 95(4) EC*) allowed a Member State to maintain a higher level of protection than was provided for in a Directive agreed under Article 100A(1) EC (now *Article 95 EC*). Different technical standards varying from Member State to Member State may impinge upon the operation of the Internal Market: first, by operating as an import restriction, hindering the free movement of goods; second, because it is generally less expensive for a manufacturer of goods to satisfy lower rather than higher technical standards. This may distort competition where technical standards are an important cost factor between the Member States. For this reason *Article 95 EC* (ex Article 100A EC) is an important tool in harmonising costs factors between the Member States. But *Articles 95 EC* and *137 EC* (ex Articles 100A EC and 118A EC) come into conflict. Measures taken under *Article 95 EC* (ex Article 100A EC) are usually directed towards the placing of goods on the market whereas the measures taken under *Article 137 EC* (ex Article 118A EC) place obligations upon employers. In the absence of Community harmonising legislation it may be lawful for a *manufacturer* to market a product and for it to be freely circulating in the Internal Market. It may not always be lawful for an *employer* to use the product in the working environment where, for example, he or she attempts to use it to replace a safer product which is more expensive.[15]

Maduro[16] argues that the Court of Justice has only imposed limits on Member State regulation not *public* regulation. The Court has assumed the role of judging the compatibility of Member State action with the tenets of the Internal Market. An example where there is a fundamental clash of values, now managed at the Community level, is the infringement action against France. This action, and the ensuing Community legislation, is a potential threat to the ability of trade unions to take collective measures. For several years the Commission had received complaints that France had failed to take adequate steps to curtail industrial action against foreign products, particularly those in the agricultural sector. The Commission

---

15   Under Article 6(f) of the Framework Directive 89/391/EEC, an employer has the overall duty to replace the dangerous with the non-dangerous or the less dangerous. This is called the substitution principle.

16   *Supra* n. 1.

eventually commenced an infringement action against France.[17] The Court found that France was in breach of *Articles 28* EC (ex Article 30 EC) and *Article 10 EC* (ex Article 5 EC) by failing to adopt all necessary and proportionate measures in order to prevent the free movement of fruit and vegetables from being obstructed by actions of private individuals. This opened up France to possible actions for damages brought by individuals who had suffered loss as a result of France's inability to secure the free movement of goods into her territory as well as further action and the possibility of penalties being imposed by the Court itself. In November 1997, one month before the Court's ruling, the Commissioner with responsibility for the Internal Market, Mario Monti, issued a draft Regulation[18] proposing to require national courts to award damages against the Member State if it failed to clear illegal trade blockages. This was adopted by the Council, with amendments, on 7 December 1998 in the form of Regulation 2679/98 and the accompanying Resolution on the free movement of goods.[19] This Regulation creates new processes for the regulation of the Internal Market. Where there is an obstacle or the threat of an obstacle to the free movement of goods a Member State must inform the Commission of the obstacle and also explain what it is doing to remove the obstacle. Article 4(1)(a) states that a Member State must 'take all necessary and proportionate measures so that the free movement of goods is assured in the territory of the Member State in accordance with the Treaty'. The Commission may request the Member State to take such measures. Article 2 of Regulation 2679/98/EC recognises the right to strike in the Member States as well as other labour law rights:

> This Regulation may not be interpreted as affecting in any way the exercise of fundamental rights as recognised in Member States, including the right of freedom to strike. These rights may also include the right or freedom to take other actions covered by the specific industrial relations systems in the Member States.

The ILO has also recognised a core of collective labour law rights as fundamental rights. Arguably, if such rights are elevated into fundamental or constitutional rights they are non-negotiable and should be respected and given a preferential status even over market freedoms.

6.2 Competition policy

The Member States' intervention in competitive markets is also regulated under the private competition rules of *Articles 81* and *82 EC* (ex Articles

---

[17] Case C-265/95 *Commission* v *France* [1997] ECR I-6959.
[18] OJ 1998 C 10/14.
[19] OJ 1998 L 337/8.

85 and 86 EC) and by special rules relating to state activity in the form of public monopolies, state aids and public procurement. In each of these areas there has been soft law, legislation and Court rulings on the effect of state intervention in the labour market.

There has been some discussion as to whether trade unions can be considered as undertakings within the context of the *Articles 81* and *82 EC* (ex Articles 85 and 86 EC). The Court has given a broad interpretation to the concept of an 'undertaking' encompassing every entity engaged in an economic activity regardless of the legal status of the entity and the way in which it is financed.[20] It can be argued that a trade union is not an undertaking as it does not carry on a commercial activity. It is also noted that in some Member States trade unions are given immunity from aspects of economic law.[21]

Cases have arisen under competition law, particularly in relation to the abuse of a dominant position under *Article 82 EC* (ex Article 86 EC) and the regulation of state monopolies under *Article 86(1) EC* (ex Article 90(1) EC). *Article 86(2) EC* (ex Article 90(2) EC) seeks to reconcile the Member States' interest in using certain undertakings as an instrument of economic or social policy with the Community's rules on competition and the Internal Market. Since *Article 86(2) EC* is a derogation from the Treaty rules it must be interpreted strictly.[22] This provision has produced case law which is complex and far from clear. For the purposes of our discussion the cases can be divided into different groups.

In *Höfner and Elser* v *Macrotron GmbH*[23] the legality of German rules which placed people looking for work with potential employers through a state-licensed agency with exclusive rights to do this were challenged as being contrary to *Article 86 EC* (ex Article 82 EC) which forbids the abuse of a dominant position in the EC and *Article 86(1) EC* (ex Article 90(1) EC) which allows Member States to grant undertakings exclusive rights in derogation of the competition rules. The Court ruled that a public undertaking entrusted with providing services of a general economic interest is subject to the obligation imposed on all undertakings not to abuse its dominant position on the market, but the application of *Article 86 EC* should not obstruct the performance of the particular task assigned to it. A Member State will be liable where it has granted the undertaking the

---

[20] See Case C-41/90 *Höfner* v *Macrotron* [1991] ECR I-1979.
[21] Desai, K., 'E.C. Competition Law and Trade Unions' (1999) 6 *European Competition Law Review* 175. See the Opinion of Advocate General Jacobs of 28 January 1999 in Case C-67/96 *Albany International BV* v *Stichting Bedrijfspensioenfonds Textielindustrie*, and the ruling of the Court on 21 September 1999.
[22] See Case 157/94 *Commission* v *Netherlands* [1997] ECR I-5699, para 37.
[23] Case C-41/90 [1991] ECR I-1979.

exclusive right to carry out the particular economic activity where it creates a situation in which the public undertaking cannot avoid infringing *Article 82 EC* (ex Article 86 EC). The Court explained why *Article 82 EC* applied in this situation. First, the exclusive right to employment procurement activities extended to executive recruitment activities. Second, the public employment agency was manifestly incapable of satisfying demand prevailing on the market for such activities. Third, the actual pursuit of those activities by private recruitment consultants was void. Fourth, the activities in question may apply to nationals, or to the territory, of another Member State, thereby interfering with the principle of free movement of persons.

In *Job Centre Coop*[24] the Italian government actively enforced a similar employment procurement monopoly through criminal proceedings. The applicant, a co-operative society with limited liability, was being established to provide public placements. A preliminary ruling was sought as to the compatibility of the public placement offices with the competition rules of the EC Treaty. The Court confirmed that, pursuant to *Article 86 EC* (ex Article 90 EC), such bodies were subject to the competition policy of the EC and that any measures which a Member State introduced and maintained in force which created a situation in which public placement offices cannot avoid infringing the Treaty, and in particular the abuse of a dominant position under *Article 82* (ex 86) *EC*, would be incompatible with the Treaty. One example of an abuse of a dominant position under *Article 82(b) EC* (ex Article 86(b) EC) is the limiting of the provision of services to the prejudice of consumers. The Court ruled that in an extensive and differentiated market such as the employment market public placement offices may be unable to satisfy a significant proportion of all the requests for services. By prohibiting any activity as an intermediary on the employment market, unless carried out by the public placement offices, a Member State creates a situation in which the provision of a service is limited, contrary to *Article 82 EC* (ex Article 86(b) EC) if the offices are manifestly unable to satisfy demand on the employment market for all types of activity. There was a potential effect on intra-Community trade since the placement of employees by private companies may extend to nationals of other Member States or to the territory of other Member States. In these two cases the State did nothing more than grant an exclusive right, but the Court found that owing to the specific economic context and the nature of the services involved the monopolist could not avoid abusing its dominant position by constantly 'limiting production, markets or technical development to the prejudice of consumers'. These were seen as exceptional

---

[24] Case C-55/96 [1997] ECR I-7119.

circumstances where the Court felt justified in challenging the Member States' freedom to grant exclusive rights.

The interplay with competition rules is also seen in the dock-work cases from Italy. In *Raso*[25] the Italian dock-work scheme granted dock-work companies an exclusive right to supply temporary labour to certain undertakings and also enabled those companies to compete with undertakings which depended upon their services. The Court found that a conflict of interest was inevitable since merely by exercising its monopoly, the dock-work company would distort competition on the market in its favour. There was thus a breach of *Articles 86* and *82 EC* since the monopolist was led to abuse its dominant position by virtue of a discriminatory state policy. In *Merci Convenzionali Porto di Genova*[26] Italian legislation which reserved dock work to Italian nationals was held to be contrary to *Article 39(2) EC* (ex Article 48(2) EC) and could not be justified as a 'public service' under *Article 39(4) EC* (ex Article 48(4) EC). The Court also looked at the application of *Article 86 EC* (ex Article 90(1) EC) and *Article 82 EC* (ex Article 86 EC), ruling that a Member State may be in breach of these Articles where the public undertaking in question merely by *exercising* the exclusive rights granted to it cannot avoid abusing its dominant position *or* when such rights are liable to create a situation where the public undertaking is induced to commit such abuses. In this case it was argued that dock work was not, in principle, a service of general economic interest, bringing the undertaking in question within the remit of *Article 86 EC* (ex Article 90 EC). An abuse of a dominant position was found in this case. A monopoly to perform dock work had been created which induced the undertaking to demand payment for services which had not been requested, to charge disproportionate prices, to refuse to use modern technology and to grant price reductions to certain consumers and to offset the reductions by increasing charges to other consumers. In these cases it was not the monopoly itself which infringed *Articles 86(1)* and *82 EC* but the monopoly *in conjunction* with additional features which made abuses very likely. Structural measures beyond the granting of an exclusive right led the undertaking in question to abuse its dominant position. Only then was there justification for holding the state at least partly responsible for the anti-competitive behaviour of the monopolist.

A different dimension to theses cases is seen in *Becu*.[27] A number of criminal prosecutions had been taken against individuals and firms who

---

[25] Case C-163/96 [1998] ECR I-533.

[26] Case C-179/90 *Merci Convenzionali Porto di Genova Spa* v *Siderurgica Gabrielli Spa* [1991] ECR I-5889.

[27] Case C-22/98 *Jean Claude Becu, Annie Verweire, NV Smeg, NV Adia Interim*, judgment of 16 September 1999.

were accused of using unrecognised dock workers in breach of a Belgian law of 1972 on the organisation of dock work. The working conditions and matters of pay of recognised dockers were governed by a collective agreement. The lower court had acquitted the defendants arguing that the Belgian law was contrary to *Article 86(1) EC* in conjunction with *Article 82 EC*. It held that the difference between the hourly wage of the workers employed by the defendants and that of the recognised dock workers was unfair. On appeal the court found that the facts were very similar to those of *Merci* but that there was a fundamental difference between the two cases: the Belgian legislation merely recognised the occupation of dock workers who were solely allowed to carry out dock work in defined areas and the legislation did not confer a monopoly on undertakings or on trade associations. The Public Prosecutor's Office appealed against this finding and the Belgian appeal court referred two questions to the Court of Justice. The first question asked whether individuals could acquire rights under *Article 86(1) EC* in conjunction with the old Article 7 EC (now repealed) and *Articles 81* and *82 EC* (ex Articles 85 and 86 EC).

The Court confirmed its earlier case law, stating that *Article 86(1) EC* gave rise to direct effect in the national courts, but *Article 86(1) EC* only applies to 'undertakings'. The dock workers were engaged on fixed-term contracts working under the direction of undertakings which employed them. They were, therefore, to be considered as 'workers', not undertakings and the defendants could not have recourse to *Article 86(1) EC* to oppose the Belgian legislation fixing their pay and conditions of work.

The second question asked if the recognised dock workers could be regarded as being entrusted with the operation of services of general economic interest within the meaning of *Article 86(2) EC* who would not be able to carry out their special duties if *Article 86(1) EC* were applied to them. This question became redundant in the light of the Court's answer to the first question.

A different set of cases has challenged the monopoly rights enjoyed by social security schemes in the Member States. As social security budgets have come under pressure in the Member States, new forms of private social security have emerged. The issue arises as to how far the introduction of competition in the social security market should also attract the application of the competition rules. In particular, should particular groups of workers be allowed to choose social security schemes which are more favourable and opt out of compulsory state monopolies for the supply of social security?[28] The Court has resisted such attacks on Member States'

---

[28] See Winterstein, A., 'Nailing the Jellyfish: Social Security and Competition Law' (1999) *European Competition Law Review* 324.

schemes by resorting to the notion of 'social solidarity'. Ideas of social solidarity can be traced back to the French Revolution, representing a belief in the protectionist role of the state against market forces. The justification for modern ideas of social solidarity is explained in *Garcia*:

> ... Social security systems such as those in issue in the main proceedings, which are based on the principle of solidarity, require compulsory contributions in order to ensure that the principle of solidarity is applied and that their financial equilibrium is maintained.[29]

In *Poucet and Pistre*[30] two self-employed workers refused to pay into compulsory social security schemes in France, arguing that they should be free to take out private insurance. They argued that the state social security schemes abused their dominant positions. The Court considered compulsory affiliation to the schemes to be indispensable for maintaining solidarity both as between persons insured and as between different schemes. In *FFSA* the Court concluded that a supplementary optional retirement scheme for self-employed French farmers did not display sufficient characteristics to meet the solidarity principle and the competition rules could apply.[31]

Bercusson sees the use of the principle of social solidarity as another indicator that principles of collective labour law are found in EC labour law. The principle is used in Commission Communications as one of the defining features of the Member States, and hence the EU, social model. For example, in the 'economic' White Paper, *Growth, Competitiveness, Employment: The Challenges and Ways Forward in the 21st Century,*[32] the Commission defends the principle.[33] Bercusson argues that the case of *Poucet and Pistre* reveals how collective labour ideas of social protection found in the Member States are filtered through Community processes to create Community concepts and legal principles of collective labour law.[34]

In *Albany*[35] a number of undertakings challenged the compulsory affilia-

---

[29] Case C-238/94 *Garcia/Mutuelle de prévoyance sociale d'Aquitaine and Others* [1996] ECR I-1673.

[30] Joined Cases C-159 and 160/91 [1993] ECR I-637.

[31] Case C-244/94 *Fédération Française des Sociétés d'Assurances* [1995] ECR I-4013. The Conseil d'Etat subsequently found an infringement of *Articles 82 EC* and *86 EC* as a result of the monopoly rights in the form of tax privileges given to the undertaking.

[32] COM (93) 700.

[33] See the interview with Commissioner Diamantopoulou, *Financial Times*, 4 November 1999.

[34] Bercusson, B., 'The Collective Labour Law of the European Union' (1995) 1 *European Law Journal* 157, 176.

[35] Case C-67/96 *Albany International BV v Stichting Bedrijfspensioenfonds Textielindustrie* judgment of 21 September 1999. See also Joined Cases C-180-184/98 *Pavlov*, pending, and Case C-222/98 *van der Woude*, pending.

tion to sectoral pension funds established in The Netherlands. The Court of Justice recognised that the supplementary pension scheme at issue fulfilled an essential social function because of the limited amount of the statutory pension which was calculated on the basis of the minimum statutory wage. The Court pointed out that if the exclusive rights to manage the supplementary pension scheme were removed:

> ... undertakings with young employees in good health engaged in non-dangerous activities would seek more advantageous insurance terms from private insurers. The progressive departure of 'good risks' would leave the sectoral pension fund with responsibility for an increasing share of 'bad' risks, thereby increasing the cost of pensions for workers, particularly those in small and medium-sized undertakings with older employees engaged in dangerous activities, to which the fund could no longer offer pensions at an acceptable cost.[36]

The Court found that there was a high degree of solidarity in the pension scheme and that to strip it of its exclusive rights would render it impossible for it to perform its tasks of a general economic interest. Thus, although the supplementary pension scheme was caught by *Article 86(1) EC*, it obtained an exemption from the application of the competition rules by virtue of *Article 86(2) EC*.

6.3 Merger control

In 1989 a Regulation was enacted to control Mergers within the EU.[37] A proposed merger must be notified to the Commission and the Commission must assess whether the merger is compatible with the Common Market. The Commission must take into consideration the social effects of the proposed merger and if they are liable to affect the social objectives of the EC referred to in Article 2 EC, including the strengthening of the Community's economic and social cohesion referred to in Article 130a EC (now *Article 158 EC*). Under Article 18(4) of the Merger Regulation 4064/89/EEC the representatives of the employees of the undertakings concerned are entitled, upon application, to be heard. It has been pointed out by the Economic and Social Committee[38] that the Merger Regulation is not complemented by social law provisions and the Committee made the suggestion that the Commission's approval of a merger should be made conditional upon the establishment of a European Works Council in the undertaking.[39]

---

[36] Para 108.
[37] Regulation 4064/89/EEC, OJ 1989 L 395/1.
[38] OJ 1989 C 329/35.
[39] See Council Directive 94/45/EEC, OJ 1995 L 254/64.

Employee representatives may have *locus standi* under *Article 230(4) EC* (ex Article 173(4) EC) to challenge a Decision of the Commission ruling on the compatibility with EC law of a proposed merger. In *Grandes Sources*[40] and *Vittel*[41] the Court of First Instance ruled that such a Decision is of *individual* concern to the employee representatives recognised in national law simply because the Merger Regulation refers to them as being one of the 'third parties' showing a sufficient interest to be heard by the Commission during the procedure for investigation of the proposed merger, regardless of whether they have actually taken part in the procedure, but the CFI ruled that, in the absence of exceptional circumstances, the Decision is not of *direct* concern to the employee representatives. This is because a Decision authorising a merger does not have any effects on the rights of the employee representatives. Secondly, the Decision does not directly affect the interests of the workers concerned since, in accordance with the Directive on the transfer of undertakings, the merger itself cannot bring about a change in the employment relationship, as regulated by the contract of employment and collective agreements.

The Court went on to rule that since the employee representatives have been given *procedural rights* under Regulation 4064/89/EC and those rights can, in principle, be given effect to only at the stage of judicial review of the lawfulness of the Commission's final decision, the employee representatives must be given a limited remedy to protect their procedural rights. However, when that remedy is exercised, only a substantial breach of the procedural rights of the employee's representatives, as opposed to a plea based on the substantive breach of the rules laid down in Regulation 4064/89/EC, may lead to an annulment of the Commission's decision.

In the *Grandes Sources* case a trade union had made an application for interim measures to suspend the operation of a Decision authorising a merger between undertakings. The CFI ruled that if it is alleged that the application is manifestly inadmissible it is for the judge hearing the application for interim measures to establish that there are prima facie grounds for concluding that there is a certain probability that it is admissible. The granting of interim measures would amount to suspending the Commission's authorisation of a merger and would upset the functioning of the undertakings. Where the application was to challenge the refusal to allow a merger to go ahead this would prolong the existence of a dominant position which could have irreversible repercussions on competition in the sector concerned. It is thus incumbent upon the court hearing the application for interim measures to balance all the interests concerned. Thus, not

---

[40] Case T-96/92 [1995] ECR II-1213.
[41] Case T-12/93 [1995] ECR II-1247.

only the applicant and the Commission's position must be taken into account, but also the interests of third parties, in particular the undertakings concerned. In such circumstances, the grant of interim measures can be justified only if it appears that without them the applicants would be exposed to a situation liable to endanger their future. In the *Grandes Sources* application, the CFI felt that the contested Decision could not have repercussions on the rights of employees of the undertakings or expose them to the risk of a loss of rights which would justify interim measures.

The ineffectiveness of the labour law rights dimension in competition matters is revealed in this case. The Court is unclear about the status of fundamental rights of workers to the preservation of their jobs and the right of their representatives to be informed and consulted.[42] One way of enhancing the role of information and consultation rights of workers and their representatives would be to use the references to fundamental rights clauses in the new *Article 136 EC* as teleological tools of interpretation.[43]

6.4 State aid

Article 87 EC (ex Article 92(1) EC) imposes a prohibition on any aid granted by a Member State (or through state agencies/resources) in any form which distorts or threatens to distort competition by giving a special status, or favour, to certain undertakings (or the production of certain goods) in so far as the state aid affects trade between the Member States. Given that all the Member States have used, and continue to use, state aid as preferences for economic/political policies, the EC Treaty had to acknowledge that some *forms* of state aid are necessary and may be compatible with the Common Market. Under *Article 87(2)* and *(3) EC* (ex Article 92(2) and (3) EC), certain forms of state aid are lawful, in certain circumstances: aid having a social character, aid granted to individual consumers (provided that the aid is granted without discrimination to the *origin* of products), and aid to make good damage caused by natural disasters or other exceptional occurrences, aid to promote the economic development of areas where the standard of living is abnormally low or where there is serious underemployment, and aid to facilitate the development of certain economic activities or of certain economic areas. The state aid must not adversely affect trading conditions to an extent which is contrary to the common interest.

---

[42] *Cf.* the ruling of the French Court in the Renault closure discussed in Chapter 2 where a fundamental rights perspective is adopted.

[43] Note also the proposal to make strategic decisions null and void where there is a failure to consult worker representatives: COM (1998) 612 final *(supra* p. 37, n. 26).

State aids are of relevance to EC labour law and the new European Employment Strategy where they assist the creation or protection of jobs in regions or particular sectors in the Member States as well as where horizontal state aid is granted to promote particular goals such as training or job creation. In 1995 the Commission adopted Guidelines[44] for the evaluation of employment aid which were a response to the White Paper on *Growth, Competitiveness and Employment*.[45] The Guidelines show that the Commission does not approve of state aid measures which maintain jobs in an undertaking since such aid constitutes an operating aid which it is felt has the effect of preventing or delaying the necessary changes to make the undertaking (or the particular sector) economically viable. Such aid is not ruled out totally; it may be given for a limited period of time or given to economically disadvantaged regions in need of aid generally. There is some controversy over aid towards job creation. Such aid may reduce labour costs but it may also create jobs where there is no economic demand.[46] Thus, the Commission will not approve a state aid which has the effect of reducing labour costs without meeting special needs or promoting EU policies.[47] Cox has criticised the Commission's policy arguing that there is not sufficient transparency and clarity between general measures for labour costs reduction which are allowed and social measures which are disallowed under Commission policy.[48]

The Commission's discretion to regulate national employment policies is powerful, showing again that the public regulation of policy has been transferred from the national to the EU level. It is not only the Member States' values which come into conflict with this new form of re-regulation: private interests may also be affected. In *Matra SA v Commission*[49] Portugal had notified a state aid scheme to the Commission under *Article 88(3) EC* (ex Article 93(3) EC). The scheme intended to grant aid from 1991–5 to Newco, an undertaking established by Ford and Volkswagon to set up a factory for multi-purpose vehicles in Portugal. The state aid was in the form of a regional subsidy and also envisaged a training programme for employees organised by the Portuguese government and Newco. In

---

[44] Guidelines on Aid to Employment, OJ 1995 C 334/4. See also Commission Notice on Monitoring State Aid and Reduction of Labour Costs, OJ 1997 C 1/5.

[45] COM (93) 700.

[46] See Layard, R. and Nickell, S., 'The Case for Subsidising Extra Jobs' (1980) 90 *The Economic Journal* 51; Szyszczak, E. *Partial Unemployment* (Mansell, London, 1990).

[47] Details of Commission's policy can be found in the annual reports on competition policy.

[48] Cox, G., 'Horizontal Guidelines: Do They Facilitate Job Creation? The Example of Employment Subsidies' in Bilal, S. and Nicolaides, P. (eds) *Understanding State Aid Policy in the European Community* (Kluwer, The Hague, 1999).

[49] Case C-225/91 R [1991] ECR I-5823.

addition, there were various investments in the infrastructure. The Portugese government was to finance 90% of the programme. Matra complained that the state aid infringed *Article 87 EC* and that Ford and Volkswagon had infringed *Article 81(1)EC*.

Matra was heard by the Commission but the Commission allowed the Portuguese scheme to go ahead. Interim relief was refused. The Court refused an annulment of the Commission's Decision. Since the Commission had a wide discretion as to how to apply the competition rules, the Court was limited to determining as to whether the Commission had exceeded the scope of its discretion by a distortion or manifest error of assessment of the facts, misuse of powers or abuse of process.

A number of challenges have come before the Court on whether certain policies constitute a state aid. The demarcation between national and different Community policies is sometimes a fine one. In *Viscido* Advocate General Jacobs points out:

> It might be asked why, given their potential effect on competition, Article [87(1)] does not cover all labour and other social measures which by virtue of being selective in their impact might distort competition and thereby have an equivalent effect to a state aid. The answer is perhaps essentially a pragmatic one: to investigate all such regimes would entail an inquiry on the basis of the Treaty alone into the entire social and economic life of a Member State.[50]

Nevertheless, issues relating to state aid in the employment field have occurred in a number of guises. In *Sloman Neptun*[51] a German Works Council had refused to recognise an agreement whereby German shipowners could employ third-country nationals and pay them only 20% of German wages. One of the arguments put forward was that this was a violation of the state aid provisions since the German government lost revenue from income taxes by allowing the underpayment of wages. The Court, by looking at the object and general structure of the German shipping registration scheme, concluded that the scheme did not seek to create an additional advantage amounting to an additional burden on the state. The scheme merely altered the framework in which contractual relations were drawn up between shipowners and employees, to the benefit of the former.

In *Kirsammer-Hack* v *Sidal*[52] the applicant sued her employer for unfair dismissal but the German legislation excluded employers with fewer than five employees from the scope of unfair dismissal law. The applicant

---

[50] Cases C-52/97 to 54/97 *Epifanio Viscido v Ente Poste Italiane* [1998] ECR I-2629 para 16.
[51] Joined Cases C-72/91 and C-73/91 [1993] ECR I-887.
[52] Case C-189/91 [1993] ECR I-6185.

argued that this was an illegal state aid under *Article 87 EC* (ex Article 92 EC), but the Court was not inclined to agree with her.

The Commission issued a Decision against Belgium finding that a scheme, 'the Maribel Scheme', which allowed for reductions in social security benefits for manual workers, was a state aid and contrary to the EC Treaty. Belgium challenged the Decision under *Article 230 EC,* arguing that the scheme was a general policy measure.[53] Temporary budgetary difficulties prevented the scheme from being extended to all economic sectors. The Court disagreed. It found the scheme to constitute a financial advantage in the form of aid. The aid was selective in that it was limited to certain sectors of economic activity. The reductions were granted unconditionally, without any direct social or economic compensatory payment on the part of the recipient undertakings. The reductions were not linked to the creation of new jobs in small or medium-sized undertakings or the hiring of certain groups of workers who were having difficulty entering or re-entering the labour market.

One area of state aid policy which affects labour markets is the area of tax competition. The Commission has proposed a Draft Code of Conduct and would like to adopt further Communications in order to make fiscal policy as transparent as possible, so ensuring that decisions are predictable and that equal treatment is guaranteed.[54]

6.5 Flanking policies of the European Employment Strategy

As part of the European Employment Strategy (EES), the EU has used the structural funds to create 'flanking policies'. After reforms in 1999 the structural funds are charged with promoting a high level of employment.[55] A new approach was introduced for all the structural funds whereby all Funds switched to favouring a global system of integration leading towards the goal of economic and social cohesion. Reforms were made to the European Social Fund (ESF) by Regulation 1260/99 which are justified in the Preamble in the light of the new European Employment Strategy.[56] Article 2 of Regulation 1262/99 lists five priority areas which the ESF can support. The areas mirror the four pillars of the Employment Guidelines.

---

[53] Case C-75/97 *Belgium* v *Commission*, judgment of 17 June 1999.
[54] *Communication From The Commission to the Council, Towards Tax Co-ordination in the European Union. A Package To Tackle Harmful Tax Competition* COM (97) 495 final.
[55] Regulation 1260/1999 of 21 June 1999 laying down general provisions on the Structural Funds, OJ L 161/1, Preamble 5.
[56] European Commission, ESF 2000: A Guide to the New Structural Fund Regulation, http://europa.eu.int/comm/dg05/esf/en/news/esfnewre.htm

The European Regional Development Fund has also been revamped. Article 1 of Regulation 1261/99 states that the Fund shall contribute to promoting sustainable development and the creation of sustainable jobs. The determination of eligible regions for aid has as its crucial feature the assessment of total unemployment and long-term employment whereby the problems are to be analysed at the national and European level.

The European Investment Bank (EIB) has also been harnessed into the EES. At the Amsterdam Summit of 1997, the European Council called upon the EIB to place greater emphasis on initiatives creating employment opportunities. In response, the EIB launched the Amsterdam Special Action Plan within a few weeks of the Summit.

6.6 Public procurement

Public procurement is the system where the state, public bodies and local government procure services or goods through competitive tendering. The primary purposes of regulating public procurement are to ensure first of all the creation of competitive conditions in which public contracts are awarded *without discrimination* through the selection of the best bid tendered; secondly, to give suppliers access to a single market; thirdly, to ensure competitiveness of European suppliers. Opening up public procurement to competition within the Internal Market was one of the aims of the Commission's White Paper of 1985.[57] The sheer scale of public procurement in the EU, some 11.5% of the Member States' GDP,[58] makes it an influential tool in promoting other policies favoured by either the Member States or the EU.[59] For example, social policy objectives can be pursued by requiring employers to observe labour law conditions when performing a contract. Some of these ideas were first addressed as long ago as 1949 by the ILO where Article 2 of the Labour Clauses (Public Contracts) Convention No. 94 requires public contracts to include clauses ensuring compliance with local working conditions and Article 2 of Recommendation No. 84 of 1949 provides a similar obligation.[60] More recently, the South African government has introduced a successful reform of procurement

---

[57] COM (85) 310 final; *cf.* the Commission's White Paper, *Growth, Competitiveness and Employment. The Challenges and Ways Forward Into the 21st Century*, COM (93) 700 final, where it is argued that the public procurement regime should be targeted to promoting sustainable growth.

[58] Green Paper, *Public Procurement in the European Union: Exploring the Way Forward*, COM (96) 583.

[59] See Fernadez Martin, J. *The EC Public Procurement Rules* (Clarendon Press, Oxford, 1996), especially Ch 2.

[60] See Nielsen, H., 'Public Procurement and International Labour Standards' (1995) 4 *Public Procurement Law Review* 94.

policy, which has constitutional standing, in order to integrate people previously disadvantaged into the socio-economic structure of the new society.[61]

In the Commission's Green Paper on Public Procurement (1996)[62] the Commission asked whether the use of public procurement to promote social policies should be clarified by a Communication and whether further measures are needed to use the procurement policy to achieve social goals effectively. There would seem to be a number of issues which need to be addressed, before public procurement regulation can be used as a tool for promoting social goals.[63] One issue is how to implement such policies. It is lawful under the EU regime of public procurement to exclude an otherwise qualified tenderer because of non-performance with a labour/social clause in an earlier public contract. Equally employment criteria may be used as proof of professional/technical capability, as well as economic/financial standing. Another technique is to require successful tenderers to comply with social labour law obligations when performing contracts awarded to them.[64] One difficulty with this approach is the divergence of labour law/social policies between Member States and the lack of a harmonised social/labour law across the EU. In Member States with a history and well-developed system of such practices, employers will have a competitive advantage over employers from other Member States where such ideas are not developed. Thus, indirect discrimination may occur in the tendering process. The Commission, in its Green Paper, argues that the current state of EU law based on the concept of 'economically most advantageous tender' precludes social considerations from being taken into account on the award of public contracts. The Court has not given a clear ruling on this issue. In *Beentjes*[65] the applicant claimed that the decision of the Dutch Ministry of Agriculture and Fisheries not to accept its tender, which was the lowest, was in breach of an EC Public Procurement Directive. The successful tenderer was preferred since it was able to employ the long-term unemployed. The Court ruled that it was possible to

---

[61] For details see: www.pwdprocure.co.za

[62] *Supra* n. 58.

[63] See the discussion in Arrowsmith, S., 'Public Procurement as an Instrument of Policy and the Impact of Market Liberalisation' (1995) 111 *Law Quarterly Review* 235; Krüger, K., Nielsen, R. and Bruun, N. *European Public Contracts in a Labour Law Perspective* (DJØF, Copenhagen, 1998); Arrowsmith, S., 'The Community's Legal Framework on Public Procurement: "The Way Forward At Last?"' (1999) 36 *Common Market Law Review* 13.

[64] See McCrudden, C., 'Social Policy Issues in Public Procurement: A Legal Overview' in Arrowsmith, S. and Davies, A. (eds) *Public Procurement: Global Revolution* (Kluwer, The Hague, 1998); Bovis, C., 'A Social Policy Agenda in European Public Procurement Law and Policy' (1998) 14 *The International and Comparative Labour Law and Industrial Relations Journal* 137.

[65] Case 31/87 *Gebroeders Beentjes BV v The Netherlands* [1988] ECR 4635.

have such a condition within the tender specification provided that it has no direct or indirect discriminatory effect on tenderers from the other Member States. The specific condition must, however, be mentioned in the contract notice. There is, therefore, a strong argument that employment criteria are lawful as contract terms when it will be economically most advantageous to accept a bid from the tenderer which is best equipped to comply with it or at least disqualify a tenderer who cannot fulfil the criteria. In *Randstad*[66] the Court held that it is lawful to take the ability to pay high wages into consideration when determining which tender is most advantageous.

Arguments can be advanced that *Beentjes* has been overtaken by later judgments of the Court. For example, in *Commission* v *Italy*[67] Italian legislation required that, first, the main contractor for certain public works contracts should reserve a certain percentage of the work for undertakings whose registered office was in the region where the work was to be carried out (i.e. a local contractor). Second, in certain cases in deciding which undertakings from a group of undertakings should be invited to submit bids, authorities should give preference to consortia and joint ventures which involved undertakings carrying out their main activity in the local area where the work was to be executed. The Court ruled that both qualifications were contrary to the free movement of services provisions contained in *Article 49 EC* (ex Article 59 EC). In another case, *Commission* v *Denmark (Storebaelt)*[68] the Court ruled that a clause in a tender specification stating that a contractor was obliged, as far as possible, to use Danish materials, goods, labour and equipment was incompatible with the free movement of goods (*Article 28 EC*, ex Article 30 EC), labour (*Article 39 EC*, ex Article 48 EC) and services (*Article 49 EC*, ex Article 59 EC) provisions of the Treaty.

It is useful to point out that in the context of posting of workers (i.e. when an employer takes its own labour force to fulfil a contract in another Member State) the Court has stated that the Treaty provisions do not prevent a host Member State from extending its legislation and collective agreements to that posted labour force.[69] This would allow a Member State to stipulate compliance with its own social/labour laws in the pro-

---

[66] Case 56/77 *Agence Européenne d'Interims SA* v *Commission* [1978] ECR 2215.

[67] Case C-360/89 [1992] ECR I-3415. See Arrowsmith, S., 'The Legality of "Secondary" Procurement Policies under the Treaty of Rome and the Works Directive' (1992) 1 *Public Procurement Law Review* 408, who considers *Beentjes* to be overturned.

[68] Case C-243/89 [1993] ECR I-3353.

[69] Case 62-63/81 *Seco SA Eri and Desquenne and Giral* [1982] ECR 223; Case C-113/89 *Rush Portuguesa Lda* v *ONI* [1990] ECR I-1417. The Court's case law has been consolidated: Council Directive 96/71, OJ 1997 L 18/1.

curement procedure, but in the absence of a coherent code of EC labour law, problems of indirect discrimination can arise. Where a Member State has developed proactive labour market policies, for example positive action for underrepresented groups, an employer in another Member State with no experience of such policies may find it more difficult to comply with such labour laws.

The Commission's Green Paper was followed up by a Communication, Public Procurement in the European Union.[70] In Paragraph 4.4 the Commission stresses the importance of social policy for the EU and accepts that public contracts may constitute a significant means of influencing the behaviour of economic operators. The Commission indicates that it intends to clarify the principles, which can be applied to allow social factors to be taken into account. The Commission also pledges to use its own procurement policy to develop social policy objectives and encourages the Member States to do the same.[71]

Public procurement rules may also clash with the transfer of undertakings Directive, discussed in Chapter 5. Where there is contracting out of public services there may be a conflict of values between the costs envisaged by contracting out and the necessity to observe the transfer of undertakings Directive protection of employment rights.

---

[70] XV/5500/98-EN, 11 March 1998.
[71] See also the Commission Action Plan Against Racism, COM (98) 183, para 2.3.7.

CHAPTER 7

An EC labour law?
Binding the themes

The preceding chapters have revealed that the fractured legal base, the different political and legal traditions of the regulation of labour law issues between and within the Member States, together with a tacit acceptance of 'subsidiarity' from the early days of the Common Market, begin to explain why EC labour law cannot be presented as either a coherent, unitary or complete system of EC regulation. Equally the divorce of EC labour law from EC social law is messy with a 'clean break' impossible to achieve. What we have discovered is that EC labour law is about substantive and procedural legal rights at both the individual and collective levels. It embraces regulatory aspects as well as fundamental social rights aspects. There are apparent tensions both within and between the Member States on the nature and role of labour law and this is manifested in the multi-tiered sites of decision making across the EU. During the 1990s, however, labour law has taken on a new dimension at the European level and has become inevitably intertwined with social policy motives and economic constraints and ultimately is driven by an EU agenda set at moulding economic and political integration. In this concluding chapter, I want to tease out some of the underlying themes which have contributed to the quilting of EC policies into a distinctive model of EC labour law and policy.

7.1 The European social model – does it exist?

In the White Paper on Social Policy[1] the Commission argues that an EC social model exists based upon a set of shared social values.[2] Such values embrace individual rights, democracy, free collective bargaining, equality

---

[1] *European Social Policy – A Way Forward For the Union*, COM (94) 333.

[2] For a discussion of social values in Community law, see Hepple, B., 'Social Values and European Law' (1995) 48 *Current Legal Problems* 39; Sciarra, S., 'Social Values and the Multiple Sources of European Social Law' (1995) 1 *European Law Journal* 60; Kenner, J., 'Citizenship and Fundamental Rights: Reshaping the European Model' in Kenner, J. (ed.) *Trends in European Social Policy* (Dartmouth, Aldershot, 1995).

of opportunities, social welfare, social solidarity and market economies. An argument can be put forward that a 'European social model' exists which is distinctive from, say, Japanese or American models and also rests independently but uneasily alongside national social models. The Member States differ widely in their regulation of labour markets and provision of social benefits. For example,[3] government expenditure on social protection is one-third of GDP in Sweden and only one-sixth in Portugal.[4] There is a strong sense of social solidarity within the Member States but not necessarily across the Member States. Arguments can also be put forward that the EU exhibits a number of distinctive features which distinguish the 'European model' from other systems of capitalist organisation which are found in the United States and Japan. Gough,[5] for example, argues that the European model is more statist and more corporatist than either the American or Japanese model and that the dominant European model is characterised by a number of features: high levels of spending (especially on transfers), insurance-based social programmes, high inter-generational solidarity (with modest to high vertical distribution), breadwinner model, good social investment in human and social infrastructure, moderate to low levels of poverty and inequality.

One of the difficulties of moulding a social model for the EU is how far characteristics of the individual Member States can be moulded into the process on European integration and how far the particular characteristics will be lost to the dynamics of integration. Streeck[6] has argued that the evolution of an EU social policy can only be understood by analysing its role in the process of European integration rather than as a steadily evolving system of a 'European welfare state' replicating the role of a welfare state at the national level.

Many of the distinctive features found in the national systems are being attacked as a result of the effects of Economic Monetary Union (EMU),[7] the unsustainability of social security schemes[8] and differing conceptions

---

[3] 'Social Protection in the EU' *Eurostat Statistics In Focus*, Population and Social Conditions, No. 14/98.

[4] Esping-Andersen, G. *The Three Worlds of Welfare Capitalism* (Polity Press, Cambridge, 1990) identified a number of different patterns of social programmes in Europe: *corporatist model*: Germany, France, Benelux, Austria; *liberal model*: UK, Ireland; *social democratic model*: Nordic states; *southern model*: Italy, Spain, Portugal, Greece.

[5] Gough, I., 'Social Aspects of the European Model and Its Economic Consequences' in Beck, W. *et al.* (eds) *The Social Quality of Europe* (Kluwer, The Hague, 1997).

[6] Streeck, W., 'Neo-Voluntarism: A New European Social Policy Regime?'(1995) 1 *European Law Journal* 1.

[7] Teague, P., 'Monetary Union and Social Europe' (1998) 8 *Journal of European Social Policy* 117.

[8] Disney, R., 'Crisis in OECD Pension Programmes: What Are the Reform Options?' (2000) 110 *Economic Journal* F1.

of the role of the state in a global economy.[9] While social policy has come to play an increasingly prominent role in the EU policy agenda, the underlying tensions of the aim of a social policy in the EU bubble under the surface. Grahl and Teague[10] argue that the European social model (which they understand to be a specific combination of comprehensive welfare systems and strongly institutionalised and politicised forms of industrial relations) is in serious crisis as a result of general economic developments which have undermined the European social model's functionality. Grahl and Teague argue that an important index as to whether influential political forces will be able to modernise the European social model will be the strength and process of European integration. At the time of writing, the immediate impact of meeting the convergence criteria for EMU has tested the Member States' commitment to the 'European social model' leaving a hiatus as the big three Member States – Germany, France and the United Kingdom – resolve their differences as to the future direction of policy in this area.

What then, are the distinctive features of the 'European social model' and how do they mould the development of an EC labour law? Schulte[11] offers a description which I will adapt and use as a framework for an analysis of EC labour law.

7.1.1 A constitutional system

Schulte identifies the first distinctive feature of the Community system as a constitutional system, based upon democratic foundations. The case law of the Court of Justice has conferred the notion of a 'constitutional charter' on the EC Treaty.[12] From the early days of its jurisprudence, the Court had a clear vision of the primacy[13] of Community law over conflicting national law in a new, autonomous legal order.[14] The effectiveness of that legal order is developed through ideas of direct[15] and indirect effect[16] and the

---

9   See the essays in Teubner, G. (ed.) *Global Law Without A State* (Dartmouth, Aldershot, 1997).

10   Grahl, J. and Teague, P., 'Is the European Social Model Fragmenting?' (1997) 2 *New Political Economy* 405.

11   'Juridical Instruments of the European Union and the European Communities' in Beck, W. *et al.* (eds) *The Social Quality of Europe* (Kluwer, The Hague, 1997).

12   See Szyszczak, E., 'Social Rights As General Principles of Community Law' in Neuwahl, N. and Rosas, A. (eds) *The European Union and Human Rights* (Nijhoff, The Hague, 1995).

13   Case 6/64 *Costa v ENEL* [1964] ECR 585.

14   Case 26/62 *Van Gend en Loos* [1963] ECR 1.

15   See, for example, Case 43/75 *Defrenne v Sabena (No. 2)* [1976] ECR 455.

16   Case 14/83 *Von Colson and Kamann v Land Nordrhein-Westfalen* [1984] ECR 1891.

partial intrusion of Community law into the national procedural and remedial arena.[17] The Court has also stressed that the Community is a legal order based upon the rule of law.[18] The development of a clear and coherent set of fundamental social rights is still rudimentary and fragmentary.[19] The reference to the 1989 Charter of Fundamental Social Rights of Workers, as well as the European Social Charter 1961 in *Article 136 EC* serves as an important teleological tool, but to date references to broad principles of non-discrimination are only found in the Preambles to new legislation, and presumably will remain of interpretative, rather than of substantive, value until *Article 13 EC* is fleshed out. A decision was taken at the EU Summits of Cologne and Tampere in 1999 to begin drafting an EU Charter of Fundamental Rights.[20]

A number of commentators speak of the Treaty of Amsterdam and the Court of Justice 'constitutionalising' aspects of EU labour.[21] Such descriptions tell us little about what is involved in this constitutionalisation process. For some commentators, even after Maastricht and Amsterdam, the EU represents no more than a free trade area.[22] Others argue that the development of regulation by the EC has remodelled the contours of the role of the state and intervention in the market at both the national and supranational level and that the search is on to describe, rationalise and

---

[17] See Hoskins, M., 'Tilting the Balance: Supremacy and National Procedural Rules' (1996) 21 *European Law Review* 365.

[18] See Case 294/83 *Parti Ecologiste Les Verts* v *European Parliament* [1986] ECR 1339.

[19] Sciarra, S., 'From Strasbourg To Amsterdam: Prospects for the Convergence of European Social Rights Policy' in Alston, P. (ed.) *Human Rights in the EU* (OUP, Oxford, 1999); Hepple, B., 'Towards A European Social Institution' in Engels, C. and Weiss, M. (eds) *Labour Law and Industrial Relations at the Turn of the Century. Liber Amicorum in Honour of Professor Roger Blanpain* (Kluwer, The Hague, 1998).

[20] The Platform of European Social NGOs and the ETUC has set out a number of conditions to be met in the drafting process. One of these is accession of the EC to the ECHR and the additional Protocols and revised Social Charter and a full set of rights, particularly the economic and social rights guaranteed in the ECHR 1951, the revised Social Charter of 1960 and 1996, the Community Charter on Fundamental Social Rights of Workers 1989, the ILO Declaration on Fundamental Principles and Rights at Work 1998, the UN Convention on the Rights of the Child 1989 and the UN Convention for the Elimination of all forms of Discrimination Against Women 1979. Such rights are to be a minimum, and a non-regression principle should be applied to existing rights in the EU or in the Member States. http://europa.eu.int/comm/dg05/fundamri/news/tampere-en.htm

[21] See, for example, Liebfried, S. and Pierson, P., 'Multitiered Institutions and the Making of Social Policy' in Pierson, P. and Leibfried, S. (eds) *European Social Policy. Between Fragmentation and Integration* (Brookings, Washington, 1995); Barnard, C., 'The United Kingdom, the "Social Chapter" and the Amsterdam Treaty' (1997) 26 *Industrial Law Journal* 275.

[22] Mortelmanns, K.,'The Common Market, The Internal Market and The Single Market, What's In a Market?' (1998) 35 *Common Market Law Review* 101.

explain the nature of state, and supranational or inter-governmental intervention.[23]

The EC Treaty has been analysed from the perspective of ordo-liberalism.[24] The argument runs that economic freedoms – freedom to trade, to enter into transactions, freedom to own and use property – are as important as the protection of traditional civil and political rights. The Internal Market is viewed from the perspective of an incipient economic constitution whereby law is used to regulate state power which might restrict the economic freedoms. While attractive in its simplicity and determinism the characterisation of the EC as an ordo-liberal regime has been challenged by other theories.[25]

Majone,[26] in contrast, argues that the work of the EU is essentially regulatory. While the EU undertakes a number of functions undertaken by the Member States it also is reluctant to undertake the classic functions of the state, such as policing, public order or re-distributive roles. This is largely due to the EU's limited fiscal capacity and the process of policy pre-emption as a result of the institutional structure of the EU. Majone, therefore, describes the EU as a 'regulatory state'. This analysis is persuasive[27] when we look at the second criterion put forward by Schulte which is the view of the 'European social model', an economic system oriented towards principles of market economy, with the state intervening to make corrections on socio-political grounds. The idea of free movement of labour and the establishment of the Social Fund and the later structural funds are examples of this model. More recently, the new mix of Community/Member State/new political actors' strategies under the new Employment Chapter and the Luxembourg, Cardiff and Cologne Processes are examples of how competing interests can be channelled to meet Community objectives.[28]

---

[23] See Chalmers, D and Szyszczak, E. *European Union Law Two: Towards A European Polity?* (Ashgate, Aldershot, 1998), Ch.1.

[24] See Chalmers, D., 'The Single Market: From Prima Donna to Journeyman' in Shaw, J. and More, G. (eds) *New Legal Dynamics of European Union* (Clarendon Press, Oxford, 1995).

[25] See Sauter, W. *Competition Law and Industrial Policy in the EU* (Clarendon Press, Oxford, 1997).

[26] Majone, G., 'The European Community Between Social Policy and Social Regulation' (1993) 31 *Journal of Common Market Studies* 153.

[27] Although it is also open to challenge, Liebfried and Pierson *op. cit.* argue that Majone overstates the case in the extent to which reliance upon regulatory techniques implies a shift in the goals of social policy. They argue that the traditional redistributive social policies can be implemented through regulatory mandates on lower tiers of either government, local government or even private actors, employers without the need for significant spending at the central level.

[28] See Teague, P., 'Monetary Union and Social Europe' (1998) 8 *Journal of European Social Policy* 117; Szyszczak, E., 'The Evolving European Employment Strategy' in Shaw, J. (ed.) *Social Law and Policy in an Evolving European Law* (Hart, Oxford, 2000).

Although it is still early days, an argument can be made that the European Employment Strategy is a significant step from the EU merely acting as a regulatory tier and a move towards a more interventionist role for the EU. The outcome may undermine the principles of a market economy set out in *Article 4 EC*.

7.1.2 Welfare of citizens

The third feature identified by Schulte is that state objectives are directed towards the welfare of citizens. As we have seen, this feature is now challenged by the disintegration of the 'traditional' European social model, particularly in the 'privatisation' of traditional public welfare and the cut-backs in public expenditure in a number of Member States in the run up to EMU.[29] Social exclusion as a priority area of EU action has received a mixed reception, because of the lack of unanimity between the Member States on how to proceed as well as a clear legal base on which the EC can proceed. It has also been relegated to soft law. Balanced against this we have seen the Court developing ideas of social solidarity in cases, arguing for market principles to be applied to social security, the use of the concept of social solidarity in the Commission's 'economic' White Paper, *Growth, Competitiveness and Employment – The Challenges and Ways Forward in the 21st Century*,[30] of unemployment and social exclusion included in EU Essen Priorities' policy agenda and the new European Employment Strategy. In an interview, the newly appointed Commissioner for Social Affairs, Anna Diamantopolou, stated that:

> Competiveness is my first aim, because we need a dynamic European economy. But we must combine it with a strong inclusive social model. I do not believe in the US model of competition without social cohesion.[31]

7.1.3 Anti-discrimination

A fourth feature of the European social model is a broad field of socio-political activities which are aimed at reducing discrimination and creating possibilities for personal development and integration of all members of society. Here the EU has been partially successful. The equal treatment programme in relation to sex equality is the most developed programme but it is not without its critics. Until *Article 13 EC* is utilised other areas of discrimination are consigned to soft law and rhetoric in Preambles.

---

[29] Guild, E., 'How Can Social Protection Survive EMU?' (1999) 24 *European Law Review* 22. See also Traversa, E., 'The Consequences of European Monetary Union on Collective Bargaining and National Social Security Systems' (2000) *The International Journal of Comparative Labour Law and Industrial Relations* 47.

[30] COM (93) 700 final.

[31] *Financial Times*, 4 November 1999.

Discrimination on the grounds of nationality can be challenged under *Article 12 EC* (ex Article 6 EC) and it is a right vigorously defended and expanded[32] by the Court of Justice, but the Court has also limited the scope of *Article 12 EC* to exclude TCNs, creating a hole in the blanket of protection offered by EC law.

7.1.4 Social protection

Linked to the third and fourth features is the idea of a well-developed system of social protection, providing compensatory action where risks materialise. Here the European social model is under most pressure, particularly in changes in political culture which have pressed for changes in the public/private mix of providing for social protection.[33] This finds expression in the Commission's policy documents in euphemisms such as the need to 'reform and modernise' social security.[34]

7.1.5 Procedural rights

Finally, Schulte identifies a legal system which guarantees the possibility for all citizens to participate in social measures and benefits on the basis of law and especially in the form of individual legal entitlements. Throughout the chapters of this book we have seen the growth of individual remedies and the use of the direct and indirect effect of EC law to allow for the pursuit of EC-based rights in the national courts both against the state and private employers. Equally, we have seen the development in conceptual thinking away from pure 'market-citizen' rights to recognising rights to citizenship away from market-based activities.[35] The latter ideas are nascent and the challenge for the next millennium is to develop social-citizenship rights away from market-based participation in European society.[36]

In this chapter, I want to expand upon Schulte's framework and elicit other aspects which, we might argue, have contributed to the emergence of a discrete area of EC labour law.

---

[32] See Case C-85/96 *Martínez Sala* v *Freistaat Bayern* [1998] ECR I-2691; Case C-274/96 *Horst Otto Bickel, Ulrich Franz* [1998] ECR I-7637.

[33] Paganetto, L. (ed) *Social Protection and the Single European Market. The Evolution of the Social Security Systems and Free Circulation: Problems and Perspectives* (CEIS Tor Vergata, Rome, 1997).

[34] Communication From the Commission. *A Concerted Strategy for Modernising Social Protection*, COM (99) 347 final.

[35] Shaw, J., 'The Many Pasts and Futures of Citizenship in the European Union' (1997) 22 *European Law Review* 554.

[36] Bercusson, B. *et al.*, 'A Manifesto For Social Europe' (1997) 2 *European Law Journal* 189. See also the Commentaries by Lo Faro, A. (1998) 3 *European Law Journal* 300 and Larrsson, A. (1998) 3 *European Law Journal* 304; Shaw, J., *ibid.*; Moebius, I. and Szyszczak, E., 'Of Raising Pigs and Children' (1998) *The Yearbook of European Law* 125.

7.2 The interaction of economic and social policies

The first feature is in fact seen as a weakness of EC labour law. The weakness of not having a tightly defined legal base for an EC labour law is that where aspects of labour law permeate into other areas of economic activity under the EC Treaty labour law policies may be lost in the competition with other EC goals, particularly competition policy itself, which aims to correct distortions of competition in the Internal Market. This may create further regulatory tensions, particularly where principles of competition and de-regulation conflict with Member States' policies of employment protection and employment promotion.

Although the EU, for obvious reasons, has had economic policy objectives it was, surprisingly, not until the TEU that a social and labour market policy was created as an independent policy area in Article 3 EC.[37] The mix of social and economic policies as interdependent, mutually reinforcing rather than conflicting policies, is stressed in the Commission's White Paper[38] and in the Medium-Term Social Action Programme 1995–97.[39] The interaction and tension of social and economic policies has appeared in rulings handed down by the Court of Justice. Particularly in relation to *Article 86 EC* (ex Article 90 EC) we see a willingness by the Court not to extend all aspects of economic activity to market principles. In a number of cases relating to the fundamental freedoms of the Internal Market we see the dominance of the market-citizen where Community law has a particularly empowering effect of establishing fundamental rights which can be used to override national labour law and policy. In contrast, the imperatives of an Internal Market show a clear conflict between the economic policy of the Community and national labour law in the ruling of *Commission* v *France*.[40]

7.3 Institutional dynamics: the role of the Court of Justice

A second distinctive feature of EC labour law relates to the pro-active role of the Court of Justice. There is a tendency to see the development of EC labour law as a conflict between the Commission and the Council. But the institutional dynamics[41] contributing to the development of an EC labour

---

[37] *Cf.* Case 43/75 *Defrenne* v *Sabena (No. 2)* [1976] ECR 455.
[38] COM (94) 333.
[39] COM (95) 134.
[40] Case C-265/95 *Commission* v *France* [1997] ECR I-6959 (see p. 148).
[41] See Hoskyns, C. *Integrating Gender* (Verso, London, 1996); Hervey, T., 'Sex Equality in Social Protection: New Institutionalist Perspectives on Allocation of Competence' (1998) 4 *European Law Journal* 196.

law are complex and, after the Treaty of Amsterdam, involve new policy-making actors. The Court has established itself as a key actor,[42] not only in the interpretation of EC labour law, but also in the legislative process as well as maintaining a dialogue with the national courts.[43] It was with some scepticism that we greeted the ruling in *Grant* v *SW Trains*[44] when the Court refused to extend the principle of non-discrimination on the grounds of sex to cover discrimination on the grounds of sexual orientation, arguing that such an extension belonged to the realms of the legislature and not the Court. The Court has frequently laid the ground for legislative change, for example in relation to employment protection rights for pregnant workers,[45] part-time workers[46] and the partial reversal of the burden of proof in sex discrimination claims. In relation to occupational social security, the Court has even cut across *Article 141 EC* (ex Article 119 EC) and secondary legislation bringing in its wake much political concern and economic problems. While the Court has been criticised[47] for not taking a stronger stance and recognising that the role of women in European society is not homogeneous, the Court has opened up for scrutiny a number of assumptions about the role of women in the labour market, particularly in relation to part-time work and pregnancy.

The Court has played a pivotal role in elevating certain social rights, particularly in the area of free movement and the equal treatment of men and women, into fundamental rights protected by EC law and binding upon the Member States.[48] It has, for instance, utilised the general principles of Community law (the principles of proportionality, equality, non-discrimi-

---

[42] See Fredman, S., 'Social Law in the European Union: The Impact of the Lawmaking Process' in Craig, P. and Harlow, C. (eds) *Law Making in the European Union* (Kluwer, The Hague, 1998). *Cf.* Simitis, S., 'Dismantling of Strengthening Labour Law: The Case of the European Court of Justice' (1996) 2 *European Law Journal* 156.

[43] Kilpatrick, C., 'Community or Communities of Courts in European Integration? Sex Equality Dialogues Between UK Courts and the ECJ' (1998) 4 *European Law Journal* 121.

[44] Case C-249/96 [1996] ECR I-621.

[45] Case C-177/88 *Dekker* v *Stichting Vormingscentrum voor Jong Volwassenen* [1990] ECR I-3941, followed by Council Directive 92/85/EC.

[46] Case 170/84 *Bilka-Kaufhaus* v *Weber* [1986] ECR 1607. This case was followed by more cases on indirect discrimination and part-time work and gave the Commission the confidence to continue with its proposals to regulate 'atypical' work which had met with resistance in the Council since the 1980s.

[47] An extensive literature exists, see Chapter 4. For a defence see: Mancini, G. and O'Leary, S., 'The New Frontiers of Sex Equality Law in the European Union' (1999) 24 *European Law Review* 331.

[48] Temple-Lang, J., 'The Sphere in which Member States are Obliged to Comply with the General Principles of Law and Community Fundamental Rights Principles' (1991/2) *Legal Issues of European Integration* 23.

nation) to enhance the effectiveness of Community law.[49] Many of the cases on remedies, sanctions, effectiveness have emerged from labour law cases brought to the Court from the national courts using *Article 234 EC* (ex Article 177 EC).[50]

Finally, the Court has been instrumental in creating links, not only between the national legal orders, but also the international legal order. In a number of cases it has referred to international human rights/social law conventions to provide inspiration for a set of Community-law social rights.[51] Vogel-Polsky[52] and Hepple,[53] in the disillusion felt over the limitations of the 1989 Social Charter, went further and suggested that the fundamental rights nature of the labour law and its global uniformity could be enhanced further by the Community acceding to international social law conventions. Given the nature of the Opinion delivered by the Court on the accession of the Community to the ECHR,[54] it is most unlikely that the Community, or the Court, would cede its autonomy or supremacy to a higher international legal order.

7.4 EC labour law and global competition

EC labour law must be placed in the context of the growth of multinational companies which Castells points out 'transcend national boundaries, identities and interests', and are the 'power-holders of wealth and technology in the global economy'.[55] Too much regulation and increased labour costs may induce such companies to switch production or sub-contract or outsource to low labour costs/low unionised areas, particularly in the Pacific Rim and the central and eastern European states. One response has been the fragmentation of national European labour markets with a corre-

---

[49] See Arnull, A. *The General Principles of EEC Law and the Individual* (Frances Pinter/Leicester University Press, 1990); Tridimas, T. *The General Principles of EC Law* (OUP, Oxford, 1999).

[50] Case 43/75 *Defrenne* v *Sabena (No. 2)* [1976] ECR 455 (vertical/horizontal direct effect); Case 14/83 *Von Colson* [1984] ECR 1891 (indirect effect); Case 152/84 *Marshall* [1986] ECR 723 (effective remedies); Joined Cases C-6/90 and 9/90 *Francovich and Bonifaci* v *Italy* [1991] ECR I-5357 (state liability).

[51] Case 149/77 *Defrenne* v *Sabena (No. 3)* [1978] ECR 1365; Case 24/86 *Blaizot* v *University of Liège* [1988] ECR 379; Case 222/84 *Johnston* v *RUC* [1986] ECR 1651; Case 36/75 *Rutili* v *Minister for the Interior* [1975] ECR 1219.

[52] Vogel-Polsky, E., 'What Future is there for a Social Europe following the Strasbourg Summit?' (1990) 19 *Industrial Law Journal* 65.

[53] Hepple, B., 'The Implementation of the Community Charter of Fundamental Social Rights' (1990) 53 *Modern Law Review* 643.

[54] *Opinion 2/94* [1996] ECR I-1759.

[55] Castells, M. *The Rise of the Network Society* (Blackwell, Cambridge, MA, 1996), p. 192.

sponding reduction in the level of employment protection rights.[56] These moves towards 'flexible labour markets' have put the role and form of labour law in a state of flux: it has become a hybrid in nature, 'torn between its old protective function and the new aspiration towards flexibility'.[57] Hepple[58] argues that the impact of globalisation poses a dilemma for labour law. A growing proportion of world trade is between states with different levels of labour costs. Thus, labour law, to be effective, must achieve a balance between protecting individual and collective rights and not destroying the very jobs it is designed to protect. There is an argument that high labour standards may produce better productivity and a long-term competitive advantage, and this is indeed is one of the arguments utilised by Deakin and Wilkinson.[59] Their argument runs that low labour costs are but one factor in locating capital and investing in industry.[60]

One response to increased competitiveness in the global market is to combine ideas of competition with standards of ethics. This is the idea of using social clauses in international trade agreements. The EU has incorporated ideas of making aid and trade to developing countries conditional upon observing human rights.[61] Attempts to incorporate social clauses into trade agreements at a global level have met with differing responses from economists asked to assess the impact of such clauses and from the political élites, often backed by multinationals, in the developing countries themselves. A report published by the OECD[62] concluded that by improv-

---

[56] Standing, G., 'Globalisation, Labour Flexibility and Insecurity: The Era of Market Regulation' (1997) 3 *European Industrial Relations Journal* 7.

[57] Sciarra, S., 'How Global is Labour Law? The Perspective of Social Rights in the European Union' in Wilthagen, T. (ed.) *Advancing Theory in Labour Law and Industrial Relations in a Global Context* (North-Holland, Amsterdam, 1998). On the impact of globalisation on decision-making processes, see Bercusson, B., 'Globalizing Labour Law: Transnational Private Regulation and Countervailing Actors in European Labour Law' in Teubner, G. (ed.) *Global Law Without A State* (Dartmouth, Aldershot, 1997).

[58] Hepple, B., 'New Approaches to International Labour Regulation' (1997) 26 *Industrial Law Journal* 353; *Labour Laws and Global Trade* (Hart, Oxford, 2000).

[59] Deakin, S. and Wilkinson, F., 'Rights vs Efficiency? The Economic Case for Transnational Labour Standards' (1994) 23 *Industrial Law Journal* 289.

[60] Lee, E., 'Globalisation and Employment: Is Anxiety Justified?' (1996) 135 *International Labour Review* 485.

[61] Cremona, M., 'Human Rights and Democracy Clauses in the EC's Trade Agreements' in Emiliou, N. and O'Keeffe, D. (eds) *The European Union and World Trade Law* (Wiley, Chichester, 1996); 'The European Union and the External Dimension of Human Rights Policy' in Konstadinidis, S. (ed.) *A People's Europe Tuning A Concept to Content* (Ashgate, Aldershot, 1999).

[62] See OECD, *Trade and Labour Standards. A Review of the Issues* (1995) and *Trade, Employment and Labour Standards. A Study of Core Workers' Rights and International Trade* (OECD, Paris, 1996).

ing labour standards the economic efficiency in developing countries might improve and that the concern for the negative effects on their economic and international competitiveness was unfounded, but a report commissioned by the World Bank[63] argues that using trade sanctions is a crude form of addressing the question and such sanctions are often counter-productive. ETUC is pressing for a working party to examine the use of ILO Conventions as a core set of fundamental social rights which should be respected in world trade agreements. Malmberg and Johnsson[64] argue that a core of fundamental labour rights has emerged, the content of which draws a consensus from the legal base of ILO Conventions as well as being recognised in the ECHR and the UN Declaration of Human Rights. The core is composed of the freedom of association, prohibition of forced labour, non-discrimination in employment, prohibition of child labour. The ILO has subsequently re-affirmed this core of fundamental rights in the adoption of a Declaration on Fundamental Principles and Rights at Work on 18 June 1998.[65] Kellerson argues that there is intrinsic value in this solemn Declaration in that it represents a reaffirmation, by governments and both social partners, of the universality of fundamental principles and rights at a time of widespread uncertainty and questioning of those rights.[66]

Another way of implementing such measures is through persuading multinational companies to adhere to codes of conduct.[67] An example of such a code is the one drawn up by the Swedish multinational, IKEA and the International Federation of Building and Wood Workers (IFBWW) in Geneva on 25 May 1998. An example of a sectoral agreement is the Social Partners Charter for the European Textile/Clothing Sector, signed in Brussels on 25 September 1997.

The importance of these approaches is also felt much closer to western Europe. The penetration of Western capital into the newly opened competitive markets of Eastern and Western Europe has brought with it fears that unless the same labour standards are applied on 'a level playing field' all

---

[63] Maskus, K., 'Should Core Labor Standards Be Imposed through International Trade Policy?' *The World Bank Development Research Group, Policy Working Paper 1817* (1997). See the discussion in Malmberg, J. and Johnsson, D. *Social Clauses and Other Means To Promote Fair Labour Standards in International Fora – A Survey* (Arbetslivsinstitutet, Stockholm, 1998).

[64] *Ibid.*

[65] See the *Special Issue: Labour Rights, Human Rights* (1998/2) 137 *International Labour Review*.

[66] Kellerson, H., 'The ILO Declaration of 1998 on Fundamental Principles and Rights: A Challenge for the Future' (1998) 137 *International Labour Law Review* 223.

[67] See Muchlinski, P. *Multinational Enterprises and the Law* (Blackwell, Oxford, 1995), Ch. 13.

the attempts to combat unemployment in the new provisions of the Treaty of Amsterdam will be lost.

7.5 The 'worker-citizen' – 'citizen-worker'

A third distinctive feature of EC labour law is related to the fact that many of the labour law issues addressed by the EC have a 'citizenship' dimension to them. The EU has increasingly turned its attention to developing rights of European citizenship.[68] While the focus of citizenship in the twentieth century has tended to be on civic and political notions of 'citizenship rights', a new element in the socio-economic domain has emerged, including what Marshall[69] has termed 'industrial rights'.[70] Many of these rights have found expression in international human/social rights covenants. The EU still does not have a fully comprehensive code of either 'citizenship' rights or 'human' rights, but within the EC legislation on labour law and through rulings of the Court of Justice a number of concepts of 'citizenship' in relation to labour law issues are emerging.[71] According to the Commission's White Paper on Social Policy:

> ... there are a number of shared values which form the basis of the European social model. These include democracy and individual rights, free collective bargaining, the market economy, equality of opportunity for all and social welfare and solidarity. These values ... are encapsulated by the Community Charter of the Fundamental Social Rights of Workers.[72]

This Charter has been criticised since the conceptualisation of rights in terms of citizenship was seemingly distorted towards workers' rights,[73] but as Everson[74] points out, the initial conception of EU citizen was that of the 'market citizen'. A person was only included within the citizenship notions of the early Common Market by exercising an economic activity within the

---

[68] See Chalmers, D. and Szyszczak, E. *European Union Law Two. Towards a European Polity?* (Ashgate, Aldershot, 1998), Ch. 2.

[69] Marshall, T. H. *Citizenship and Social Class and Other Essays* (Cambridge University Press, Cambridge, 1950).

[70] *Cf.* Giddens, A., 'Class Division, Class Conflict and Citizenship Rights' in Giddens, A. (ed.) *Profiks and Critiques in Social Theory* (Polity Press, Cambridge, 1982). Giddens refers to such rights as 'economic civil rights'; Held, S., 'Citizenship and Autonomy' in Held, S. and Thompson, J. (eds) *Social Theory of Modern Societies: Anthony Giddens and his Critics* (Cambridge University Press, Cambridge, 1989). Held refers to the rights as 'economic rights'.

[71] See Bercusson, B. *European Labour Law* (Butterworths, London 1996), especially Title IV.

[72] *European Social Policy – A Way Forward for the Union*, COM (94) 333, para 3.

[73] Bercusson, B. *European Labour Law* (Butterworths, London, 1996) 601.

[74] 'The Legacy of the Market Citizen' in Shaw, J. and More, G. (eds) *New Legal Dynamics of European Union* (OUP, Oxford, 1995).

sphere of (economic) competence of the Treaty of Rome,[75] the most notable example, for our purposes, being the exercise of the right to free movement of workers – and their (extended) families. Notions of 'citizenship' rights are found throughout the historical development of EC social law. Yet, there has been a tendency to dismiss such rhetoric as purely symbolic.[76]

There is an attempt to create a notion of 'citizenship' rights within EC labour law which is very different from national ideas of the scope and content of labour law. Some of these 'citizen-worker' rights are seen in the language used either in legislation or in rulings by the Court of Justice. For example, the 'soft law' provisions relating to sexual harassment at work talk about 'the protection of the dignity of women and men at work'.[77] In *P v S* [78] Advocate General Tesauro in his Opinion cites the right to respect for private life enshrined in Article 8 ECHR and already recognised by the Court in a staff case, *X v Commission*.[79] This coaxed the Court to rule that in relation to discrimination against transsexuals:

> To tolerate such discrimination would be tantamount, as regards such a person, to a failure to respect the dignity and freedom to which he or she is entitled, and which the Court has a duty to safeguard.[80]

The principle of the right to dignity is seen in attempts to respect the private life of workers, for example in reconciling occupational and family obligations.[81] This issue permeates the Commission's Action Programmes on Equal Opportunities for Women and Men,[82] is found in the new Employment Guidelines and finds expression in some of the Court's case

---

[75] *Cf.* the earlier description of rights to free movement as embryonic citizenship rights: Plender, R., 'An Incipient Form of European Citizenship' in Jacobs, F. (ed.) *European Law and the Individual* (North-Holland, Oxford, 1976).

[76] Shaw, J., 'Twin-Track Social Europe – the Inside Track' in O'Keeffe, D. and Twomey, P. (eds) *Legal Issues of the Maastricht Treaty* (Wiley/Chancery, Chichester, 1993).

[77] Resolution OJ 1990 C 157/3. The inspiration for this language was from the report by Rubenstein, M. *The Dignity of Women at Work* (Commission of the European Communities, OOPEC, 1988). See Rubenstein, M., 'Sexual Harassment: European Commission Recommendation and Code of Practice' (1992) 21 *Industrial Law Journal* 70.

[78] Case C-13/94 [1996] ECR I-2143.

[79] Case T-121/89 and T-13/90 [1992] ECR II-2195; on appeal: Case C-404/92P *X v Commission* [1994] ECR I-4737.

[80] *Ibid.*, para 22.

[81] See the Recommendation on Child Care 92/241/EEC, OJ 1992 L 123/6 and the Parental Leave Directive 96/34/EC, OJ 1996 L 145/4. Note also under the Employment Guidelines this is seen as an important issue under the fourth pillar of equal opportunities.

[82] See EC Commission, *White Paper on Social Policy,* COM (94) 333; Fourth Medium-Term Action Programme on Equal Opportunities for Women and Men (1996–2000), COM (95) 381 final.

law protecting pregnant women at work.[83] Similarly, maternity is accorded special status in the health and safety sphere in Council Directive 92/85/EEC.[84] In addition to employment protection, the employer must assess the nature, degree, duration of exposure to physical, chemical and biological agents in order to determine the risks to the health and safety of a pregnant worker and so decide what measures to take.

Equally, EC labour law recognises that while women's caring responsibilities often prevent them from participating fully in public economic life, men have also traditionally found it difficult to participate fully in private (domestic) economic life. Thus, the Directive on Parental Leave,[85] though very limited in scope, is a first step in redressing this imbalance.

EC labour law also recognises that young people also have a right to private life: a right to a childhood and education free from interference from economic work obligations which might encroach upon that time. As a health and safety measure, a Council Directive on the protection of young people at work has been enacted.[86] In the preparatory documents, the Commission cites studies showing that young people are more likely to be affected by occupational risks such as local muscular or cardio-respiratory or sensory or general fatigue with young people suffering twice as many accidents as adults during their first year of work.[87] The Directive aims to ensure that the minimum working age is not lower than the minimum full-time compulsory school leaving age (or 15 years, whichever is higher) and to regulate the way work is carried out by young people. The Directive also imposes obligations on employers to take the necessary measures to protect the health and safety of all young workers permitted to work by the Directive. This includes a risk assessment before a young person starts work and if there is any major change in their working conditions. The Directive does not implement all the ideals set out in Articles 20–23 of the 1989 Social Charter. Article 21 requires that young people in gainful

---

[83] The reception of these ideas is mixed. See: Case 177/88 *Dekker* [1990] ECR I-3941; Case C-32/92 *Webb* v *EMO Cargo* [1994] ECR I-3567 and compare with Case C-179/88 *Hertz* [1990] ECR I-394 and Case C-400/95 *Larsson* v *Fotex* [1997] ECR I-2757. *Cf.* these cases with Case C-394/96 *Brown* v *Rentokil* [1998] ECR I-4185. The Court is encumbered with its notorious statement in Case 184/83 *Hofmann* v *Barmer* [1984] ECR 3047 that EC law did not alter the division of responsibility between parents in raising children. *Cf.* Case C-243/95 *Hill* v *Stapleton* v *IRC* [1998] ECR I-3739. For a critique see Szyszczak, E., 'Community Law on Pregnancy and Maternity' in Hervey, T. and O'Keeffe, D. (eds) *Sex Equality Law in the European Union* (Wiley, Chichester, 1996); Wintemutte, R., 'When Is Pregnancy Discrimination Indirect Sex Discrimination?' (1998) 27 *Industrial Law Journal* 23.

[84] OJ 1992 L 348/1.

[85] OJ 1996 L 145/4.

[86] Council Directive 94/33/EC, OJ 1994 L 216/12.

[87] COM (191) 543 final.

employment must receive equitable remuneration in accordance with national practice and Article 23 provides that following the end of compulsory education young people must be entitled to receive initial vocational training of a sufficient duration to enable them to adapt to the requirements of their future working life.

Issues of privacy are addressed from another perspective in a Directive on the Protection of Individuals with Regard to the Processing of Personal Data and the Free Movement of Such Data.[88] Again, the Community's response mirrors developments in international law.[89] Simitis and Lyon-Caen[90] argue that in no other area is personal data so systematically gathered and processed as in the employment relationship. The practical reasons for the development of more detailed, sectoral rules for employment data can be made out, given the growing mobility of employees and the increasing centralisation of processing of personal data in multinational companies. The Community Directive is only a first step[91] and the Commission's White Paper on Social Policy argues the case for further initiatives in this area.[92]

7.6 EC labour law as a 'floor of rights'

Hepple[93] criticises the Community for not establishing a central 'core' of employment rights despite the lip-service paid in the new *Article 136 EC* to the 1989 Social Charter and the European Social Charter 1961. He gives examples to show that the 'European model' is still in its infancy: worker participation has neglected fundamental social rights associated with collective bargaining, cross-border mergers are not adequately protected and local management may shield behind the failure of the undertaking taking the decision to provide information.

The concept of the European model has met with criticism. It is different

---

[88] Council Directive 95/46/EC, OJ 1995 L 281/31. Simitis, S., 'From the Market to the Polis: The EU Directive on the Protection of Personal Data' (1995) 80 *Iowa Law Review* 445.

[89] See Council of Europe, Convention for the Protection of Individuals with Regard to Automatic Processing of Personal Data, 28 January 1981; Recommendation No. R (89) 2 of the Committee of Ministers to Member States on the Protection of Personal Data used for Employment Purposes. See Simitis, S., 'Developments in the Protection of Workers' Personal Data' (1991) 10/2 Conditions of Work Digest Workers' Privacy, Part I: Protection of Personal Data (ILO, Geneva, 1992).

[90] Simitis, S. and Lyon-Caen, A., 'Community Labour Law: A Critical Introduction to its History' in Davies, P. *et al.* (eds) *European Community Labour Law* (Clarendon Press, Oxford, 1996).

[91] Paragraph 68, Recitals of Council Directive 95/46/EC.

[92] COM (94) 333.

[93] 'New Approaches to International Labour Regulation' (1997) 26 *Industrial Law Journal* 353.

from national models, thereby changing radically some of the ideas of how to regulate labour and labour markets but also, for some Member States, diluting hard won rights on both the employer and the employee side. EC labour law begins to fit into the classic EU regulatory process of 'de-regulation' of national laws with 're-regulation' at the EU level. The perceived neglect of the collective dimension to labour law at the Community level is often criticised as is the predominant focus of EC intervention upon competition. In the early days of the Common Market this was inevitable given the limited legal base upon which labour law measures could be proposed. Even in the nascent equal opportunities legislation we see the Commission invoking the free movement of persons principle as the justification for the Community intervention. In later developments measures are justified to facilitate cross-border trade and market integration; for example, the proposals on worker participation and consultation are made to ensure a harmonious functioning of the internal market and to avoid distortions of competition. The Court of Justice frequently reinforces this view that labour law intervention is there to harmonise costs. Wedderburn[94] and Mancini[95] summarise the situation: competition is upstream from welfare.

Deakin argues that EC labour law has a dual function. In 'harmonising costs' of labour law it, inevitably, has laid down a 'floor of rights'.[96] At the Community level the phrase is used to describe the processes whereby labour law establishes a broad level of basic rights which Member States and employers must grant to workers. As we have seen, this floor may be established at a low level and may not provided full coverage. The economic arguments for a 'floor of rights' are set out by Deakin and Wilkinson[97] in that by investing in a set of basic employment protection rights, the EC may retain comparative advantage in terms of a skilled and efficient workforce.

Deakin[98] draws upon the work of Sengenberger[99] who classifies the term 'labour standard' as having two distinct forms. The first form refers to

[94] 'Consultation and Collective Bargaining in Europe: Success or Ideology?' (1997) 26 *Industrial Law Journal* 1.

[95] 'Labour Law and Community Law' (1985) 20 *Irish Jurist* 1.

[96] Deakin, S., 'The Floor of Rights in European Labour Law' (1990) 15 *New Zealand Journal of Industrial Relations* 219.

[97] Deakin, S. and Wilkinson, F., 'Rights vs. Efficiency? The Economic Case for Transnational Labour Standards' (1994) 23 *Industrial Law Journal* 311.

[98] Deakin, S., 'Integration Through Law? The Law and Economics of European Social Policy' in Addison, J. and Siebert, W. (eds) *Labour Markets in Europe* (Dryden Press, London, 1997).

[99] Sengenberger, W., 'Protection – participation – promotion: the systematic nature and effects of labour standards' in Sengenberger, W. and Campbell, D. (eds) *Creating Economic Opportunities: The Role of Labour Standards in Industrial Restructuring* (International Institute for Labour Studies, Geneva, 1994).

actual terms of employment, quality of work and protection of workers at a particular location and point of time. The second form is a normative or prescriptive one relating to ideas of collective organisation and action as well as prescriptive levels of protection such as working time hours, minimum wages as well as rules of conduct and dispute resolution. Deakin, writing with Mückenberger,[100] has argued further that as far as normative standards are concerned a further distinction between substantial and procedural regulation should be drawn. Substantive regulation relates to the use of particular levels of minimum protection into the employment relationship which replace individual bargaining. These norms may be either compulsory or what is described by Wedderburn[101] as 'inderogable' norms which are impossible to contract out of, for example minimum wage legislation, or there may be the opportunity to derogate in limited circumstances to facilitate 'flexibility' in specific sectors/workplaces. Procedural regulation establishes the *process* of bargaining (that is, it does not *set* any particular standards). In both the substantive and procedural sphere of labour standards there may also be examples of 'controlled derogation' which provides for limited exceptions from substantive norms which are agreed and monitored collectively or by a regulatory body.[102]

A third form of labour standard can be identified as a 'promotional standard'. This is found in vocational training, worker placement schemes and is designed to channel economic activity through the provision of public support services or subsidies.

Harmonisation of standards as norms does not necessarily lead to uniformity of standards across the EU. According to Deakin, the debate over the 'social dimension' to the EU has suffered by failing to recognise this distinction. The harmonisation of social policy has been aimed at achieving a 'level playing field' between the Member States to establish 'parity of costs' which have occurred as a result of (different) regulatory systems of the Member States. This idea is set out by the Court in *Commission* v *United Kingdom* where the Court ruled that the Community legislature intended both to ensure comparable protection for workers' rights in the different Member States and to harmonise the costs which such protective rules entail for undertakings.[103]

---

100 Mückenberger, U. and Deakin, S., 'From Deregulation to a European Floor of Rights: Labour Law, Flexibilisation and the European Single Market' (1989) 3 *Zeitschrift für ausländisches und internationales Arbeits-und Sozialrecht* 157.

101 Lord Wedderburn, 'Inderogability, Collective Agreements and Community Law' (1992) 21 *Industrial Law Journal* 245.

102 Lord Wedderburn and Sciarra, S., 'Collective Bargaining as Agreement and as Law: Neo-Contractualist and Neo-Corporative Tendencies of our Age' in Pizzorous, A. (ed.) *Law in the Making* (Springer-Verlag, Berlin, 1988).

103 Case C-382/92 [1994] ECR I-2479, para 15 and C-383/92 [1994] ECR I-2479, para 16.

The Commission has taken a differentiated approach drawing distinctions between direct and indirect wage costs and charges (social security/ tax payments) and argued for harmonisation on the basis of 'relationships between costs levels and the relative weight carried by the factors of production'.[104] As Deakin points out, neither the Court nor the Council of Ministers when enacting legislation envisages the EU achieving either uniformity of social law provision or the static parity of costs. Thus, Deakin argues that the EU process should not be viewed in terms of a static endpoint in which Member States provide parallel forms and levels of protection. He argues that it is potentially much more useful to see it as a *dynamic process* in which transnational labour standards interact with the economic integration to produce a continuous upwards movement in social provision.

Evidence for this analysis of EC labour law is seen in Directives promulgated before and after the SEA 1987, the old Article 118A EC, the ruling of the Court in *Defrenne v Sabena (No. 2)*[105] and the subsequent 'levelling up' interpretation of Article 119 EC (now *Article 141 EC*) and the Commission's Green Paper on Social Policy.[106] Deakin and Wilkinson,[107] argue that the 'floor of rights' approach also embraces the promotion of labour as a productive resource, giving a role for law, and other forms of transnational regulation, in channelling economic activity in the direction of productive efficiency and social cohesion.

As Chapter 4 on Equal Treatment and Chapter 5 on Employment Protection reveal, the floor of European labour law rights is only partial with significant moves towards allowing the Member States a measure of discretion as to how the floor is constructed at the national level. Thus, not only is the floor of rights flimsy but the ceiling for such rights is set at a low level, particularly in the employment protection arena. In contrast, the elevation of equal treatment between the sexes and the right to free movement as fundamental rights in EC labour law have created a higher level of substantive and procedural rights for workers in the Community.

There are other problems with Deakin's analysis, which are acknowledged by Deakin himself. Throughout Europe, and within Central and Eastern Europe, a new political order is forging a different consensus on the role of state intervention in 'welfare' systems and labour markets. This has led Deakin and Mückenberger to call for a *re-regulation* at the

---

[104] Commission, Explanatory Memorandum on the Proposals for Directives Concerning Certain Employment Relationships, COM (90) 228.
[105] Case 43/75 [1976] ECR 455.
[106] COM (93) 551.
[107] *Supra* n. 97.

European level, described 'in the sense of a European social order which increases the requirements of equality, individual freedom and welfare within a network of collective security and participation'.[108]

7.7 Conclusion

The challenges to the creation of an EC labour law and policy are not only political but economic. Unless there is a consensus on the role of labour law and labour market policy within the new geo-political boundaries of Europe, there are opportunities for economic factors to gain the upper hand. Equally, until there is consensus on the role of labour standards in the European market, there are incentives for European and multinational capital to relocate in the emerging competitive labour markets of Central and Eastern Europe as well as to the developing countries. The pressures of EMU have created new forms of political governance where the regulation of labour markets and labour market institutions has become a key item on the agenda. The institutional arrangements for the new forms of dialogue are being created on the hoof. There are also countervailing tendencies whereby the success of the Internal Market programme has created new forms of *transnational* economic and political arrangements which cannot be accommodated in the traditional hierarchy of multi-level decision making. Doubts are being expressed as to how far traditional values respected at the national level and, to some extent, at the Community level will be respected in the new forms of dialogue and political governance that are emerging. The interaction of the new Chapter on Employment Policy with the new legal base for labour law in the Treaty of Amsterdam combined with the legacy of social fundamental rights and new ideas of citizenship rights reveals the complexity of the dynamics involved in creating an EC labour law.

---

[108] Mückenberger and Deakin, *supra* n. 100; see also: Shaw, J., 'The Many Pasts and Futures of Citizenship' (1997) 22 *European Law Review* 554; Bercusson, B. *et al.*, 'A Manifesto For Social Europe' (1997) 3 *European Law Journal* 189.

INDEX

184